Contemporary Development Issues in Nigeria

Contemporary Development Issues in Nigeria

Edited by

A.O. Olutayo, A.O. Omobowale
and Olayinka Akanle

Cambridge
Scholars
Publishing

Contemporary Development Issues in Nigeria

Edited by A.O. Olutayo, A.O. Omobowale and Olayinka Akanle

This book first published 2015

Cambridge Scholars Publishing

Lady Stephenson Library, Newcastle upon Tyne, NE6 2PA, UK

British Library Cataloguing in Publication Data
A catalogue record for this book is available from the British Library

ISBN (10): 1-4438-7268-7
ISBN (13): 978-1-4438-7268-3

This book is dedicated to Prof. A. O. Olutayo, the contemporary Father of Development Sociology in the Department of Sociology, Faculty of the Social Sciences, University, Nigeria, from whose well of knowledge, scholarship and mentorship all contributors in this book drank.

TABLE OF CONTENTS

CONTRIBUTORS

Olutayo, A.O. Ph.D. is a Professor at Department of Sociology, Faculty of the Social Sciences, University of Ibadan. He was the immediate past Head of the Department and current Dean of the Faculty. He has published widely in local and international journals, contributed to various edited volumes and authoured and co-authoured many books. His post-doctoral research interests include the Sociology of Development, Rural Sociology and Social Theory.

Dr. Olayinka Akanle holds a PhD degree in Sociology (2012) from The University of Ibadan, Nigeria. He is a lecturer in the department at the moment. Dr. Akanle is a Nigerian and has won some scholarly awards like; 2013. World Social Science Fellow (WSSF) of The International Social Science Council (ISSC), Paris, France, 2013. Department of Sociology, University of Ibadan award for staff research, 2012 Laureate. Council for the Development of Social Science Research in Africa Council (CODESRIA) Child and Youth Institute, Youth, Social Transformation and Development in Africa. Dakar, Senegal, 22 October-09 November and 2012 University of Ibadan Postgraduate School Prize for publication. Dr. Akanle has attended many local and international scholarly conferences and has published widely in local and international journals, books, technical reports and encyclopedia. He has over 60 publications and not less than 20 conferences to his credit. His Post-Doctoral research interests include: Sociology of Development/Development Studies, Rural Sociology, Social Theory, Sociology of Religion, Migration and Diaspora Studies, Child, Youth, Gender and the Family in Post-Colonial Africa.

Dr Olabisi Sherifat Yusuff is a lecturer at the Department of Sociology, Lagos State University. She recently bagged her PhD degree from Department of Sociology, University of Ibadan. Nigeria. Her research interest includes Sociology of Development, Gender/Women Studies and Rural Development. She has published in Foreign and Local Journals

Dr. Busari Dauda is a lecturer in the Department of Sociology, Faculty of the Social Sciences, University of Ibadan, Nigeria.

Dr. Busuyi I. Adeniran holds a PhD in Sociology. He is presently a lecturer/researcher in Sociology at Obafemi Awolowo University, Nigeria and a visiting researcher at The Harriet Tubman Institute, York University, Canada. He is a recipient of the International Sociological Association (ISA) doctoral scholarship (South Africa, 2011); Africa Initiative (AI) research grant (Canada, 2011) and CODESRIA's Comparative Research Network (CRN) grant (2012). He has published widely in renowned outfits locally and internationally. He recently co-edited a book: 'Regional Economic Communities: Exploring the Process of Socio-economic Integration in Africa' (CODESRIA, 2014).

Dr. Enaikele, M.D. holds a PhD in Sociology from the University of Ibadan. He is currently a staff in the Department of General Studies, Federal College of Fisheries and Marine Technology, Lagos, Nigeria.

Dr. Godwin Odok obtained his doctoral degree in the department of Sociology, University of Ibadan, Nigeria. He works through research and community organizing to address poverty, social inequality, cultural & environmental change. Godwin holds a Masters' degree in Sociology (University of Ibadan); Law Diploma (University of Jos), a Certificate in Political Economy Analysis (PASGR), and a Global Classroom Certificate in 'Foundations of Sustainable Development' (Earth Institute). Godwin had participated in several conferences/workshops within and outside Nigeria, including the 2012 International Sociological Association (ISA) Ph.D students' laboratory in Taipei, Taiwan; the Medical Research, Development, and Memory in Colonial and Postcolonial Nigeria Workshop, Nsukka, organized by the London School of Hygiene and Tropical Medicine (LSHTM) and IFRA-Nigeria; and the Political Economy Analysis (PEA) course, Nairobi, organized by the Partnership for African Social & Governance Research. Godwin is currently an assistant lecturer in the department of sociology, Federal University, Dutsin-Ma, Katsina State, Nigeria.

Dr. Nurudeen Aliyyu holds a Ph.D. in Sociology from the University of Ibadan and currently lectures at the Department of Sociology/Psychology, Olabisi Onabanjo University, Ago Iwoye, Ogun state Nigeria. He is the current Head of the Department.

Ayokunle Olumuyiwa Omobowale holds a Ph.D. in Sociology from the University of Ibadan. He has interest in scholarly African issues related to the Sociological fields of Development, Cultural, Rural, Political, Medical and Urban studies. He has won the University of Ibadan Postgraduate

School Award for scholarly publication, 2007, IFRA (French Institute for Research in Africa) Research Fellowship 2009, American Council of Learned Societies-African Humanities Programme Post-Doctoral Fellowship 2010 and African Studies Association Presidential Fellow 2014. Dr Omobowale was also at the Centre for African Studies as a Visiting Scholar in November 2014. He was a lecturer at the University of Lagos, Lagos, Nigeria, from April 2007 to May 2008. At present, he is a lecturer in Sociology at Nigeria's Premier University; the University of Ibadan, Ibadan. Dr. Omobowale also served on the Board of Editors of the *International Encyclopaedia of Revolution and Protest* published in March 2009 by Wiley-Blackwell Publishing, Oxford. He has published articles in top journals and he is the author of *Tokunbo Phenomenon and Secondhand Economy in Nigeria* (Peter Lang, Oxford 2013).

Dr Yetunde A. Aluko is a Senior Research Fellow in the Social and Governance Policy Research Department, of the Nigerian Institute of Social & Economic Research, (NISER) Ibadan, Nigeria. She specializes in Gender and Development Studies, and Industrial Sociology focusing on women's sexuality and empowerment, reproductive health and rights, women in management/leadership positions among other areas. She has many publications to her credit which have appeared in both local and international journals as well as chapters in books. She is a member of a number of professional bodies and associations including: International Industrial Relations Associations (IIRA), Nigerian Anthropological and Sociological Practitioners Association (NASA), Nigerian Institute of Personnel Management (NIPM), Nigerian Industrial Relations Association (NIRA), African Sociological Association (AFSA), Pan–African Gender and Peace Research Group (PAGPRG), and International Association for Feminist Economics (IAFFE). She has participated in some international conferences/workshops in the United Kingdom, U.S.A, South Africa, Senegal and Nigeria

Abisoye, A.O. PhD, is a Senior Lecturer in Political Sociology/ Development at the Department of Social Sciences, (Sociology Programme) Crawford University, Igbesa Nigeria. He is currently the coordinator of Pre-Degree/Foundation Programme, Crawford University.

Dr. Olawuyi holds a Ph.D. in Sociology from the University of Ibadan.

Comfort Erima Ugbem holds a Ph.D. in Sociology from the University of Ibadan and currently lectures at the Department of Sociology, Benue State University, Nigeria.

Dr. Dokpesi holds a Ph.D. in Sociology from the University of Ibadan and currently lectures at the Department of Sociology, University of Benin, Nigeria.

ACKNOWLEDGEMENTS

We appreciate all the contributors who made this groundbreaking book possible, who, despite being very busy, made time to contribute to its success. We also acknowledge our students for their probing questions.

FOREWORD

It takes tremendous effort and courage to write a book. This is more so where the attempt is to proffer a solution to the question of development. Almost every scholar and politician is a development specialist. As such, there seems to be a cacophony of voices with regards to the prescriptions being proffered. The unpleasant mixture of these prescriptions requires that we begin to untangle the complexity of development. It is not just the prescriptions that have failed to be implemented that is the major concern here, but also the fact that Nigeria, nay Africa, continues to be poor, yet rich in terms of human and material resources. Though the permutations for Africa becoming a beacon of hope in the twenty-first century seem rife, the horizon remains bleak! This is why there is a need for further interrogation of why development remains elusive in the largest black continent.

Although the chapters address a number of different issues, the overarching concern is the issue of Nigeria's development question, which remains, for all practical purposes, unanswered. As long as Nigeria remains among the worst performing countries on the Human Development Index (HDI), this book remains a must read for all development scholars, students and practitioners. Though all the chapters emanated from the supervision of Professor Olutayo at doctoral level, they are not only empirical studies but also deal with various aspects of development and the independent opinions of the authors. This is why Olutayo also had to present his own point of view which may, to a large extent, differ from those of other authors. The interest is therefore to present various ideas without which societies cannot develop. There are always alternatives contrary to the former "belief" of TINA (There Is No Alternative) in the development paradigm foisted on the Third World societies towards the end of the twentieth century, and which, ironically, is plaguing the European Union.

This is the first edition and there is a conviction that it will soon be revised as more issues emerge. The book comprises fourteen chapters and an introduction written by the editors. These chapters are independent of each other and therefore no one is more important than the other. Consequently, the ordering of the chapters does not signify quality but an organizational necessity, with each containing practical development corridors for both Nigeria and other developing nations.

Prof. A. O. Olutayo.
2015.

INTRODUCTION

A. O. OLUTAYO, A. O. OMOBOWALE AND AKANLE OLAYINKA

Development is a critical issue confronting the world today as every country and every person sincerely desires development. Yet, the meaning and pathways to development are not always straight. The routes, processes, trajectories and dynamics of development are complex and confounding, necessitating detailed, broad-based, multi-facetted and continuous specialized study. This is more so as, according to Martin & Kandal (1989, 3), development "is a product of history, and in the modern world is increasingly conditioned by the structures of the capitalist economy." The history of a people is thus very important in comprehending and achieving development. This is why it is often maintained that development is the most crucial, complicated and contentious contemporaneous issue, even in the realms of academia, policy and practice. It is the complications and necessities of development that lead to the emergence, development and institutionalization of development studies as a unique area of study.

Development studies, in a contemporary sense, although a fledging discipline, is certainly forcefully establishing itself across the world given its relevance and capacities relative to unravelling the "mysteries" of development (Akanle 2012). Development studies engage many critical, practical and provocative questions, like: What is development? Why is development necessary and important? Why do poor countries remain poor while the rich get richer? Why are rich nations becoming poor and indebted in contemporary terms, while some poor countries are getting out of poverty? How can development be measured? What are the theoretical and analytical praxes of development? Thus, development studies examines and explains the dynamics of socio-economic, physical, environmental and political life in human societies through scientific and theoretical processes, models and frameworks to understand how people can reach and be at their objective best in terms of wellbeing and standards of living (Akanle & Adebayo 2013; Akanle 2012). In other words, development studies is concerned with understanding and explaining how societies can achieve optimal health, the best of useful knowledge, optimal resources utilization for the common good, appropriation of their participation rights and the achievement of optimum standards of living without external impositions. Within the postmodern construct, micro-national issues are better explored for galvanizing articulated development.

Although it is common to locate development studies within economics—because development is, erroneously, often seen in economic terms only—development studies goes beyond economics, as development is also beyond economic improvement, connecting the social structure of societies. Development studies is usually multidisciplinary as it appropriates frameworks, tools, methodology and theories from a number of related and unrelated disciplines to reliably explore the difficult subject of development across the world. It is a very comprehensive area of knowledge and a broad discipline, and development experts are also very broad-minded, exactingly critical and analytical in making contributions with practical usefulness to national and global development.

Unfortunately, however, the impact of development studies is yet to be felt in Nigeria in particular and Africa in general, as development issues are very diverse and yet to be sufficiently understood. Development studies is mostly left to the mercy of economists using mathematical models devoid of critical, contextual and ethnographic accounts of local dynamics and trajectories that determine and moderate development efforts. Hence, Nigeria remains dangerously rooted in underdevelopment with little or no appreciable contributions from development studies. Few development experts exist in Nigerian universities, while specialized diagnostic development texts that confront practical development issues are lacking. Texts and scholars with capacities for dispassionate engagement and interrogation of contemporary development issues in the country are regrettably few.

This book is thus intended to fill the identified vacuum in scholarship and practice and be a theoretical and pragmatic contribution to development studies and practical development efforts at policy domains across the world, and especially Nigeria. The book therefore acts as an interventionist and disciplinary compass, and is intended to be groundbreaking. It has chapters that capture the overarching picture of the nexus of development and underdevelopment in Nigeria by teasing out practical development issues in manners that illuminate the development realities. This is very important, as Nigeria today is among the least developed nations of the world with little or no sign of developing, and remains a development paradox with at least a 70% poverty level even in the midst of abundant human and material resources (Akanle 2013a; 2013b). The chapters in this book engage trajectories of definitive development issues in Nigeria in manners that demonstrate the profoundness of the development challenge. With the exception of Prof. Olutayo's contribution, they are all the PhD theses of the contributors. Hence, all theses were supervised by Prof. Olutayo over the course of a decade and address the profoundly definitive development problems facing the nation.

The chapters are arranged in no particular form of significance, but collectively give a situational snapshot of the development position of the country. They are intended to drive policies and studies on Nigeria and sub-Saharan Africa. The world recently experienced what came to be known as a "global financial crisis" or "global meltdown, " and Nigeria and Africa were not insulated from it. Even though many have argued that Nigeria and Africa did not experience the negative ripple effects of the meltdown as the financial situations of the country and continent were actually already comatose, African nations could not wriggle out of the consequences of problems they did not create. Hence, African nations still find it difficult to chart alternative development pathways for themselves even when it has become obvious that the current development framework given by Euro-American scholarship cannot guarantee universal development and is not foolproof, as the meltdown demonstrated. Prof. Olutayo's chapter sets the tone and theoretical background for the chapters in this book by using practical TINA (There is No Alternative) to engage Africa's development quagmire (Olutayo, Olutayo & Omobowale 2008). He engages the issue demonstratively through the analytical window of the global economic meltdown.

Dr. Aluko's chapter engages the gendernomics of nation building and national development in Nigeria. She explores the gender components of the Nigerian development problems, demonstrating the critical nature of gender in the national development equation. If gender is not sufficiently factored into the development process, development may continue to be a mirage in the nation. The political process is equally important. This has a strong historical existence in Nigeria, especially against the now very important socio-political history of sub-Saharan Africa as codified in the statement "seek ye first political independence (power, control) and other things shall be added onto you." Africans cherish politics, not only because it enables authoritative allocation of scarce resources and values, but also because it is a veritable avenue for embezzlement, corruption and a sure leeway out of poverty, with an intergenerational aspect. Also, politics in Nigeria and many African countries builds influence and patronage, as demonstrated in the celebrated book by Richard Joseph, *Democracy and Prebendal Politics: The Rise and Fall of the Second Republic* (2014). Dr. Omobowale's chapter demonstrates, through rich ethnographic data, how "institutionalized" clientelism held sway and affected development in southwestern Nigeria. This chapter also has relevance for the whole of sub-Saharan Africa where political power mixed with extreme poverty is used to build huge followings and support bases for politicians in the communities (Omobowale & Olutayo 2007; Omobowale 2008; Omobowale & Olutayo 2010).

In chapter four, Busari Dauda engages with the knotty issues in information technology and education in Nigeria. As the world goes virtual and conventional pedagogical approaches are deconstructed, how prepared is Nigeria and what are the issues? The chapter is very practical yet contentious given the sometimes opposing views that lecturers and students have on the subject. This chapter is, however, able to find the balance on the issues and makes useful contributions to the sociology of education and the interface with development. If sustainable development is possible, education must be in tune with global dictates and development in education especially relative to the academy. Also, if there is to be development the civil service must be in tune with contemporary developments in service delivery. This is more so as the civil service is the administrative organ of government, especially in democratizing regimes. If the civil service is unsupportive of government programmes and state policies, there can never be sustainable development. This is why Dr. Abisoye's work is key. He engages public service delivery in Nigeria, demonstrating the trajectories and practical implications for national development.

Agriculture used to be the mainstay of Nigeria's economy and development before the discovery of oil in 1958. In fact, the sector employed at least 70% of the population. In the era of global food insecurity and a national agricultural and food deficit, a sociological consideration of agriculture is needed, especially when the nation is already noted to be insecure in this respect. It has also already been noted that oil can never bring sustainable development to Nigeria as the proceeds only breed more corruption and environmental degradation. This is why attention is being given to agriculture. Dr. Enahikele's chapter addresses these issues through the window of aquaculture as an innovative method, demonstrating that oil has been a curse rather than a blessing, a tragedy rather than a development solution, as experiences in Nigeria over the past fifty years have shown.

The ways people construct themselves affect how they relate to their nation and contribute to national development. Identity constructions are thus very important, especially in a globalized world and societies where identity becomes an object of negotiation for scarce resources. Comfort Erima Ugbem's chapter confronts this salient yet profoundly important issue among "minority groups." The chapter is both very demonstrative and pragmatic, as well as professionally and dispassionately written, even though it addresses a very sensitive issue. International migration is another major issue in Nigeria. In fact, Nigerians are among the most migratory in the world. When migrations north from Africa and developing nations are considered, Nigeria ranks among the highest (Akanle 2013a).

Whether in terms of regular or irregular/illegal migrations, Nigeria has a profound impact. Of interest, however, is the comprehension of the trajectories, nuances and drivers of these migrations and how they affect development of the country. These are what Olayinka Akanle engages with in his chapter. Busuyi Adeniran engages with the issues of movement of people and lifestyles across the Economic Community of West African Nations (ECOWAS) corridor to influence its policies. This is particularly important as ECOWAS is moving from one of nations to one of people, yet the daunting development and security of lives and properties confront the commission. This chapter is very relevant to policy and practice, particularly in the era of unprecedented smuggling, terrorism and transborder banditry, along with the development challenges they pose to nations in the ECOWAS corridor.

Augustine Okhobo Dokpesi, in his chapter, engages with the paradigm of resource curse in developing nations. It is against this background that he empirically interrogates the interface of oil as a resource and the development paradox of Nigeria. The ultimate research question of the chapter is to what extent has oil positively driven the development of Nigeria?

Street begging (alms giving) is a visible problem in Nigerian societies. Every society/city in the country has an army of beggars, signalling the level of poverty and helplessness of the people in the face of an excruciating development deficit and survival threats. Dr. Adewuyi looks at this problem from a scholarly angle and gives a useful account of the problem as a demonstrative development deficit.

Still within the context of popular disempowerment construct, Dr. Nurudeen Alliyu engages with the challenge of property rights and development with a structural approach. The issues and contours engaged with have serious development implications, and the author is able to show the variability, nuances and dynamics in manners that make developmental sense.

Godwin Odok's chapter is an interrogation of the ligaments of rural development and climate change. He examines the implications of rural processes for the understanding of climate change from a development perspective.

Yusuff Olabisi's chapter shares a unique commonality with that of Odok as both wrote from within the prism of rural sociology, but Yusuff's adds a gender dimension within the informal economy interrogating challenges of women rural entrepreneurs.

It is important to note that we are not pretending that this book addresses *all* the development issues in Nigeria and Africa, and we are not in any way suggesting that the chapters have watertight solutions to all the problems of Nigeria. Nigeria's development debacle is far greater than any single book can totally explore. What we have provided, however, is a very practical, useful and scholarly book that addresses some critical development issues in Nigeria with implications for sub-Saharan Africa. And, as already noted in age-old proverbs and wise sayings, "the best way to eat up an elephant is to eat it in bits." In this way, this book has taken a giant stride towards a sustainable understanding of Nigeria's development problems.

References

Akanle, O. 2013a. *Kinship Networks and International Migration in Nigeria.* U.K: Cambridge Scholars Publishing.

—. 2013b. "The Development Exceptionality of Nigeria: The Context of Political and Social Currents." *Africa Today.* 59 (3): 31–48.

Akanle, O. & Adebayo, A. A. 2013. "Sociology of Development." In *Essentials of Sociology*, edited by Aborisade, R., Omobowale, A. O. & Akanle, O., 395–412. Ibadan: Ibadan University Press.

—. 2012. "Introduction to Development Studies." *The Basics of Social Sciences*, edited by Ogundiya, I. S. & Amzat, J., 45–68. Sokoto: Usmanu Dan Fodio University.

Ake, C. 1979. *Social Science as Imperialism: A Theory of Political Development*. Ibadan: Ibadan University Press.

Martin, M. T. & Kandal, R. K. 1989. "Introduction." In *Studies of Development and Change in the Modern World*, edited by Kandal, R. K. & Martin, M. T., 3–21. New York and Oxford: Oxford University Press.

Olutayo, A. O., Olutayo, M. A. O. & Omobowale, A. O. 2008. "'TINA', Aids, and the Underdevelopment Problem in Africa." *Revista de Economia Politica: Brazilian Journal of Political Economy* 28 (2): 239–248.

Omobowale, A. O. 2008. "Clientelism and Social Structure: An Analysis of Patronage in Yoruba Social Thought." *Africa Spectrum.* 43 (2): 203–224.

Omobowale, A. O. & Olutayo, A. O. 2007. "Chief Lamidi Adedibu and Patronage Politics in Nigeria." *Journal of Modern African Studies* 45 (3): 425–446.

—. 2010. "Political Clientelism and Rural Development in South-western Nigeria." *Africa* 80 (3): 453–472.

CHAPTER ONE

CAUSE WITHOUT CAUSE: AN ANALYSIS OF THE ECONOMIC MELTDOWN AND THE IMPLICATIONS FOR AFRICA

A.O. OLUTAYO

Introduction

The financial crisis which the developed nations are facing does not seem to have an end in sight. This is in spite of various attempts, including fiscal stimuli, monetary policy expansion and institutional bailouts, as well as austerity measures of spending cuts and tax increases. Strikes and demonstrations on the streets of these nations have become daily occurrences and their governments are seemingly incapable of crafting relevant policies to bring an end to their people's sufferings. The strikes and protests by the erstwhile docile Western populations have been described as the most extreme since the world upheaval of 1968.

> From Seattle, where protesters shut down the talks of the World Trade Organization in December, to Washington DC, when authorities recently had to go to super-extraordinary lengths to prevent a shutdown of the World Bank and International Monetary Fund annual meetings, unrest is in the air. (http://acade-mic.brrokylyn.cuny.edu/education)

Perhaps of great relevance is the inability of these nations to go back to the **cause** of the meltdown. It has become very clear that the free market economy cannot freely give answers to the problems at hand. Yet, if they care to remember, the present dilemma cannot be dissociated from their attempts at deregulation which started in the United States in the 1970s. The fervour with which the rational person is encouraged in the neoliberal economy seems to have blinded governments to the limits of the human as a thinking being, interested not only in the welfare of others but also of their nations! With deregulation, less oversight is given to the state as the "watchdog." As such, policy makers could not easily recognise the increasing roles of the free market, especially the financial institutions, such that they were not subject to regulations; rather, they were "bailed-out" of the problems instead of allowing them to fade away (Geithner-Speech Reducing Systemic Risk in a Dynamic Financial System, Newyorkfed.org 2008).

Stated succinctly, the financial crisis and the eventual world recession may be traced to the inadequate, poorly designed, impractical and inconsistent financial regulations across institutions and market systems, leading to accumulated debt in the world's centres of advanced economies of Europe and the United States of America (Rowe 2012; Kodres & Narain 2012). Even with massive policy interventions, recovery is very slow, discouraging and subject to—in the words of the International Monetary Fund (IMF) Managing Director, Christine Lagarde—"serious downside risks" (2012). Even where the 2013 forecast gives an average of 2% growth to the United States, the assumptions are that regulations will be put in place (World Economic Outlook 2013).

While economic recession is not a new incidence in the Capitalist World Economy—there have been three others since the end of World War II in 1975, 1982 and 1991—the concern now is that the economic recoveries from earlier episodes were faster than the current one, which is "still much worse than the typical recovery of the last six decades" (Rampell 2012), including the recessions after World War I. The result of the present recession has therefore been negatively impactful on ordinary citizens. Of significance is the level of unemployment affecting all age groups (Dietrich 2012). In the United States, high levels of unemployment have negatively affected the incidence of hunger and poverty, with about 15% of the population, 11.8% of families, 13.7% of people between aged 18–64, 22% of children under 18, and 9% of people aged 65 and older categorised as poor in 2011 (DeNavas-Walt, Proctor & Lee 2011). The overall poverty rate, according to the Research Supplemental Poverty Measure 2010 (2011), is 16%, as compared with the official poverty rate of 15.1% and the 2011 9% estimate of the CIA World Factbook, as well as the World Bank's 9.6% estimate (World Bank 2013). Indeed, these figures are not unexpected, with the US government having more government debt per capita than Greece, Portugal, Italy, Ireland and Spain (IMF Data 2013), and its attempt to reduce the debt with the "fiscal cliff" dilemma arising from the controversy surrounding how to reduce debt through tax hikes and massive spending cuts.

What comes to mind from all these mind-boggling statistics is how these nations have come to find themselves in these scenarios, given that emerging and less developed nations seem to be experiencing contrary scenarios? The position of this chapter is that, as argued elsewhere, a neoliberal economy with the assumption of the rational human would continue to experience these hiccups (Olutayo, Olutayo & Omobowale 2008). How did we arrive at this conclusion? In answering this question, we may have to go back to the cause of the present recession in the United States, even though this seems obvious. Nonetheless, this is of significance because the rationale behind the "economic human" thesis continues to hold sway. As it was applied as the "drug" for "curing" the developing nations' "ailment" through the Structural Adjustment Programme (SAP) in the 1980s, with little or nothing to show for it, the intention of the developed world for giving more space to the private sector and increasingly "rolling back" the state by relaxing the rules of engagement between the state and the private sector will only delay the further crisis that would emerge if and when this is solved.

The Cause—Rolling back the State

Until "reregulation" (Kodres & Narain 2012) was introduced in 2009, the United States embarked on reckless privatisation beginning in the 1970s and early 1980s, in spite of ambiguous claims for its efficiency (Kosar 2006). Indeed, in the world over, the language and programmes of privatisation have been likened to a revolution or a boom (Young 1987; Dunleavy 1986). With roots in free market economic theory and public choice theory, exponents of privatisation argue against the concentration of power in the hands of the government with a view to protecting individuals, it is argued, from political power. They therefore posit that the free market is the most efficient means of producing goods and services. By implication, from the public choice perspective public bureaucrats are criticised as self-seeking rather than being public-spirited (Tullock, Seldon & Brady 2002). The argument is that the government should be rolled back as it is presumed to be doing what it should not (Bockman 2013). On the contrary, Lopez-de-Silanes, Shleifer & Vishny (1995) have found that the political trade-offs that politicians face in the United States between the in-house provision of public services, which gives them political benefits, and higher government spending, which gives them political costs, determine the decision to privatize government services to a significant extent. Nonetheless, ideological and efficiency factors are built into their decisions on privatization.

In the United States, the Ronald Reagan administration overtook all other nations that began the privatisation process from the late 1980s by targeting programmes and assets for privatisation early in the decade. Since this period, much intellectual groundwork has legitimised privatisation, with a tremendous amount of literature broadening the concept, leading to further privatisation. Thus, both theory and idea have found a place in the political landscape for shaping policy agenda (Henig 1989–1990). Of course, as Henig further asserted, the American public had accepted the basic elements of the welfare state before Reagan. Nonetheless, the need to "refurbish" *laissez faire* philosophy and the redefinition of pre-existing local government practices, through an exercise of intellectual imperialism, gave impetus to the privatisation movement. Thus, the idea found fertile ground in which to grow. This, of course, was not the same in most developing nations, and we will return to later.

Suffice to say that, according to one of Reagan's advisers on privatisation, and R. W. Poole (2004), the founder of the Reason Foundation and an intellectual imperialist, Reagan's position on privatisation was mostly a remedy for what he thought was wrong with socialist countries rather than his being a global privatisation revolutionist. As such, it was for Reagan an ideological battle to be won at all costs. The former UK Prime Minister Margaret Thatcher was usually seen as the chief launcher of privatisation as a result of British indebtedness in the coal, steel, oil, and electricity industries. By the 1990s, the former USSR began privatisation with the assistance of the World Bank, the United States Agency for International Development (USAID), the German *Treuhand*, and other governmental and nongovernmental organizations.

Perhaps Poole's position needs to be further re-emphasized given Reagan's educational legacy as the governor of California. Clearly evident was his intolerance of public schools from his utterances loaded with revulsion for alleged communist thinking. Specifically, he set the tone of his educational reform by, according to Clabaugh (2004):

(a) calling for an end to free tuition for state college and university students
(b) annually demanding 20% across-the-board cuts in higher education funding
(c) repeatedly slashing construction funds for state campuses
(d) engineering the firing of Clark Kerr, the popular President of the University of California
(e) declaring that the state "should not subsidize intellectual curiosity"
(f) consistently called student protesters derogatory names, and
(g) consistently and effectively opposing additional funding of basic education, leading to classroom overcrowding, worn-out textbooks, crumbling buildings and demoralized teachers.

These were his credentials as governor which he transferred to his presidency. From here, Reagan presided over the collapse—or what was known as the "rolling back"—of the Soviet Union, which he publicly called the "evil-empire, " to him a basically immoral and foolish society. To achieve this, he increased military spending to prevent Soviet expansion in South Vietnam (while the United States was wallowing in its post-Vietnam defeat), Cambodia, Laos, South Yemen, Angola, Mozambique, Ethiopia, Nicaragua, Grenada and Afghanistan. He initiated a $1.5 trillion dollar military build-up, "the largest in American peacetime history" (D'Souza 2003), to draw the Soviets into an arms race which, he knew, they could not win. Along with his free-market ideology of expanding privatization, Reagan increased the federal deficit from $100 billion in 1981 to $3 trillion by 1989 when he left office (Simkin 2004; D'Souza 2003). Rather than expending the profits made from the selling of arms to the Islamic fundamentalist government in Iran (popularly known as Iran-gate) to cushion the American economy, his priority was to sponsor the anti-Marxist guerrillas fighting in Nicaragua.

Simply put, the "rolling back of the state" under Ronald Reagan had more of an ideological than economic purpose—first and foremost, this was the need to push global American dominance to the fore. The privatization exercise became, in a way, the instrument presenting an alternative to state dominance. Through this state dominance, the USSR was becoming more relevant as *the* recognised world power, especially with its military. This was discomfiting to the United States and its allies, and thus all arsenals were gathered to "roll back the state, " first in the USSR and later those nations within which the state was becoming dominant.

In fact, Reagan was only playing out the already dominant ideological position of America in the world. This resulted in the Cold War period (1945–1980), and the US government policy of containment of the USSR and its rollback toward the Third World (Bodenheimer & Gould 1989), a fall-out from the defeat of Germany by the allies (the United States, USSR, Great Britain and France) in the Second World War. It should be recalled that one of the main reasons for fighting Germany was its insistence that the classical political economy of Adam Smith did not consider the culture of different societies before developing the concept of the "rational man." The German historical school of economics, the dominant political ideology, vehemently resisted this, positing that what is rational is defined by each society, adding that the materialistic concept of the human is too general, over-assuming and over-committed to the *laissez faire* doctrine (Olutayo 2001–2002; Marshall 1972).

The disagreement between the Soviet Union and the United States with the remaining allies (Great Britain and France), having shared the war booty from the destruction of Germany, was over the best way of governing, with the US and its allies identifying with the "freedom of man" and the USSR emphasizing the "irrational man." Without going to war, as with Germany, Soviet Russia was capitulated through the final push of Reagan's policies and the "active" connivance of Mikhael Gorbachev, the then Soviet President. As today, China seems to be on the path of confrontation with the US and its former allies, now including Germany and other European nations as well as other developing nations, as the state versus private dominant ideologies continue to contest for superiority.

To be sure, the financial deregulation constituted the major albatross resulting in the financial meltdown with which this chapter is concerned. Nonetheless, our position is that all this had a great impact on what happened later, which was that the need to "roll back the state, " an extension from the need to "contain" the USSR, was sustained after Reagan and the following administrations further deepened the process.

The current crisis, as has been variously alluded to, resulted from the weak financial regulations in the United States and Europe, which gave impetus for deregulated "shadow banks" operating outside the banking regulatory system (Kodres & Narain 2012). In their words:

> Much of the activity at the heart of the global crisis occurred between the shadow system and the more formal banking system. U.S. broker-dealers, bank-sponsored special investment vehicles and conduits, money market mutual funds, hedge funds, and an assortment of financial institutions interacted to spawn a growing systemic mismatch between longer-term assets and the short-term liabilities that funded them.

The deregulation processes which made it possible for these institutions to achieve this were themselves a direct conspiracy between the regulating agencies, politicians and the business outfits (Levin-Coburn Report 2011; Sherman 2009; Moseley 2009; Amy n.d.). Amy presents the names of people appointed during Bush's tenure to help slash budgets, weaken rules and relax the enforcement of regulations. As Amy observes, during the Bush administration the staff of the Minerals Management Services (MMS) of the Director of the Interior, overseeing oil operations, was compromised, partying with executives and accepting gifts, and allowing British Petroleum (BP) to get a waiver from conducting an environmental impact analysis. To further the collusion, BP was encouraged to not use the relevant advanced blowout technology, claiming that it was too expensive.

As Amy further shows, the overseeing Director of the MMS was later compensated with a plum job as head of the National Oceans Industries Association. Amy's assertions were confirmed in the words of the Levin-Coburn Report that the crisis resulted from:

> high risk, complex financial reports; undisclosed conflicts of interest; the failure of regulators, the credit rating agencies, and the market itself to rein in the excesses of Wall Street.

Perhaps the worst repercussion from all this was the BP oil spill of April 20, 2010. Apart from the after-effects of the spill, it was never certain how the dispersants would affect the environment and people (Jackson 2010; Venosa 2010). The "spill" has been described as the biggest in recent US history, claiming eleven lives and releasing oil into the Gulf of Mexico, destroying not only the environment but also disturbing the livelihoods of millions of people.

Such was and would always be the expectation where rules are deregulated—a thesis based on the rational human. This is more so in a capitalist system where businesses do everything to ensure the sustenance of not just the company but also its profits, which are prioritized over prudence (Moseley 2009). Indeed, with the relaxation of rules, "sharp practices" became the norm, as adumbrated above, leading to the crisis, first in the housing sector, and later extending to other sectors. This was more so where any business could claim bankruptcy and still be compensated for running itself aground, even though the pre-existing rationale was that privately run businesses are very efficient, will always encourage growth, maintain safe working conditions, protect workers, compensate government "failures" and excess bureaucracy, and be competitive, leading to better production and the supply of good and services. While some of these claims have been justified, the recent realities tend to negate the facts!

Human beings in any capitalist society with little or no regulation would go beyond the limits to exploit whatever situation they find themselves in for the sustenance and furthering of benefits. The current banking crisis alone ranks among the costliest crises in terms of fiscal outlay and output losses (Laeven & Valencia 2012). If this can happen in the banking sector, the livewire of any capitalist system, the implication for the whole system is too obvious, as is being currently witnessed. Indeed, by the third quarter of 2012 international investment continues to dry up as the trust in the system seems to have been shattered. According to the OECD Observer 2012, as the euro crisis drags on:

> Europe is expected to experience the largest drop in outward investment, a staggering 48%. Investments by Africa and the Middle East, North America and Asia are also expected to drop significantly. Latin America had seemed to be bucking the trend as intra-regional deals in airlines, steel, telecommunications and retail buoyed activity. However, IM&A into Latin America is set to fall by 30% in 2012. (oecd.org 2012)

Implications for Africa

The Reagan regime began the rollback of the state as he publicly declared that his policy was to support "freedom fighters" trying to overthrow Third World "communist tyranny." Even though this had been the US policy before him, his was more open to the worldwide rollback policy with the aim of shrinking the "Soviet empire" at its periphery. This was branded "democracy" as we know it today in the Third World, Africa inclusive. The establishment of democracies, however, was never the intention but a blatant and abrasive method of rolling back the state which, it seemed, was in tune with the Soviet-type government.

Indeed, as Bodenheimer & Gould (1989) observe with clear evidence, it was in the character of the US governments to attempt to overthrow "Communists" whenever and wherever they existed. For instance, they point out the case of Guatemala, which was a democracy elected in 1954 but through which the US installed a military regime. In 1956, the United States supported the cancellation of elections and backed another repressive South Vietnamese leader, who took power through coups and assassinations. In the Dominican Republic in 1965, the United States prevented the installation of the elected president to prevent the creation of a Communist state. In Chile, a covertly organised bloody military coup by the United States robbed Salvador Allende of his democratically won victory in 1973. In 2012, the Muslim Brotherhood was democratically elected in Egypt, but in the eyes of the United States governmental activities were at variance with its acclaimed good governance.

This, it seems, is the normal trend when one considers US disposition to the Apartheid regime in South Africa. In so far as it did not profess a Communist manifesto, all was well. Indeed, since its interest was to defend any so-called threat from Soviet expansion, the US government under Reagan had to prevent the existence of independent revolutionary states in Africa. Thus, the Apartheid regime in South Africa had to be encouraged to undermine independent governments in Angola, Mozambique, and Zimbabwe (Bush 1985).

Before the era of privatisation and democratisation sing-song, the state was providing virtually all the welfare needs of its citizens. Rather than development, globalisation became the "buzzword, " reinforced through the Washington Consensus' preaching of privatization of state enterprises and welfare programmes through the reduction of state expenditures, deregulated trade with the developed world, and the emphasis on export orientation (Leys 2005; Tau 2008). Backed by the IMF, There Is No Alternative (TINA) became the policy wherein the conditionality for any financial assistance was adherence to the neoliberal doctrine (Wallerstein 2011).

Central to this neoliberal doctrine is the governance type under which it must be undertaken. "Democracy, " a term derived from Greek over two thousand years ago, has been the recommended prescription for engineering neoliberalism. It is believed that such a doctrine gives more room for more participants, even though its relevance continues to be suspect as even the most autocratic regimes can claim to be democratic (Schnitter & Karl 1991). Greek democracy, as conceptualised, was relevant to a specific societal context dependent on a "low level" of the means of production around which social relations of production were organised. As such, it was easy to discern a government of the people, by the people and for the people, since most were involved in production and subsequent social relations. Its meaning has however changed with the development in the means of production as new social relations have emerged around them, which has characterised the historical conditions of Western Europe and the United States (Olutayo 2002; Olutayo 1994). Consequently, the liberal doctrine of the "government of the people *by the few for the few*" became and still is the new form of democracy, since the interests of the few who now own and control the new means of production predominate in the governance democracy we now have. This is popularly referred to as "representative democracy." Thus, what we have is a more "tree top" politics.

Unfortunately, the historical experiences of Western Europe and the United States differ fundamentally from those of Africa, like most other Third World nations. Nonetheless, this idea has been foisted on them with debilitating consequences for the different nations. In most of them, the means of production are not as developed as those of developed nations. Therefore, only those with access to the control of the political institution, as a means of acquiring wealth, become, in the words of A. G. Frank (1972), *lumpenbourgeoisie*, and determine their development agendas based on the dictates from and dependency to those they derived their existence from—the controllers of the World Capitalist System.

Thus, even though the economic growth statistics tend to be positive for them, such an outcome is only dependent on the state of the world wherein the predicament of their "master" has given them a slight breathing space, or more so than where they are mainly exporters of raw materials to these masters. This has been made possible, as Wallerstein (2011) would argue, because of their peripheral statuses in the World Capitalist System. Indeed, as the Managing Director of the IMF Christine Lagarde stated for Latin America, and which was reiterated by Nigeria's finance minister Okonjo-Iweala, no country is immune to the global crisis as, due to the economic crisis in the United States and Europe, growth in Latin America and the Caribbean slowed from 4.5% in 2011 to an estimated 3.75% in 2012. She emphasised that though there are better prospects for growth in 2013, "policy slippages in advanced economies could weigh on Latin America, " especially because their source of strength derives from the stability of the advanced economies given their strong ties to them.

Like its "masters, " Africa has accepted the view that the private sector should be the engine of growth. As alluded to earlier, this was a conditionality given through the Washington Consensus. In line with this new orientation, almost all African countries have engaged in one form of privatization or another (Jerome & Rangata 2003). Yet, after decades of privatization the high expectations of the processes have, most researchers conclude, more or less remained a mirage (Nellis 2003; Ariyo & Jerome 2003; 1999; Jerome 2004).

Indeed, the unrealisable dreams of democracy and development have been pinned on the basic requirements of human rights, independent media and an independent judiciary, participatory politics, and a liberalised market economy, which most of these nations lack (Divano 1995). However, such requirements, to be sure, are pursued on a piecemeal basis rather than through a fundamental rethinking of the social structure. Such attempts tend to confirm the fact that the foundational rationale of rolling back the state continues to occupy the ultimate objective rather than a deep concern for the development of these nations. That is, the character of state occupants, in terms of their formation and historical-sociological experiences, are fundamental to the realisation of development in any nation. Such experiences are hinged on the available means of production and the attendant socio-relations of production. Where these are lacking, the ruling elites would be unlinked from their roots; that is, the substructure on which their society hinges.

Conclusion

The business of social scientists is to discern the causes and courses of social experiences to posit alternatives to challenges that such societies or groups may encounter. Unfortunately, it seems that ideas and ideologies continue to inform social science disciplines, thus limiting the understanding and the alternatives proffered, if any. The acceptance of "no alternatives" to development has beclouded the ability to explore possible alternatives, having examined the existing social situations. This is why some people are astounded when seemingly new challenges emerge, contrary to the "only alternative" proffered earlier.

While it seemed that the so-called "developed" nations had reached their zenith, their historical-sociological experiences present a contrary view as they are still "developing." Their development processes continue to show the activities of the *dramatis personae* in projecting and protecting what these people desire for their societies. In achieving such desires, their ability to control the social processes has been fundamental. Yet, their achievements in this regard are themselves predicated on their relation to the means of production. Where they own and control the means of survival of the society, it is almost inevitable that they easily determine those who depend on them for survival.

To effectively control their dependants, however, they must create rules within which to operate, where such rules are subjugated and cataclysms result. This seems to explain the crises that the United States and Europe are experiencing; unfortunately, their limited views of possible alternatives seem to have further compounded the challenges. There is never a "rational man" that does not need to be controlled and/or corrected. Indeed, the concept of rationality is itself subject to societal contexts.

These are the concerns that Africa, as much as other continents, needs to understand in delineating the socio-structural arrangements for development. There is never only one way to development—it is dependent on different historical-sociological experiences. Even in "borrowing" from other societies, there is a need for the ruling elites to own and control the means of production as well as being able to determine what is to be "borrowed, " and how such "borrowings" would be adapted to their societal contexts. Unfortunately, Africa does not seem to have people who own and control the means of production. As such, those who occupy the ruling "class" are not able to determine what is to be borrowed and on what terms.

By implication, this opportune "class" needs to create and own the means of production, or at least mobilise the populace by developing a historical-sociologically relevant "rationality" within which their actions and those of their followers would be gauged. This, perhaps, is what we may refer to as a form of ideology.

Lastly, within this ambit it becomes imperative that "outsiders" are delineated and controlled rather than being given leeway to do whatever pleases them. In the history of all hitherto existing societies, this has been one of the major factors that continue to sustain these societies.

References

Amy, D. J. n. d. "Stealth Regulation: The Untold Story, " Government is good: An Unapologetic Defence of a Vital Institution. http://www.governmentisgood.com/articles.php?aid=15&print (accessed January 28, 2013).

Ariyo, A. & Jerome, A. 1999. "Privatization in Africa: An Appraisal." *World Development* 27 (1): 210–214.

—. 2003. "Privatization in Africa: Lessons from the Ghanaian and Nigerian Experience." African Development Yearbook. Institute for World Economics and International Management (IWIM). Germany: University of Bremen.

Bockman, J. 2013. "Neoliberalism." *Contexts* 12 (14).

Bodenheimer, T. & Gould, R. 1989. *Rollback: Right-wing Power in U.S. Foreign Policy*. Boston, MA: South End Press.

Bush, R. 1985. "Reagan and State Terrorism in Southern Africa." *Crime and Social Justice* 24: 1–9.

CIA Fact book. 2013. US: CIA.

Clabaugh, G. K. 2004. "The Educational Legacy of Ronald Reagan." http://www.newfoundations.com/Clabaugh/CuttingEdge/Reagan.html (accessed January 22, 2013).

D'Souza, D. 2003. "President Ronald Reagan: Winning the Cold War." *American History Magazine*. June 12, 2006. http://www.printfriendly.com/print/v2?url=http://.hi-storynet.com/president-ronaldreagan (accessed January 22, 2013).

De-Navas, C.; Proctor, B. and Lee, C. 2011. *Income, Poverty, and Health Insurance Coverage in the United States: 2010*. U.S. Census Bureau. September.

Dietrich, H. 2012. *Youth unemployment in Europe: Theoretical considerations and empirical findings*. Germany: Friedrich-Ebert-Stiftung.

Divano, J. V. 1995. *Privatization in Developing Countries: its Impacts on Economic Development and Democracy*. Westport, Connecticut: Praeger.

Dunleavy, P. 1986. "Explaining the Privatisation boom: Public choice versus radical approaches." *Public Administration* 64.

Frank, A. G. 1972. *Lumpenbougeiosie: Lumpendevelopment*. Monthly Review Press.

Geithner, T. F. 2012. "Reducing Systemic Risk in a Dynamic Financial System." http://finance.fortune.cnn.com/2012/06/13-/financial-crisis-myths (accessed December 12, 2013).

Henig, J. R. 1989–90. "Privatization in the United States: Theory and Practice." *Political Science Quarterly* 104 (4): 649–670.

IMF Data. 2013. *Budget Summary Tables and Senate Budget Committee Calculations*. Geneva: IMF.

IMF Survey Magazine. 2012. "Interview: Africa Must Diversify to Create More Jobs, Says Okonjo-Iweala." May 16.

Jackson, L. P. 2010. "News Release—BP Spill.' Statement of Lisa P. Jackson, Administrator, U.S. Environmental Protection Agency, Testimony on Federal Response to the Recent Oil Spill in the Gulf of Mexico, Senate Committee on Environment and Public Works. Release date May 18, 2010.

Jerome, A. 2004. "Infrastructure Privatization and Liberalization in Africa: The Quest for the Holy Grail or Coup de Grace?" *4th Mediterranean Seminar on International Development*. Spain, Palma de Mallorca: University of Balearic Islands. September.

Jerome, A. & Rangata, M. 2003. *The Tortuous Road to Privatization and Restructuring of State Assets in South Africa: Lessons from African Privatization Experience*. University of Cape Town: Development Policy Research Unit.

Kodrea, L. & Narain, A. 2012. "Fixing the system." *Finance and Development* 49 (2).

Kosar, K. R. 2006. *CRS Report for Congress: Privatisation and the Federal Government: An Introduction*. USA: Congres-sional Research Service. Order Code RL 33777.

Laeven, L. & Valencia, F. 2012. "Systemic Banking Crises Database: An Update." IMF Working Paper WP/12/163 (New York: IMF).

Lagarde, C. 2012. "Building on Latin America's success." IMF direct, The International Monetary Fund's global economy forum. December 6, 2012. http://blog.imfdirect.imf.org/2012/12/06 /buildingonLatinAmerica'ssuccess (accessed December 12, 2012).

Leys, C. 2005. "The Rise and Fall of Development Theory." *The Anthropology of Development and Globalization*, edited by Edelman, M. & Haugerud, 109–125. Massachusetts: Blackwell Publi-shing.

Lopez-de-Silanes, F., Shleifer, A. & Vishny, R. W. 1995. *Privatization in the United States*. NBER Working Paper Series No. 5113. Cambridge, MA: National Bureau of Economic Research. May.

Marshall, G. 1982. *In Search of the Spirit of Capitalism: An Essay on Max Weber's Protestant Ethic Thesis*. London: Hutchinson Co.

Moseley, F. 2009. "The U.S. Economic Crisis: Causes and Solutions." *ISR.* Issue 64. March–April.

Nellis, J. 2003. "Privatization in Africa: What has happened? What is to be done?" *Center for Global Development.* Working Paper. February 25.

Neoliberalism: The New Global Economic Order
http://acade-mic.brrokylyn.cuny.edu/education/
(accessed January 18, 2013).

OECD Investment News. 2012. http://www.oecd.org/daf/inv
/investment-policy/IN18.pdf (accessed November 19, 2014).

Olutayo, A. O., Olutayo, M. A. O. & Omobowale, A. O. 2008. "TINA, Aids, and The Underdevelopment Problem in Africa." *Revista de Economia Politica: Brazilian Journal of Political Economy* 28 (2): 239–248.

Olutayo, 'Lanre. 2001–2002. "The contributions of Ralf Dahrendorf to Sociological discourse." *Ibadan Journal of Humanistic Studies* 11–12: 27–44.

Olutayo, A. O. 1994. "Poverty as a Barrier to Democracy: The Case of Nigeria." *Democracy, Democratization and Africa.* Ed. Thompson, L.A. Ibadan: Africa Link. 205–218.

—. 2002. "The Concept of Mode of Production in the Analysis of Development." In *Currents and Perspectives in Sociology*, Edited by Isiugo-Abanihe, U.C., Isamah, A.N. & Adesina, J., 138–148. Lagos: Malthouse.

Poole, R. W. (Jr.) "Ronald Reagan and the Privatisation Revolution." http://news.heartland.org/print/15469 (accessed January 18, 2013).

Rampell, C. 2012. "Is this really the worst economic recovery since the depression?" *New York Times*, http://economix.bl-ogs.nytimes.com/ 2012/08/10/is-this-reallytheworsteconomic-recession
accessed 160113
http://economix.bl-ogs.nytimes.com/2012/08/10/is-this-
reallytheworsteconomic-recession (accessed January 16, 2013).

Research Supplemental Poverty Measure. 2010. (2011) U.S. Census Bureau.

Regional Economic Outlook. 2012. *Sub-Saharan Africa: Sustaining Growth and Global Uncertainty*. Washington D.C: IMF.

Rowe, J. L. 2012. The Crisis and Beyond. *Finance and Development*. IMF. June. 49 (2).

Schnitter, P. C. & Karl, J. L. 1991. "What democracy is … and what it is not." *Journal of democracy* 2 (3).

Senate Financial Crisis Report. 2011. http://hsgac.senate.gov/ public_files/FinancialCrisisReport.pdf (accessed April 2, 2013).

Sherman, M. 2009. *A Short History of Financial Deregulation in the United States*. Washington DC: Center for Economic and Policy Research. July.

Smikin, J. 2004. "Ronald Reagan and the Cold War." http:// educationforum.iphost.com/index.php/shc (accessed January 22, 2013).

Tau, U. 2008. *The Politics of Neo-Liberal Democracy in Africa: State and Civil Society in Nigeria*. London: Taurus.

Tullock, G., Seldon, A. & Brady, G. L. 2002. *Government Failure: A Primer in Public Choice*. Washington: Cato Institute.

Venosa, A. D. 2010. "Deluge of Oil Highlights Research and Technology Needs for Effective Cleanup of Oil Spills." Written Statement of Albert D. Venosa PhD, Director, Land Remediation and Pollution Control Division, National Risk Management Research Laboratory, Office of Research and Development (ORD), U.S Environmental Protection Agency (EPA), to the Committee on Science and Technology SubCommittee on Energy and Environment U.S House of Representatives. June 9.

Wallerstein, I. 2011. "Structural Crisis in the World-System: Where Do We Go From Here?" *Monthly Review* 62 (10): 1–7.

World Bank. 2013. *Unemployment Total (% of Total Labour Force)*. The World Bank Group.

World Economic Outlook Update. 2013. "Gradual Upturn in Global Growth During 2013." Washington DC: IMF.

Young, P. 1987. "Privatisation around the world." In *Prospects for privatisation*, edited by Hanke, S. H., 205. New York: The Academy of Political Science.

CHAPTER TWO

GENDER EQUALITY, NATION BUILDING AND NATIONAL DEVELOPMENT

YETUNDE A. ALUKO

Introduction

The beginning of the twenty-first century witnessed a profusion of new thinking in gender studies across the social sciences. The philosophical and political conceptualisations of gender equality have been substantially reworked to account for new social agendas around multiculturalism and diversity while new notions of citizenship and nationhood have required a reconsideration of how to position women in modern society (Benhabib 2002; Yuval Davis 2001). This re-engagement with the theoretical foundations of gender research within the world of academia occurs at a time when gender concerns (particularly around women's empowerment through economic progress and development) are on international agendas (Nussbaum 2000; Sen 2004; Arnot & Fennell 2008).

As a result, promoting gender equality is now globally accepted as a development strategy for reducing poverty levels among women and men, improving health and living standards and enhancing efficiency of public investments. The attainment of gender equality is not only seen as an end in itself and a human rights issue, but as a prerequisite for the achievement of sustainable development (Igbuzor 2008; Ukpore 2009; Aluko 2010). Gender equality and women's empowerment continue to be central themes in global treaties, covenants and declarations because they are now acknowledged as catalysts to people-centred development strategies focussing on poverty reduction, improved standards of living, and good governments that give men and women equal voices in decision-making and policy implementation, attainment of MDGs and other global/regional targets (CEDAW, EFA, ICPD PoA, ILO, environment, reduction of HIV/AIDS, etc.).

African governments have responded positively to the burden of underdevelopment by instituting continent-specific development goals and strategies, while also recognizing the firm commitment to gender equality as the bait to development. These are expressed in the African Charter on Human and People's Rights (ACHPR), adopted in 1981 and its Women's Rights Protocol of 2003; the ECOWAS Protocol on Democracy and Good Governance, 2001; and the New Partnership for African Development (NEPAD) adopted in July 2001. These initiatives are linked with other international agreements, and especially the Millennium Development Goals (MDGs).

The above notwithstanding, the history of development policies in Nigeria has been that of a general neglect of the gender variable. The first twenty years of development planning in Nigeria as a Republic remained largely welfarist, whereby gender concerns and women's interests were subsumed within the national interest and a trickle down approach to development practice. Under such an arrangement, development policies remained gender-blind, and gender was never an issue of development planning (Odejide 1997).

Take, for instance, the NEEDS programme. NEEDS is a medium-term plan conceived to address poverty and achieve sustainable growth through home-grown strategies that aim at wealth creation, employment generation and value reorientation. It is therefore not just a macroeconomic policy, but rather addresses critical social, political and cultural problems that have short-changed Nigeria's immense growth and development potentials. Gender issues are subsumed within the latter. Ostensibly, NEEDS' claim to address gender inequality lies within this framework. The more visible aspects of NEEDS may therefore be said to be those reforms that reflect more of a gender-bias than gender sensitivity. Gender inequalities continue to influence all walks of life, women do not have *de jure* equality, and quality of life is more favourable to men than women (Ajala et al. 2002). Summarily, gender inequalities and stereotypes exist in all spheres of the Nigerian polity, preventing women from developing and exercising their full human capabilities. As a result of the inequality, it is increasingly clear that new approaches, strategies and methods are needed to reach the goal of gender relevance in the national development.

With a National Gender Policy (2006) replacing the National Policy on Women of 2000, and the introduction of the Millennium Development Goals, more vigorous global and national attentions are now drawn to pursuing gender sensitive policies. Goal 3 of the MDGs aims at achieving gender equality and women's empowerment, and is not only of intrinsic value in itself but is also central to the attainment of all the other MDGs. This is because an overarching strategy for gender equality in the development process in any nation is likely to be that which takes women and men as partners in development, and more importantly challenges the structure which continues to produce gender-based inequalities in the society, and balances power relations between women and men for growth and development both at micro and macro levels.

It is against this backdrop that this chapter examines how the National Gender Policy and the drive towards the attainment of the Millennium Development Goals have fared in promoting gender equality in nation-building and national development. The chapter addresses the following questions: What are the development frameworks at the global level that have shaped the understanding and strategies for the participation of women and men in nation-building and national development? What are the significant contributions made by women to the development of Nigeria so far? What are the strategies for improving women's roles in national development?

Re-conceptualizing Gender Equality in National Development

Gender equality may have different meanings within the various academic and non-academic spheres. Gender equality can be seen as the measurably equal representation of women and men (World Bank 2001), and occurs in a society when men and women are regarded and treated equally in respect to their rights and privileges, opportunities and obligations in every area of life. This is a situation whereby both men and women are able to share equitably in the distribution of power and influence, have equal opportunities for financial independence in work or in business, and enjoy equal access to education and opportunities in life to develop and improve personal ambition. It describes an environment in which the fair and equitable distribution of overall opportunities, benefits and resources is available to women and men and both sexes are not subjected to gender-based discrimination (UN 2005).

Gender equality does not imply that women and men are the same, but that they have equal value and should be accorded equal treatment. Therefore, the purpose of any gender policy should be to bring a gender perspective into all aspects of planning policy, developing legislation and transformation activities in any nation. In other words, a gender policy that will have a direct effect on overall development goals, not only from the context of legal equality and human or women's rights, but within a broad development context.

In conceptualizing the role of women *vis-à-vis* their male counterparts in development, it is important to note at this point that the role of either is a function of the ways different policy regimes have either reinforced gender difference or deliberately reduced them through one or more of the past development approaches. Since the differences were externally stimulated mainly through the process of colonialism and the imposed neoliberal development agenda, the amelioration has also been externally stimulated (Awe & Akanji 2010). It is, however, useful to briefly examine the past global development frameworks and their varying degrees of success and outcomes for women and men.

From WID to GAD—Conceptual shifts in the discourse on women and development

Women in Development (WID)

The term "women in development, " as originally coined by a Washington-based network of female development professionals in the early 1970s (Tinker 1990), sought to question "trickle down" theories of development by arguing that modernization was impacting differently on women and men (Razavi & Miller 1995). Instead of improving women's rights and statuses, the development process appeared to be contributing to a deterioration of their position.

A dominant strand of thinking within WID was to influence development policy with a combined argument for equity and economic efficiency. The emphasis on women's productive contributions, it was hoped, would convince planners to alter development practice so as to direct scarce economic resources to women. Although women's equity demands were thereby made relevant to the concerns of development planners and policy makers, the strategy also entailed a more controversial implication that prioritized what development needs from women over what women need from development. It advocated for greater gender equality, did not tackle the unequal gender relations and roles at the basis of women's exclusion and gender subordination, and did not address the stereotyped expectations entertained by men (Razavi & Miller 1995). Moreover, the underlying assumption behind the call for the integration of Third World women with their national economy was that women were not already participating in development, thus downplaying women's roles in household production and informal economic and political activities (Koczberski 1998). The WID was also criticized for its views that women's status will improve by moving into "productive employment, " implying that the move to the "modern sector" needs to be made from the "traditional" sector to achieve self-advancement, further implying that "traditional" work roles often occupied by women in the developing world were inhibiting self-development (Koczberski 1998).

Women and Development (WAD)

WAD arose out of a shift in thinking about women's role in development, and concerns about the explanatory limitations of the modernization theory (Parpart, Connelly & Barriteau 2000). Rather than focus specifically on women's relationship to development, WAD focuses on the relationship between patriarchy and capitalism. The approach suggests that women-only development projects were theorized to remove women from the patriarchal hegemony that would exist if women participated in development alongside men in a patriarchal culture, though this concept has been heavily debated by theorists in the field (Tietcheu 2006).

The approach also stresses the relationship between women and the work that they perform in their societies as economic agents in both the public and domestic spheres. It also emphasizes the distinctive nature of the roles women play in the maintenance and development of their societies, with the understanding that the integration of women into development efforts would serve to reinforce the existing structures of inequality present in societies overrun by patriarchal interests (Parpart, Connelly & Barriteau 2000). However, the approach has been criticized on the grounds that the women-only development projects would struggle, or ultimately fail, due to their scale and the marginalized status of these women.

Furthermore, the WAD perspective suffers from a tendency of viewing women as a class, and pays little attention to the differences among women (such as the feminist concept of intersectionality), including race and ethnicity, prescribing development endeavours that may only serve to address the needs of a particular group. While an improvement on WID, WAD fails to fully consider the relationships between the patriarchy, modes of production and the marginalization of women. It also presumes that the position of women around the world will improve when international conditions become more equitable. Additionally, WAD has been criticized for its singular preoccupation with the productive side of women's work, while it ignores the reproductive aspect of women's work and lives. Value is placed on income-generating activities, and none is ascribed to social and cultural reproduction (Parpart, Connelly & Barriteau 2000).

Gender and Development (GAD)

The Gender and Development approach focusses on the socially constructed basis of differences between men and women (Reeves 2000) and the need to challenge existing gender roles and relations (Moser 1993). This departs from WID, which perceived women's problem in terms of their biological differences rather than gender (Razavi & Miller 1995). GAD challenged the WID focus on women as an important "target group" (Moser 1993) and "untapped resource" for development (Razavi & Miller 1995). GAD marked a shift in thinking about the need to understand how women and men are socially constructed and how "those constructions are powerfully reinforced by the social activities that both define and are defined by them" (Razavi & Miller 1995). GAD focus primarily on the gender division of labour and gender as a relation of power embedded in institutions (Moser 1993). Consequently, two major frameworks, "gender roles" and "social relations analysis, " are used in this approach (Development Assistant Committee [DAC] 1998).

However, GAD has been criticized for emphasizing the social differences between men and women while neglecting the bonds between them, as well as the potential for changes in the roles. Another criticism is that GAD does not dig deep enough into social relations and so may not explain how these relations can undermine programs directed at women. It also does not uncover the types of trade-off that women are prepared to make for the sake of achieving their ideals of marriage or motherhood (Razavi & Miller 1995). Another criticism is that the GAD perspective is theoretically distinct from WID, but in practice the program seems to have elements of both. Whilst many development agencies are now committed to a gender approach, in practice the primary institutional perspective remains WID (Moser 1993).

Many women and development advocates now emphasize women's NGOs as key actors in development. The present enthusiasm for NGOs voiced by donors and governments in an effort to roll back the state should be approached with caution by women and development advocates. Women's NGOs have an important role to play in creating space for women to politicize their demands. But in encouraging NGOs to undertake projects with welfare or production objectives, in the hope that this will empower women, advocates may be neglecting the need to put pressure on the state to regulate macro-level forces in a more gender-equitable manner. It is with this goal in mind that possible points of convergence between top-down and bottom-up strategies should be explored by women and development advocates. Hence, in advocating support for women's NGOs, the objective of mainstreaming WID/GAD concerns should not be abandoned.

Women's participation in National Development

In Nigeria, awareness about the role of women in development gained momentum in the latter half of the 1980s. Awareness was further enhanced in 1995 by the effective participation of Nigerian women in the International Conference on Women in Beijing, China. However, in spite of these efforts it is appropriate to state that the role of Nigerian women in development has not been sufficiently emphasised. In highlighting the Nigerian experience, three periods—the pre-colonial, colonial and postcolonial—will be briefly looked at.

The Pre-colonial Period

In the pre-colonial era, women were not only equipped with the skill of child rearing and home management but were equally equipped with political, social, and economic skills, which they acquired through initiation, ritual apprenticeships and ceremonies. In line with the above view, Mannahein & Stewart (cited in Ojieh 2007, 28) note that "women helped significantly to shape the mental and attitudinal infrastructures of a pre-colonial past." During the pre-colonial era, Nigerian women contributed to the sustenance of the kin groups. Within these structures, although women were not always dominant in the construction of these entities, they had clearly defined roles as managers of households (Ekejiuba 1995). Within the household, a woman was a wife, mother, breadwinner, landowner, trader and political leader.

In leadership, history is replete with accounts of women of courage (Awe 1977a) who were actors in themselves rather than simply wards or wives of men. Relations among women (inter-dependence as well as class conflict) is shown by hierarchical studies of women and slavery (e.g. Awe's illustration of *Efunsetan Aniwura* [1977b]), exploits of heroines such as Queen Amina of Zaria (Sa'ad Abubakr [n. d.]), Queen Kambasa of Bonny (Alagoa & Fombo 1972) and sacrificial figures such as Daurama or Daura and Moremi of Ile-Ife (Abdullahi 1990; Ikejiani 2001).

As economic agents, women became leaders of community networks through trade and agricultural exchanges. Women were fully involved in food processing, pottery making and long-distance trading (Olutayo 2005), and dominated the hoe culture (Bryceson 1995), while men were mainly hunters. Thus, while women had full use of cultivable land, men exerted influence more over forest resources (trees, uncultivated land, forest fauna, timber and wild resources that needed male bravery to exploit them) (Guyer & Idowu 1991). Women from history in Nigeria were therefore numbered among the greatest traders, landowners, slave owners, managers of human labour, priestesses and captains of warfare (Awe & Akanji 2010).

Education in pre-colonial times was functional, enabling women to obtain a skill in order to earn a living. Obadiya (2009) observes that a woman who was without a craft or trade, or who was totally dependent on her husband, was not only rare but also regarded with contempt. Education in the pre-colonial era was regarded as indigenous knowledge and informal education, and was a natural process of growth and development, being the local knowledge unique to a given culture or society. Indigenous knowledge refers to those experiences, insights and skills applied by the people of a particular community to maintain their livelihoods (Ezegbe & Akubue 2012).

Colonial Period

The colonial economy was export oriented and seriously undermined the prestige of the traditional occupations of Nigerian women. While it placed women at a great disadvantage (Guyer & Idowu 1991), it enhanced the economic status of the British, Lebanese, Syrian and a few male Nigerian merchants (Awe & Akanji 2010). Many of the smaller markets hitherto dominated by women gradually disintegrated as a result of the emergence of expatriate firms such as John Holt, the United African Company (UAC) and Lever Brothers. Women were denied access to medium- and large-scale loans, which were vital in operating at the bulk purchase level of the colonial economy. In agriculture, cash crop incentives, technology and innovations were restricted to men (Obadiya 2009). Colonial policies and statutes were clearly sexist and biased against women, and "a defeminisation of agriculture" occurred, at least in the valued sector since trade was focused on the new industrial crops controlled by men (Awe & Akanji 2010, 625). Colonialism truncated the complementarity of men's and women's roles and relegated women's enterprises to the sphere of subsistence and the household.

Also, during the colonial period, though education was functional the curricula emphasised religious instruction and clerical skills for boys and domestic science for girls. Technological- and scientific-based education was not encouraged, and the curricula for girls enabled them to become good housewives rather than income earners (Ezeani 1998; Onwuka 2008).

As regards politics, colonialism affected Nigerian women adversely as they were denied franchises, and very few were offered any political or administrative appointments. For instance, it was only during the 1950s that three women were appointed to the House of Chiefs, namely Chief (Mrs.) Olufunmilayo Ransome Kuti (appointed into the Western Nigeria House of Chiefs), and Chiefs (Mrs.) Margaret Ekpo and Janet Mokelu (both appointed into the Eastern Nigeria House of Chiefs). It was also only in the 1950s that women in Southern Nigeria were given the franchise. Otherwise, female wings of political parties possessed very little functional relevance.

Uchendu (cited in Ikejiani 2001) noted that the economic and political suppression of women in the colonial era gave rise to the Igbo women's protest in Eastern Nigeria in 1929. This situation, however, contradicts Palmer & Almazi (1991) and Anugwom (2009), who maintain that the socio-economic improvement of nations can be achieved through the acquisition of education and the broad empowerment of women. However, despite the obnoxious policies of the colonial administration, women vehemently rejected the colonial order. The political and economic force of women in colonial times is described thus: "These women employed their traditional organization … to mobilize all women in most parts of Aba, Owerri and Opobo, etc; in order to assert their rights politically as had been during the pre-colonial era" (Ikejiani 2001). The active role played by Madam Tinubu and Mrs. Ransome-Kuti in mobilizing women against taxation cannot be forgotten.

Post-Colonial Period

While the situation remains unsatisfactory, there is a marked difference from that obtained during the pre-colonial and colonial times. During this period, Nigerian women assumed a more critical role in traditional agriculture. Particularly as a result of the large-scale exodus of able-bodied men to wage labour, Nigerian women took on an increasing portion of the burden of food production, contributing between 50% and 70% of Nigeria's food requirements (Tewe 1978). Also, the role of women in Nigeria's post-1960 politics has not been reflected sufficiently in terms of appointments to policymaking posts. In spite of the massive support given to various political parties by women, women's organisations, market women movements etc., until recently very few women benefited from political patronage.

The position of women in education in postcolonial Nigeria has not improved much. Education is seen as a powerful instrument through which national development can be attained (Federal Republic of Nigeria [FRN] 2004). In this sense, it has no gender or sex attachment because the type of development referred to in this work requires the corporate participation of members of the society, both men and women alike. The fact remains that:

> the task of nation building demands that all hands should be on deck in order to initiate ideas, make plans and participate in their actual implementation. For maximum contribution towards national development in technology and positive outcome, both sexes (male and female) should be equally interested in science and arts subjects. (Kano 1995).

The above claim simply shows the relevance of both sexes (male and female) in national development. This is why gender equality and female empowerment continue to be central themes in global treaties, covenants and declarations. They are now acknowledged as important to the people-centred development roadmap.

Judging from the situation narrated above, one can still contend that at the pre-colonial stage women in their own circle were able to acquire knowledge and skills that helped them compete with their male counterparts in all spheres of life. One can therefore argue that the decline in female education could be traced to the discriminating policy in education and training given by the early Europeans (Boserup 1970, cited in Ozigboh 1998). The Nigerian women have done a lot to escape from the cultural prejudice and male chauvinism that inhibited their progress, preferring to work in groups to enable solutions to their socio-economic, political and cultural problems. They pull their meagre resources together and are able to provide social services and infrastructures in their communities, and thereby promote development and community solidarity.

Women also form Non-Governmental Organizations (NGOs) to fight economically obnoxious policies that are against women, such as political participation, legal status, child marriage and the "osu" (caste) system. One such important female group is the National Council for Women Society (NCWS), established in 1962, made up of educated and influential women. Their objective is to assist female groups in the rural area and educate them on how to be self-reliant and thereby play important roles in their homes as mothers and contribute to nation building. The NCWS sees education as an instrument for the improvement of women's socio-economic statuses. Other women's organizations include the National Association of University Women (NAUM), Women in Nigeria (WIN), the Country Women Association of Nigeria (COWAN), the Committee on Women and Development (COWAD), BAOBAB, GADA, WRAPA and many others.

Education as an imperative for enhancing women's participation in National Development

Global awareness of the role of women in national development has made nations, individuals and groups think of strategies that enhance women's roles in national development. Education is one of the main mechanisms for promoting social change and adjusting the roles of individuals to meet the demands of social and economic change. Any nation that strives for sustainable democracy and development therefore makes an effort to provide an equitable education to all its citizens. However, the argument about gender inequities, especially in education, has perhaps been the fiercest (Olurode & Soyombo 2001), especially in recent times (Igwesi 2012). This is because the female had been the most short-changed, despite the effort of various governments to close the gap created by gender discrimination. There still exists a wide gap between men and women in public life and in all sectors. A lot of traditional and cultural factors have been claimed as limiting women educationally and economically to other opportunities. These cultural practices constituted many barriers to women's educational opportunities and are all imbedded on the political, economic and religion realities of the people (Ozigboh 1998).

This situation is in opposition to the three active steps to implementation of sustainable development given by the United Nations (2004) in Agenda 24, Chapter 21. The steps request the government take measures to eliminate illiteracy among females and expand the enrolment of women and girls in educational institutions, promote the goal of universal access to primary and secondary education for girls and women, and increase educational and training opportunities for women and girls in sciences and technology, particularly at the post-secondary level (Ukpore 2009). Although there is evidence that the federal government has established a universal basic primary and junior secondary education for both sexes, the policy has been fraught with problems. There is a need to establish and strengthen gender units or gender focal points at all levels in all ministries to ensure that the gender concerns are mainstreamed into policymaking and budgetary processes (Akosile 2008).

Denying girls and women education is synonymous to denying them the right to existence. Similarly, it is important to note that understanding women's roles, statuses and aspirations is a key element in the matrix of social revival in all fields of current national development strategies, and in both rural and urban areas of any society (Abodomore 1989). The education of women gives them the opportunity to participate and contribute to national development because it increases economic growth (Abu & Klassen 2004). Benwari & Igwesi (2009) also outlined some areas where female education can contribute to national development, including increased participation in the labour force and earning power, creating intergenerational education benefits, reducing women's fertility rates, lowering maternal mortality rates, protecting against HIV/AIDS and lowering infant and child mortality rates.

Most educated women earn more income than the uneducated. This increases the level of their contributions to the maintenance and development of themselves, their family members and the society at large. A study by Plewis, Mooney & Creeser (1990) also revealed that mothers' education has a significant positive relationship with children's educational attainment and opportunities. The education of women contributes to national development because educated women give birth to fewer and healthier children than uneducated ones. This is because their marriage is likely to be delayed on account of formal education. Lowering maternal mortality rates, protection against HIV/AIDS and lowering infant and child mortality rates are all linked to female education, because educated women not only know the importance of pre and post-natal care, seeking medical care for their children and accessing information about HIV/AIDS, but they also utilize this knowledge and understand how to translate it into practice. This ensures that they and their family members enjoy good health.

Conclusion—The Way Forward

The foregoing shows that women have the notable potential necessary for development, yet are still denied certain rights due to some factors. The Convention on the Elimination of All Forms of Discrimination against Women (CEDAW) has not been fully implemented in Nigeria. Though there seemed to be a slight improvement in female involvement in some sectors the change is not significant compared with the size of the female population in the country. Integrating gender equality in national development planning is therefore critical. Though efforts made so far have yielded some positive results, years of gender blindness through the colonial modernist period still leave their mark on the sands of progress. Therefore, efforts must be doubled to redress these development imbalances in our spectrum of development as it is prescribed worldwide. The challenge is to continue to respond to the demands of equality in development with concerns for redistribution and social inclusiveness in all areas of our polity.

References

Abdullahi, R. 1990. "Women in Politics: A psychological Appraisal." In *The Contribution of Women to Natural Development in Nigeria*, edited by Akande, J., Jegede. O., Clara, O. & Oyekannu. F.D. Nigeria Association of University Women Food Foundation.

Abodomore, E. 1989. "Women & Rural Development Equation in Nigeria." *Business Times*. Monday, May 8.

Abu, G. D. & Klassen, S. 2004. "The Economic & Human Development Costs of Missing the Millennium Development Goal on Gender Equity." World Bank Working Paper. Washington DC: The World Bank. Report No. 29710.

Abubakar, S. 1992. "Queen Amina of Zaria." In *Nigerian Women in a Historical Perspective*, edited by Awe, B. Ibadan: Sankore/Bookcraft.

Alagoa, E. J. & Fombo, A. 1972. *A Chronicle of Grand Bonny*. Ibadan: University Press.

Aluko, Y. A. 2010. "Challenges to Implementing a Robust Gender Policy in Nigeria." *NISEREEL*. Ibadan: NISER. 81–92.

Anugwom, E. E. 2009. "Women, Education and Work in Nigeria." *Education Research and Review* 4 (4). www.academicjournals.org/err/PDF/pdf/2009/apr/anugwom pdf.

Ajala, A. O., Nelson-Twakor, E. N., Obioha, E. N., Alonge, S. K. & Babatimehin, O. 2002. *Review of Quality of Life as experienced in selected domains by Nigerians from 1990–2000*. NISER.

Akosile, A. 2008. "Nigeria: Women Seek Strategies to Address Gender Concerns." *This Day Newspaper*. January 29, 2008. Lagos.

Awe, B. & Akanji, B. 2010. "Women, Gender Difference and Nigeria's National Development." *Nigeria at 50: Accomplishments, Challenges and Prospects*, edited by Akande, S. O. & Kumuyi, A. J. Ibadan: NISER. 617–659.

Awe, B. A. 1977a. "The Iyalode in the Traditional Yoruba Political System." In *Sexual Stratification: A Cross-Cultural View*, edited by Schegel, A. Columbis University Press.

Awe, B. A. 1977b. "Nigeria Women and Development in retrospect." *Women and Development in Africa*, edited by Jane L. Papart. Dalhousie African Studies Series 7. University Press of America.

Benhabib, S. 2002. *The Claims of Culture: Equality and Diversity in the Global Era.* Princeton: Princeton University Press.

Benwari, N. N. & Igwesi, B. N. 2009. "Gender Equity in Education: A Panacea for Sustainable Development." *Journal of International Gender Studies* (5): 103–112.

Boserup, E. 1970. *Women's Role in Economic Development.* New York: St. Martin's Press.

Bryceron, D. F. (ed.) 1995. "Women Welding the Hoe." In *Lessons from Rural African from Feminist Theory and Development.* Oxford: Practice, Berg.

Ekejiuba, F. I. 1995. "Down to Fundamentals. Women Centred Hearth Holds in Rural West African." In *Women Welding the Hoe; Lessons from Rural West African from Feminist Theory and Development*, edited by Bryceron, D. Oxford: Practice, Berg.

Ezeani, O. E. 1998. "Gender and political participation in Nigeria." *International Journal of Studies in the humanities (IJOSH)* 1 (1): 96–107.

Ezegbe, B. N. & Akubue, F. N. 2012. "An Appraisal of the Status of Nigerian Women: Educational Implications and National Development." *American Journal of Sociological Research* 2 (2): 27–31.

Federal Republic of Nigeria. 2004. *National Policy on Education*. Lagos: NERDC Press.

Fennell, S. & Arnot, M. 2008. *Gender Education and Equality in a Global Context Conceptual frameworks and policy Perspectives*. New York: Routledge.

Guyer, J. I. & Idowu, O. 1991. "Commercialisation and the Harvest Work of Women: Ibarapa, Oyo State, Nigeria." Women's Research and Documentation Centre. Institute of African Studies, University of Ibadan. Occasional Paper No. 2.

Igbuzor, O. 2008. "Promoting Gender Equality for Sustainable Development using the National Gender Policy." http://www-.gamji.com/article6000/NEWS7860.htm.

Igwesi, B. N. 2012. "Enhancing Women Participation in National Development through a Change in the Gender System of Nigeria." *Asian Social Science* 8 (1).

Ikejiani-Clark, M. 2001. "Gender and Culture in Nigeria." In *Studies in Gender Discrimination in the 21st century*, edited by Ogbazi, N.J., Azikiwe, U. & Ifelunni, I., 19–26. Owerri: Cape Publishers International Ltd.

Kano, T. N. 1995. "Enhancing Women's contribution to National Development through the Relevant Curriculum." In *Women Education and National Development and Crisis in Nigerian Educational system*, edited by Badmus, G. A., 33–40. The Nigerian Academy of Education, Abuja.

Koczberski, S. 1998. "Women in Development: A Critical Analysis." *Third World Quarterly* 19 (3): 399.

Moser, C. O. N. 1995. *Gender Planning and Development: Theory, Practice and Training*. London: Routledge.

Nussbaum, M. 2000. *Women and Human Development: the Capability Approach*. Cambridge: Cambridge University Press.

Odejide, A. S. 1997. "Gender Blind Economic Adjustment Policies: The Consequences for Women in Nigeria." In *Women and Economic Reforms in Nigeria*, edited by Garba, K. P., Akanji, B. & Isiugo-Abanihe, I., 33–49. Ibadan: WORDOC.

Olurode, L. & Soyombo, O. (eds.). 2001. *Sociology for Beginners* (2nd Ed.). Ikeja: John West Publications.

Olutayo, O. 2005. "Women in Informal Long-Distance Trade: The Family and the Rural-Urban Market Nexus in South-western Nigeria." *Ibadan Journal of the Social Sciences* 3 (2): 67–76.

Onwuka, U. 2008. "Igbo women in Education." In *New Brides, More Hopes: Igbo Women in Socio-Economic Change*, edited by Otagburuagu, E. & Afigbo, A. E., 49–63. Institute of African Studies, University of Nigeria Nsukka, Nsukka.

Ojieh, M. E. N. 2007. "Education: An Imperative for Women empowerment and Impact in Nigeria Development." *A Journal of Today's Education* 10 (3): 28–32.

Ozigboh, F. U. 1998. "Women's Education in Nigeria: Issues and Problems." *International Journal of Studies in the Humanities (IJOSH)* 1 (1): 66–75.

Obadiya, J. O. 2009. "Nigerian Women and Development: Yesterday, Today and Tomorrow." http://obadiyajohn.blogspot-.com/2009/11/nigerian-women-and-development.html.

Palmer, A. & Almazi, E. 1991. *Women Development and Educational Reforms: An Ethiopian Perspective.* Radchff College.

Parpart, J. L., Connelly, P. & Barriteau, E. 2000. *Theoretical Perspectives on Gender and Development.* Ottawa: International Development Research Centre.

Plewis, I., Money, A. & Creeser, R. 1990. "Time on Educational Activities at home and Educational Progress among Infant School Children." *British Journal of Educational Psychology* 60 (1): 64–73.

Razavi, S. & Miller, C. 1995. "From WID to GAD: Conceptual shifts in the Women and Development discourse. United Nations Research Institute." *Occasional Paper Series* (United Nations Research Institute for Social Development) 1 (2).

Reeves, H. 2000. *Gender and Development: Concepts and Definitions*. Brighton: University of Sussex.

Sen, A. 2004. *Development as Freedom*. Oxford: Oxford University Press.

Tewe, B. 1978. "The Role of Women on Farm Labour Supply: Case study from Western Nigeria." Thesis. University of Ibadan.

Tietcheu, B. 2006. "Being Women and Men in Africa Today: Approaching Gender Roles in Changing African Societies." http://trendytraveller.com/sitesearch.php?rt=Bertrand%2c+Tietcheu+%282006%29.+%22Being+Women+and+Men+in+Africa+Today%3a+Approaching+Gender+Roles+in+Changing+African+Societies%22 (accessed November 19, 2014).

Tinker, I. (ed.). 1990. *Persistent Inequalities: Women and World Development*. Oxford: Oxford University Press.

Ukpore, B. A. 2009. "Sustainable Development in Nigeria: Roles of Women and Strategies for their Improvement." *Journal of Sustainable Development in Africa* 10 (4).

UN. 2005. *Progress Towards the Millennium Development Goals, 1990–2005*. Secretary-General's Millennium Develop-ment Goals Report. June 13, 2005.

World Bank. 2001. "Engendering Development: Through Gender Equality in Rights, Resources, and Voice." World Bank Policy Research Report No. 21776.

Yuval-Davis, N. 2001. "Nationalism, Feminism and Gender Relations." In *Understanding Nationalism*, edited by Hutchinson, J. & Guibernau, M., 120–141. Cambridge: Polity Press.

CHAPTER THREE

ETHNOGRAPHY OF CLIENTELISM AND DEVELOPMENT AMONG THE YORUBA OF SOUTHWESTERN NIGERIA

AYOKUNLE OLUMUYIWA OMOBOWALE

Introduction

The primary focus of this chapter is a presentation of the ethnography of clientelism and its impact on development in southwestern Nigeria. It presents clientelism as an integral aspect of the culture of the predominantly Yoruba southwestern Nigeria and shows its dynamism through the main historical epochs of pre-colonial, colonial and post-colonial Nigeria. The chapter thus traces the changes in the clientelistic structure as well as its practice in southwestern Nigeria from the pre-colonial to the post-colonial period.

Clientelism has often been described as a system or structure of exploitative relationships, through which the elite or dominant groups and individuals extract the support and loyalty of the downtrodden and powerless groups through gift giving and protection (Roniger 2004; Wantchekon 2003; Clark 2002). As much as clientelism may be exploitative, it is worth stating that it is a form of exchange relationship in which the so-called dominated may exert some assertive powers on the dominant in the process of negotiations and exchange (Omobowale & Olutayo 2010; Omobowale 2006). This chapter thus defines clientelism as a form of exchange relationship between dominant and dominated groups and individuals, in which one actor/party provides the valued resources of the other and vice-versa (Omobowale & Olutayo 2010; Omobowale 2006). The valued resources may be the patrons' protection, finance, offices, positions and other productive resources for the clients' loyalty (and/or votes) (Gërxhani & Schram 2009; Omobowale & Olutayo 2007; Lazar 2004; van de Walle 2003).

Clientelism, as a social issue, has attracted much attention in scholarly literature. In fact, a review of literature shows extensive discourses of clientelism across societies, irrespective of the ideological and modernity divides. Marantzidis & Mavrommatis's (1999) research in modern Greece reveals how socially excluded Gypsies in the town of Sofades utilize clientelistic structures with traditional and modernist tones to access resources. Harney (2012) discusses how Ukrainian migrants in Italy utilize clientelistic networks and structures to access economic resources and security, while Osipian (2012) studied "loyalty as rent" in Russian universities. Likewise, Charle (2008) discusses the contribution of clientelism to elite formation in the Western European countries of France, Great Britain and Germany in the nineteenth century. Keefer & Vlaicu (2008) posit that clientelism is a bane to development in newly democratizing Third World nations bedevilled by inept corruption. Concerning Argentina, Auyero, Lapegna & Poma (2009) conclude that clientelism is integral to collective action, and by extension social inclusion. This is evident in political and economic networks, patrons' influence, overt and covert support and individual actions and inactions within the clientelistic system. Lee's (2012) research in Taiwan traces how the Taiwanese professional baseball system is encapsulated in the global Taiwanese clientelistic system (see also Wang 2007). He concludes that political clientelism in Taiwan allows diverse interest groups to pursue and achieve their purposes, and that clientelism is unlikely to end in Taiwan soon. Likewise, Henry & Nassis (1999) discuss political clientelism and its impact on sports policy in Greece between 1981 and 1993. Henry & Nassis categorically claim that political parties utilized clientelistic relations in sports policy formulation and support for national governing bodies of sporting activities. Finally, Thies (2007) describes the political economy of state building in Africa as predatory, heavily clientelistic and rather antithetical to development.

Pre-colonial and Colonial Patronage Systems

Prior to colonialism, the indigenous system evolved forms of patronage system ensuring some sort of dyadic asymmetric relationship with the patron providing protection and resources to clients who gave loyalty in return. The relationship was guided by certain normative thoughts, as Omobowale (2008) has shown. Principally, the patron normatively serves as a mentor and model to the protected clients who are inclined to yield loyalty in return. Patronage normative thoughts are enshrined proverbs, idioms and songs prescribing the kind of relationships that should ensue between patrons and clients. Starting with *Iya ni wura, baba ni dingi* ["mother is gold, father is the mirror"], the Yoruba depict the preciousness of the mother as the "vehicle" of the journey to the world, who also catered and nursed an individual into adulthood. The father represents the model and/or standard to which an individual must aspire. This explains why the father is described as a mirror—the mirror reflects the socially acceptable standard to which an individual seeks to conform.

The Yoruba term for patron is *babaisale* ["father at the base"].[1] The *babaisale* is thus regarded as a father who provides "grounded" support, which when used here goes beyond material support. Along with material support, the *babaisale* must eschew good virtues that would present him as a role model (Omobowale 2008; 2007; 2006; Omobowale & Olutayo 2010; 2007). *Babaisale* also takes on the role of the elder (*agba*). The Yoruba attribute enormous social value to the elder, considered the repository of knowledge and in the best position to ensure social order through advice and truthfulness, irrespective of the situation at hand (Salawu 2011; Omobowale 2008; Dopamu & Alana 2004). Hence, a proverbial song says "*e w'ole f'agba, agba nii gba ni, l'ojo isoro, agba nii gba ni, l'ojo airije, agba nii gba ni*" ["bow to the elders, they rescue in the times of trouble, they rescue in the times of want, they provide"] (Omobowale 2008, 215). This song depicts the socially assumed capability of the elder to save irrespective of the circumstances, providing material, nonmaterial and moral assistance (Omobowale 2008). An elder who fails in social expectations becomes the ignoble elder [*agba langba*] (Omobowale, forthcoming). Hence, the social structure provides checks and balances and normative frames which guide the pre-colonial patronage system. Indeed, the patron formerly provided material support as well as the moral lead and was a role model, otherwise becoming ignoble. This was to change during the colonial period.

Southwestern Nigeria gradually came under British colonial rule with the annexation of Lagos in 1861 (Mann 1991). Subsequently, most of the Yorubaland gradually came under British rule after the signing of the Protectorate Treaty in 1893 (OyoProf 2/3 File No. C. 42). By 1910, most of the communities in Yorubaland had capitulated under British rule. British adoption of the Indirect Rule System significantly and phenomenally altered the patronage system that had subsisted until then. Whereas the precolonial administrative and patronage systems ensured a degree of accountability to client-followers, indirect rule demanded accountability principally to colonial officials. Hence, native administrations were equipped with political, economic and coercive powers with which

[1] In pre-colonial Ibadan, the term for patron was babaogun (father-at-war). It is a reflection of the warlike nature of Ibadan in pre-colonial times (Omobowale 2007; Watson 2005).

the populace was subdued to both native administrators and colonial officials at the pain of punitive sanctions. Native administrators as "renewed" patrons became autocratic, usurping land and perverting justice at will (Omobowale 2006). The draconic reorientation of native administrators was confirmed in a report prepared by the Colonial Chief Commissioner of the Western Provinces in a document dated September 19, 1942, which states:

> In Oyo we hear of the useful and democratic custom of sending an Oba who had lost popular confidence a parrot's egg as a hint to remove himself, while in Benin City and in Abeokuta we find the existence of Guilds and Township Councils which formed units for the expression of popular opinion … It is my opinion, shared I believe by many Western Provinces officials, that our administration, applying the Northern Emirate model to the Western Provinces, was responsible for giving the principal Obas an autocratic position which was foreign to Yoruba custom and constitution. (OyoProf 2/3 File No. 154A: 5–6)

The reference to the autocratic power of the Oba [king] alluded to above was a reflection of the reality of draconic powers held by all native administrators, who also doubled as patrons. They had the powers on purpose, ensuring that the locals (clients) were loyal to the colonial regime. Hence, in another report dated April 28, 1948, the Oyo Province Senior Resident submitted:

> Nobody would wish to lessen in any way the political power or the prestige of the senior chiefs, and it is most important that it should not be lessened … They are a valuable bulwark against disruptive tendencies …. (OyoProf 2/3 File No C59:22)

Native administrators remained powerful patrons as long as they were useful to the colonial administration; otherwise, they were expelled. However, as independence approached in the 1950s, colonial officials started a programme of democratization which would usher in the new independent Nigeria. The major criteria for participation in politics were no longer titles acquired through claim to some traditions, but literacy and economic buoyancy (Omobowale 2006; Lloyd 1951). Hence, the educated and economic elites emerged as the new patrons in 1951. On August 11, 1952, the Minister of Local Government in the Western Region, Chief Obafemi Awolowo, hinted what the role of native administrators would be in the new dispensation:

> … under the new dispensation, our traditional rulers will be called upon to play an entirely new role … It will be the duty of our traditional rulers to

> use their tremendous influence to promote harmony, decency and morality in the affairs of the several areas under their respective control …. (MLG (W) 3 File No 253 Vol. 1: 6)

This policy was implemented via an order issued by the Western Region Government on September 23, 1954 that stripped native administrators of the economic, coercive and political powers. The order placed under the authority of the newly created District Local Councils:

> … all sums of money, streets, open spaces, lands, buildings, waterworks, bridges, piers, ferries, vehicles, goods and all other property whatsoever … [and] the rights, interests, obligations and liabilities under contract or instrument of native authorities …. (IbaDivl/1 File No 2642 Vol. II: 217)

With control over economic, political and coercive powers, the educated and economic elite became the new patrons. Some particular individuals among these elite emerged as ground patrons controlling huge masses of clients to whom they provided protection and resources in exchange for loyalty. Prominent among them are Alhaji Adegoke Adelabu and Chief Lamidi Adedibu.

Adelabu and Adedibu

Alhaji Adegoke Adelabu and Chief Lamidi Adedibu were two prominent patrons who reigned about three decades apart from one another. Adelabu lasted from 1951 until his death in 1958, while Adedibu came to prominence as a patron in about 1990 until his death in 2008 (Omobowale & Olutayo 2007; Post & Jenkins 1973). Both were popular among clients and politicians as politicians of high pedigree and political brokers. Ibadan, the capital of the old Western Region, was their primary base. Both politicians also prioritized Ibadan interests and consciousness as the primary fulcrum of their political engagements. As the early administrative, political and economic capital of colonial and immediate post-colonial southwestern Nigeria, Ibadan was a major centre of political development and participation (Watson 2005; Falola 1984). In spite of the strategic position of Ibadan, its indigenous population was largely disadvantaged in South-Western Nigeria's political calculation due to the high illiteracy level among Ibadan indigenes (Omobowale 2006). Adelabu thus built on the political disadvantage of the Ibadan masses to build a clientele that aimed at advancing Ibadan interest.

Adelabu founded the Mabolaje Party in the early 1950s, making the Ibadan mass conscious of their domination by those he perceived as alien Ijebu, who were in control of the ruling Action Group (AG) led by Chief

Obafemi Awolowo (Omobowale & Olutayo 2007). By prominently espousing his Islamic faith and providing goods to needy clients, Adelabu endeared himself to the poor Ibadan Islamic majority as a benevolent patron. He aligned with the opposition National Council of Nigeria and Cameroon (NCNC). Adelabu was elected the chairman (mayor) of the Ibadan District Council. This position afforded him a veritable base to engage the ruling AG and provide goods for clients, seemingly illicitly, from the public treasury. His belligerent opposition to the ruling AG attracted the attention of the government to corrupt practices in the Ibadan District Council. A consequent commission of inquiry presided over by a colonial official appointed by the AG government found Adelabu culpable, and he was forced to resign from all political appointments in 1956. Notwithstanding this, Adelabu remained the main political patron in Ibadan until his demise in a ghastly motor accident in 1958. It is noteworthy that close to six decades after his death, Adelabu's legacy is still annually celebrated by the Ibadan political class and intelligentsia. This attests to the popularity and acceptance of Adelabu's political relevance in the political consciousness and "liberation" of the Ibadan public from the rule of supposed aliens.

It took another three decades for an Ibadan patron with the charisma of Adelabu to emerge. At the age of 27, the young Lamidi Adedibu gradually built his political career as from 1951, pitching his political allegiance with Chief Obafemi Awolowo, who was at that time Adelabu's arch political opponent (Adedibu 1997; Akinyemi & Laoye 1997a; 1997b). During the forty years of military rule in Nigeria, Adedidu was largely in the "shadows, " though he was a government contractor. His political pedigree and sagacity became obvious during Nigeria's preparation for its Third Republic. Adedibu gradually built his clientelistic base using the wealth gained through government patronage (Omobowale & Olutayo 2007; Omobowale 2006). Hence, after the 1991 elections, Adedibu's candidates, Chief Kolapo Ishola and Alhaji Busari Raji, won the governorship and party chairmanship respectively under the Social Democratic Party (SDP). Again, Chief M. K. O. Abiola, Adedibu's preferred candidate for the SDP prudential ticket, won the party's primaries in 1993. These elections were organized under a diarchical system orchestrated by General Babangida, who remained the military president. Adedibu was able to establish himself as a political patron and broker because he had mastered the art of providing for people's basic needs.

Aside from providing daily meals for the large throng of the underprivileged who visited his mansion at Molete, Ibadan, Adedibu also had a huge number of poor children under his sponsorship while providing economic empowerment for those who needed it. Besides this, Adedibu provided the infrastructural needs of rural communities where he had networks and assumed the personality of one who meet the development needs where the government defaults on them.

Adedibu's reign in the 1990s was, however, short lived. He made a miscalculation in supporting General Abacha after the military leader annulled the June 12, 1993 presidential election which Chief Abiola was poised to win (Ukiwo 2003). Consequently, Adedibu lost the respect of the larger majority of the Yoruba political class and intelligentsia. The eventual campaign of calumny against Adedibu demonized him and presented him as a military apologist. During the subsequent riots, Adedibu's properties were attacked and damaged by members of the under-privileged class comprising his clients. At this stage, Yoruba consciousness and self-determination outweighed whatever good Adedibu had to offer. Adedibu was further isolated following General Abacha's sudden demise on June 8, 1998 (Omobowale & Olutayo 2007). This opened the doors for the democratization process and Nigeria thus returned to civil rule on May 29, 1999. Adedibu was sidelined in the Alliance for Democracy (AD), which won elections in southwestern Nigeria. His resources were largely drained, while it was reported that Adedibu resorted to snail farming since neither contract nor regular financial patronage were forthcoming from the government treasury (Omobowale & Olutayo 2007). During this period, Adedibu aligned with the All Nigeria's Peoples Party (ANPP).

As the 2003 general election approached, Chief Adedibu joined the ruling People's Democratic Party (PDP). With a mandate from President Olusegun Obasanjo to secure southwestern Nigeria for the PDP, Adedibu enjoyed economic, political and coercive resources from them. The AD was successfully ousted from power while Chief Ladoja of the PDP was installed as governor after an election that was fraught with irregularities. On the one hand, an astute and shrewd businessman, Ladoja viewed whatever assistance and/or brokerage Adedibu provided as a business deal, which terminated with his successful election as governor (Omobowale & Olutayo 2007). On the other, Adedibu expected continual returns from the state treasury. Ladoja's refusal to budge pitched him against Adedibu. As governor, Ladoja was largely protected until he voiced his opposition to President Obasanjo's third term bid. Again, Adedibu became a ready tool to ensure the removal of Ladoja. With Obasanjo's support, federal economic and coercive resources were released to Adedibu. Adedibu secured the support of the majority of the members of the Oyo State House of Assembly in exchange for material gifts, such as upmarket Toyota cars. Governor Ladoja was thus impeached on January 12 2006 and replaced by his deputy, Chief Alao Akala, an Adedibu loyalist and apologist. Ladoja was out of power until he was reinstated by the Supreme Court in November 2006. Already out of favour, he was voted out of power in the 2007 general elections, while Alao Akala was elected as the governor. Akala ensured the continuous patronage of Adedibu and access to state resources as the undisputed patron of Ibadan until his sudden death at the age of 84 in Ibadan while processing papers to travel out of the country. Since his demise another patron of his clout is yet to emerge in southwestern Nigeria. However, Chief Bola Tinubu, the acclaimed leader of progressive politics in the region, is assuming the status of a prime patron and his profile deserves scholarly scrutiny in the nearest future.

Democratization and Contemporary Clientelism

Following the first bloody military coup of January 15, 1966, where the Prime Minister Alhaji Tafawa Balewa and other political leaders were killed, Nigeria remained under military rule for about four decades, except during a short period between 1979 and 1983 when civilians ruled in the second republic (Lewis 1994; Oyediran & Agbaje 1991). The four-decade rule of the military entailed a period of gross abuse of power and fundamental human rights, gross corruption, official ineptitude, an abysmal economic downturn and paralysation of the Nigerian state in international politics (Falola & Heaton 2008; Olutokun 2004). Pro-democracy groups constantly advocated for a return to civil rule and enlightened the populace to the benefits of democracy. The then military president General Babangida initially rolled out an elaborate plan aimed at a return to civil rule by the year 1992. He subsequently postponed it to 1993, claiming that the political class was ill-prepared.

In 1993, Babangida annulled the June 12 presidential election which Chief M. K. O. Abiola was posed to win (Omobowale & Olutayo 2007). The annulment resulted in widespread demonstrations, eventually leading to Babangida's resignation from office. For the first time, Nigerians who had readily and joyfully welcomed the military in an earlier *coup d'état*, were up in arms against the military government, having been educated. Their thirst and protest for democracy hunted General Abacha's regime until his demise on June 8, 1998 (Egwaikhide & Isumonah 2001). The successive government of General Abacha quickly put in place a nine-month return to a civil rule programme, which culminated in Nigeria's return to democratic rule on May 29, 1999. The return to democratic rule has also evolved a new dimension of domesticated clientelism built in tune with the group/associational culture of the indigenous population.

Following the economic downturn of the 1980s, many Nigerians who fell below the poverty line became involved in associational groupings to find succour. The associational groupings were in the form of cooperative associations (e.g. *ajo* or *esusu*), friendship groups, neighbourhood associations and working-class groups (Omobowale 2011). These groups provided (and still provide) welfare and social security where the government would not, existing with some support from the elite class whose members serve as patrons (Omobowale 2006). Concisely, associational groups appoint willing economic and political elites as patrons, who provide support for associational groups in return for the loyalty of group members (Omobowale 2010; 2006). The patron "figure" looms large as a wealthy philanthropist who gives to the poor. The clients do not necessarily have to access the patron individually, as their needs and desires are processed through the group structure. In this way, group norms, values, ethics and social expectations keep each client in line, conforming with group expectations, including submission and loyalty to the patron. Gaining clients' support is thus simplified for the patron. Once the patron secures the support of the leadership of an association, it is very likely that every other member will follow suite. Otherwise, the dissenting member may be sanctioned with suspension, expulsion or denial of group benefits.

Associational group-based clientship is thus a local dimension to clientelism, which has allowed patrons to have much easier access to clients. Once a patron gains the support of a group, they gain the support of every member who would also consciously and unconsciously secure friends and family loyalty to the patron by relaying the apparent good deeds of the patron, symbolized by the goods they have given to clients. As group membership swells, the patron's clientelistic base also increases. The patron thus gains the support of the political class either as a broker or as a patron politician whose client base would ensure victory at the polls for the party or politician that the patron supports (Omobowale 2010). Of course, the patron transfers client loyalty to politicians and/or parties in exchange for access to economic resources, with which the clientship base is continually fuelled and supported.

Conclusion

This chapter has examined the context of clientelism among the Yoruba of southwestern Nigeria, showing that it is embedded in indigenous value and modified in line with subsisting local political and development realities. Poor, disempowered and disadvantaged in the contemporary liberal democracy of Nigeria, the poor working-class people whose membership forms the crust of the clientele depend on benevolent patrons sourced from the privileged economic and political classes to access development and survival needs. Such patrons are thus seen as noble fathers or elders as long as goods continue to flow in.

References

Adedibu, L. A. 1997. *What I Saw on the Politics and Governance of Ibadan and the Issue of June 12, 1993*. Ibadan: HUA Nigeria Ltd.

Akinyemi, A. & Laoye, S. 1997a. "Lamidi Aribiyi Adedibu: Reminiscence of 47 Years of Political Activism 1." *Daily Monitor*. October 23, 1997. 7.

—. 1997b. "Lamidi Aribiyi Adedibu: Reminiscence of 47 Years of Political Activism 11." *Daily Monitor*, October 24, 1997. 8.

Auyero, J., Lapegna, P. & Poma, F. P. 2009. "Patronage Politics and Contentious Collective Action: A Recursive Relationship." *Latin American Politics and Society* 51 (3): 1–31.

Charle, C. 2008. "Elite Formation in Late Nineteenth Century: France Compared to Britain and Germany." *Historical Social Research/ Historische Sozialforschung* 33 (2): 249–261.

Clark, T. N. 2002. "The Presidency and the New Political Culture." *American Behavioral Scientist* 46 (4): 535–552.

Dopamu, P. A. 2004. "System of Discipline." In *Understanding Yoruba Life and Culture*, edited by Lawal, N. S., Sadiku, M. N. O. & Dopamu, P. A., 175–185. Trenton: Africa World Press, Inc.

Dopamu, P. A. & Alana, E. O. 2004. "Ethical Systems." In *Understanding Yoruba Life and Culture*, edited by Lawal, N. S., Sadiku, M. N. O. & Dopamu, P. A., 155–173. Trenton: Africa World Press, Inc.

Egwaikhide, F. O. & Isumonah, V. A. 2001. "Nigeria Paralysed: Socio-political Life under General Sani Abacha." *Africa Development* 26 (3–4): 219–241.

Falola, T. & Heaton, M. M. 2008. *A History of Nigeria*. Cambridge: Cambridge University Press.

Falola, T. 1984. *The Political Economy of a Pre-Colonial African State: Ibadan, 1830–1900*. Ife: University of Ife Press.

Gërxhani, K. & Schram, A. 2009. "Clientelism and Polarized Voting: Empirical Evidence." *Public Choice* 141 (3–4): 305–317.

Harney, N. D. 2012. "Migrant Strategies, Informal Economies and Ontological Security: Ukrainian in Naples, Italy." *International Journal of Sociology and Social Policy* 32 (1–2): 4–16.

Henry, I. P. & Nassis, P. 1999. "Political Clientelism and Sports Policy in Greece." *International Review for the Sociology of Sports* 34 (1): 43–58.

IbaDiv l/l. File No 2642 Vol II. Local government law 1952, No. 1 of 1953. Ibadan: National Archives.

Keefer, P. & Vlaicu, R. 2008. "Democracy, Credibility, and Clientelism." *Journal of Law, Economics & Organization* 24 (2): 371–406.

Lazar, S. 2004. "Personalist Politics, Clientelism and Citizenship: Local Elections in El Alto, Bolivia." *Bulletin of Latin American Research* 23 (2): 228–243.

Lee, P. 2012. "Political Clientelism and Professional Baseball in Taiwan: The Merger between the two Leagues in 2003." *International Review for the Sociology of Sports* 47 (4): 475–491.

Lewis, P. M. 1994. "Endgame in Nigeria? The Politics of a Failed Democratic Transition." *African Affairs* 93 (372): 323–340.

Lloyd, P. C. 1951. *Some Comments on the Elections in Nigeria. The Western Region Election under the Macpherson Constitution*. MLG (W) 1. File No. 24870. Ibadan: National Archives.

Mann, K. 1991. "Women, Landed Property, and the Accumulation of wealth in Early Colonial Lagos." *Signs* 16 (4): 682–706.

Marantzidis, N. & Mavrommatis, G. 1999. "Political Clientelism and Social Exclusion: The Case of Gyspies in the Greek Town of Sofades." *International Sociology* 14 (4): 443–456.

MLG (W) 3. File No 253 Vol 1. *Local Government in the Western Provinces*. Ibadan: National Archives.

Olutokun, A. 2004. *Repressive State and resurgent Media under Nigeria's Military Dictatorship, 1988–1998*. Nordiaka Afrikainstitutet Research Report No. 126. Upsalla: Nordiaka Afrikainstitutet.

Omobowale, A. O. & Olutayo, A. O. 2007. "Chief Lamidi Adedibu and Patronage Politics in Nigeria." *Journal of Modern African Studies* 45 (3): 425–446.

Omobowale, A. O. 2006. *Political Clientelism and Rural Development in Selected Communities in Ibadan, Nigeria*. Thesis. University of Ibadan, Ibadan, Nigeria.

—. 2007. "Babaogun Exchange Relations and Grassroots Politics in Ibadan, Nigeria." *International Journal of Social and Management Sciences* 1 (2): 143–163.
—. 2008. “Clientelism and Social Structure: An Analysis of Patronage in Yoruba Social Thought.” *Afrika Spectrum* 43 (2): 203–224.
—. 2011. “Social Capital and Ajo System among Working Class Traders in Ibadan, Nigeria.” *Working USA: The Journal of Labor and Society* 14 (3): 333–346
—. (forthcoming) “Atari Ajanaku: An Ethnographic Textual Analysis of Ageing and the Elder’s Character among the Yoruba of South-Western Nigeria.” *Canadian Journal of Sociology*.
Omobowale, A. O. & Olutayo, A. O. 2010. “Political Clientelism and Rural Development in South-Western Nigeria.” *Africa* 80 (3): 453–472.
Osipian, A. L. 2012. “Loyalty as Rent: Corruption and Politicization of Russian Universities.” *International Journal of Sociology and Social Policy* 32 (3–4): 153–167.
Oyediran, O. & Agbaje, A. 1991. "Two-partyism and Democratic Transition in Nigeria." *Journal of Modern African Studies* 29 (92): 213–235.
OyoProf 2/3 File No. C. 42 *Ibadan-Oyo: Relations Between* Ibadan: National Archives.
OyoProf 2/3. File No 154A. *Future Political Development of Nigeria 1940–1948.* Ibadan: National Archives.
OyoProf 2/3. File No C59. Native Administration Policy Local Government Legislation. Ibadan: National Archives.
Post, K. W. J. & Jenkins, G. D. 1973. *The Price of Liberty: Personality and Politics in Colonial Nigeria*. Cambridge: Cambridge University Press.
Roniger, L. 2004. "Political Clientelism, Democracy, and Market Economy." *Comparative Politics* 36 (3): 353–357.
Salawu, A. 2011. “The Paradigm of Ethical Development for Civilized Leadership in Africa.” *Leadership* 8 (1): 17–27.
Thies, C. G. 2007. “The Political Economy of State Building in Sub-Saharan Africa.” *The Journal of Politics* 69 (3): 716–731.
Ukiwo, U. 2003. "Politics, Ethno-Religious Conflicts and Democratic Consolidation in Nigeria." *The Journal of Modern African Studies* 41 (1): 115–138.
van de Walle, N. 2003. "Presidentialism and Clientelism in Africa's Emerging Party Systems." *The Journal of Modern African Studies* 41 (2): 297–321.

Wang, C. 2007. "Dilemmas of Electoral Clientelism: Taiwan, 1993." *International Political Science Review* 28 (2): 225–245.
Wantchekon, L. 2003. "Clientelism and Voting Behavior: Evidence from a Field Experiment in Benin." *World Politics* 55 (3): 399–422.
Watson, R. 2005. *Civil Disorder is the Disease of Ibadan: Ija Igboro Larun Ibadan*. Athens: Ohio University Press.

CHAPTER FOUR

INFORMATION TECHNOLOGY AND EMERGING ISSUES IN VIRTUAL LEARNING IN NIGERIA

BUSARI DAUDA

Introduction

"Necessity is the mother of invention." This well-known maxim captures the dynamics of social change, social needs and innovations that have characterized human civilization. The twenty-first century confronts its citizenship with new choices, opportunities and challenges due to the ubiquitous presence of technology in all spheres of life, such as business and administration, government and education. Specifically, innovations have always been a result of the human's continuous attempt to understand itself and its environment, as well as meeting all attendant challenges. Thus, the human devises a plan and appropriate strategy to meet such challenges. The history of human civilization is full of instances of the fruits of such intellectual and technical skills, including but not limited to catching fish with bare hands, starting a fire with stones, fashioning a spear, bow and an arrow, the hoe, the abacus, the Igloo, the umbrella, gunpowder, the bullet, dynamite, pencil, pen, paper, printing, the typewriter, the camera, electricity, trains, aeroplanes, motor cars, television, the computer, the telephone, and the mobile phone. Thus, profound shifts in the knowledge industry must be viewed through thoughts on the new possibilities that new technologies involve.

The advent of information technology and the digital revolution has affected every aspect of existence in the knowledge-based information age. There has been a rapid shift from voice to data and analogue to digital technologies, as well as the increasing role of wireless technology that creates greater mobility and flexibility for users. Information technology may have also shaped the future of education globally, presenting a departure from the traditional mode of delivery, but nonetheless providing the assurance of mass literacy and a quality certificate recognized worldwide. The permeating presence of internet networks in all scopes of life allows unlimited access to information and the removal of time and space barriers in learning.

Traditional teaching and learning paradigms have been shaken by the impact of the integration of information and communication technologies (IT from now on) into educational practices. Teachers and students are confronted by challenges ranging from the acquisition of skills and literacy in the usage of IT to the delivery of the necessary tools, leading students to become knowledge creators and users. Thus, they become deeply immersed in the society of knowledge—a society based on the critical, rational and reflexive use of global and distributed information (Gisbert 2003, 252), in which the most outstanding communication means are virtual networks. One of the greatest challenges on our way through the twenty-first century is enabling teachers and students to achieve competency and mastery in the use of technology instead of letting them be enslaved by it.

The widespread use of IT in all areas has a direct effect upon the way in which the world is perceived. The permeating presence of virtual networks in all scopes of life allows unlimited access to information and a flexibility of time and space barriers. IT has shaken the traditional teaching and learning approaches and poses new challenges to the educational community, which emerge together with new teaching and learning environments and instructional modalities, mainly virtual. A profound integration of new technologies into education as a central means to teaching and learning processes will inevitably require changes in teachers' attitudes and teaching paradigms. Such changes will oblige them to adapt to new methodological approaches, educational concepts and management aspects, all of which will have to be set in technology-rich environments. Thus, open and flexible teaching and learning processes, interactive and bi-directional communication systems, together with the emergence of alternative spaces aimed at promoting communication, all generate new needs and expectations for educators. Using IT in education favours interaction and collaboration among participants, and the world wide web fosters new means of communicating and interacting both in real and asynchronous time, providing authentic material and resources that can be easily exploited.

Open Distance Learning and Virtual Universities

One of the most pragmatic approaches to managing the insatiable demand for information, knowledge and skills is the open distance learning education platform. Several world-class universities like Queens University, the University of Wisconsin and the University of London have been providing distance education for some time. Others involved in the provision of distance learning education include Penn State University, the University of British Columbia and Saskatchewan University in Canada. The University of South Africa (UNISA), with about 124, 000 students spread across the length and breadth of the world, has been operating a dual- or mixed-mode system delivering both traditional on-campus and distance-education modes. As Bates (2001, 20) states:

> For such institutions (UNISA), this outreach or extramural strategy was a critical extension to the original mandate of the institutions; it enabled them in to reach out to farmers, working professionals and those who cannot afford to move to a campus away from their homes or jobs.

A later development was the single-mode wall-less university whose mandate is to deliver only distance education, as in the dual-mode institutions such as the British Open University (OU), the Spanish University National de education a distance (UNED), the Chinese University, the Korean National Open University, the Indira Ghandi National Open University (IGNOU) with 600, 000 students, and the National Open University of Nigeria (NOUN) with about 30, 000 pioneer students enrolled.

In the educational history of Nigeria, the University of London, the University of Ibadan, the University of Lagos (all mixed-mode institutions) and the British Open University have had the most impact on a good number of aspiring Nigerians in the 1940s, 1950s and 1960s, respectively.

The Open University in the UK, for example, proved to be a model success story in democratizing knowledge and education in a conservative, socially stratified environment. The reform of the school system witnessed the introduction of the comprehensive General Certificate of Secondary Education (GCSE), designed to erase the profound effects of the grammar school culture on British society. But in the early attempts at providing able and willing learners living and or working at considerable distances from the centre, educational institutions relied on two basic modes of knowledge delivery: the postal system and radio communication, with or without occasional face-to-face interaction between learners and teaching staff.

The advent of colour television added great audio-visual authenticity to teaching and learning. It should be recalled that the distance learning mode proved its worth among very many West African students in the early 1940s who could not afford to travel to the UK for further studies after their Cambridge School Certificate. Such students would register as external candidates for the L.LB (Inter.) and B.Sc (Inter.) degrees of the University of London. Private students also took correspondence tuition courses from Wolsey Hall, Oxford, and the University of London for O and A level examinations. In Nigeria there were several local opportunities and providers. For example, the University of Ibadan ran a popular extramural studies outfit of the Department of Adult Education, as did the Rapid Results Correspondence College that offered postal tuition O and A levels in the 1960s and 1970s. The National Teachers Institute (NTI) Kaduna, was set up in the 1970s to enhance the qualification of elementary school teachers through correspondence and face-to-face interaction, especially since 1988 as the NCE Certificate was to become the minimum qualification for teaching in primary schools in Nigeria. The Institute soon became the largest educational outfit in West Africa, with more than 85% of Grade II teachers upgraded to the minimum level of NCE.

In the early 1970s, the University of Lagos created the first multi-site study centres where postal tuition was delivered and learners would meet study centre coordinators and tutors for face-to-face interaction. In the case of education students, supervised teaching practice was carried out in designated collaborating secondary schools located around the respective study centres. Initially called the Correspondence and Open Studies Unit (COSU), the Unit became the Correspondence and Open Studies Institute (COSIT) in the 1980s as a result of its organization, and is now the Distance Learning Institute (DLI).

The latest initiative in Nigeria is the National Open University of Nigeria (NOUN) project, which has admitted its first students. On September 27, 2000, the National Workshop on Distance Education was held, and the Nigerian government and other major Stakeholders articulated the mission of NOUN. In the words of the then Minister of Education, Professor Babalola Borishade (2002, 3), the tasks that face the education sector are herculean and capital intensive:

> Against the background of decaying infrastructure, low morale of teachers, a very widening and ever-increasing enrolment figure at all levels especially at the primary level, the need to improve the content of education, and ensure continued relevance and maintenance of quality, is the urgent need to balance access with relevance and improved quality. A potent tool for achieving this especially in a depressed economy like ours is that which provides optimal advantage at minimal cost … [and] increases and widens access without compromising quality and content.

Beyond this national initiative there is the Commonwealth of Learning (COL), founded in 1987 by the Commonwealth Heads of Government (CHG) and mandated to:

> promote the use of distance and open learning in the Commonwealth: to help them exploit open, distance and technology-mediated learning … recognizing that an investment in education and training is an investment in people, a nation's most important asset; that education is the only means to empower their people to shape their own destiny, respond to social, economic and personal challenges of the global village, and contribute to their countries' development. (Dhanarahan 2000, 9–13)

Furthermore, COL has been carrying out its mandate in collaboration with national education systems in countries of the Commonwealth, especially by helping to create or enhance the capacities of open universities in India, Pakistan, Bangladesh, Sri Lanka, Tanzania, Zimbabwe and now Nigeria with the National Teachers Institute and the National Open University. Specific actions of COL in member-countries cover:

> staff development, training, policy formulation, collaborative materials development, technology applications, knowledge sharing and the implementation of student support systems in non-formal education, basic and post-basic education, teacher training, continuing technical and professional education, skills for development or technical/vocational education, higher education. (10)

However, Nigeria's readiness to integrate new technologies in distance education has been described by Jegede (2000, 14–29) as:

> still very rudimentary with a heavy reliance on print materials. There is hardly anything that can be regarded as educational broadcasting and no attempt is being made to take advantage of the emerging and new information communication technologies ….

There are over 20 Internet Service Providers (ISPs) that focus mainly on the elite's use of email and internet services for personal and business activities. Further, educational uses have not been thought of at national or private sector levels. Nevertheless, with the beginning of academic activities in early 2004, the situation was expected to be encouraging in relation to 2000, especially with the institutional partnership provided by the National Information Technology Development Agency (NITDA). Furthermore, the National IT Policy

Document (Human Resources Development) highlights three key strategies of crucial importance to the sustainability of NOUN:

(1) Making the use of IT mandatory at all levels of educational institutions through adequate provision for tools and resources.
(2) Developing relevant IT curricula for the primary, secondary and tertiary institutions (including) the proposed digital virtual library scheme and related educational scheme. A virtual university system shall be established.
(3) Establishing facilities for electronic distance learning networks and ensuring effective internet connectivity, which will provide opportunities for educationally disadvantaged areas to educationally leapfrog into the modern era.

Jegede's (2000, 14–29) statements of the advantages of distance education for the Nigerian environment are noteworthy. Distance education:

(1) Delivers instruction independent of time, location and space.
(2) Is used for a variety of learning situations, i.e. full-time, part-time, graduate and undergraduate and continuing education.
(3) Accommodates diverse learning styles.
(4) Provides just-in-time training and courses at schools or work places.
(5) Provides access to remote and usually inaccessible under-represented groups such as women, rural and remote dwellers.
(6) Has effectiveness in coping with mass education.
(7) Sources revenues for institutions.
(8) Provides distance and open education.
(9) Lessens the financial pressure on students of full-time conventional universities or tertiary institutions.
(10) Ensures availability and affordability of emerging information technologies for efficient and effective delivery of instruction.
(11) Alleviates constraints on admission capacity of educational institutions.
(12) Promotes lifelong and life-wide education.

In order to achieve the intended results highlighted above, it is assumed that the real transformation would be brought about through the use of information and communication technologies or e-learning techniques in conjunction with the more traditional or low technology inputs (i.e. books, references, modules, blackboards etc.). The first quarter of the twenty-first century will witness even more amazing e-based learning delivery systems that higher education institutions aspiring to excellence in knowledge generation and dissemination through teaching, research and development, and service to the local and global communities, cannot possibly ignore.

But the nagging question is how higher education can, while logging on to the global village, humanize globalization without being unnecessarily drawn into the earlier discussed issues of technologies of freedom or technologies of domination? For, as the World Conference on Higher Education (ICHE 1998) rightly observed (Fact sheet 3):

> The borders between countries have become more and more open to intellectual exchanges, to solidarity networks, to trade and to the search for common solutions, as well as to organized crime, pollution, poverty and disease … In our enthusiasm over the explosion of communications, however, we often tend to overlook the dramatic consequences that this new global economy can have at the local level, particularly where it heightens existing inequities and gives rise to new ones that sovereign states too often seem incapable of overcoming. Civil society is now being called upon to take a more active role in international relations, which are also undergoing a profound change. In this connection, higher education, which has long had international and universal dimensions and aspirations, must now play an important role in giving a human face to globalization.

Guidelines adopted include the following major shifts, from mere routines of international cooperation to the internationalization of higher education through greater individual mobility of manpower, concrete UNESCO-driven support of higher education in the developing world, and the efficient and effective coordination of international cooperation.

In order to achieve this significant shift, higher education institutions will have to fulfil the following new obligations:

- establish comparable quality standards that are recognized internationally.
- promote intellectual and scientific cooperation by encouraging multilingualism and sponsoring teacher and student exchange programmes.
- create interactive networks, mobility for teachers and students and international research projects as quality indicators for higher education, and offer international learning possibilities linked to the world of work.

This envisaged shift and cluster of obligations would continue to echo the first major intervention by UNESCO to address the issues and anxieties of stakeholders, who include national governments, the private sector, student unions, intergovernmental organizations, and the World Trade Organization.

The occasion was the first Global Forum on International Quality Assurance, Accreditation and Recognition of Qualifications in Higher Education held in Paris on October 17–18, 2002. The bone of contention among participants was the need for higher education in the spirit of the UN charter. In other words, higher education, being a public good, should not be left to the vagaries of commercialization and market forces. The following excerpt from the UNESCO 2002 Report of Thematic Workshop 1 summarizes this division of interests:

> Globalization in higher education is associated with a substantial growth of international trade in global markets of higher education. This growth is driven by political, economic and technological factors and there is no reason to expect in the near future a slow down of the process. Nor is there any chance of formulating a definitive value judgment (good vs bad) on the development of international trade in higher education. On the one hand there are those who strongly opposed the treatment of higher education as a commodity or tradable service, since this would negatively affect the long standing academic values while on the other hand are those who consider that trade is already there in higher education that GATs (General Agreement on Trade in Services) exists and certain countries have already made their commitment and that it also brings about specific benefits and opportunities. Some others would also consider that the development and implications of trade and markets in higher education will depend largely on national context and policy options. (2002, 163)

The questions that this scenario raises are: To what extent are conventional universities meeting these needs and expectations using the full potential of new technologies? How are they transforming or re-engineering themselves for a very competitive learning- and knowledge-based global society and market? More importantly, do national and private local tertiary institutions meet the vast range of needs of the growing army of potential beneficiaries outside the formal sectors?

The answers lie in the basic educational institutional organization, dedicated or open-ended orientation, entrepreneurship, competitiveness, risk absorbing capacities, funding, diversification, and flexibility of academic, research and innovative service strategies on the local and international scenes. In addition are the students' or learners' capabilities to fit into the world of employment and job creation, and the degree of democratization, social accountability and technology transfer, to mention only the most decisive for higher education institutions, especially in the developing nations. As the 1996 Sao Paulo Congress of University Administrators emphasized: "It will profoundly modify mass education. But ... the challenge is not so much in technology, but in the way universities are presently organized."

Distance learning should be considered a leveller for change in both the supply and demand of education training and research, such that whether one is dealing with borderless higher education, e-leaning, distance learning or the gains or pains derivable by all stakeholders, it will be determined by the level of vision, political will and the regulatory mechanism in place to ensure not only quality education, but also to minimize the potential dangers of globalization while maximizing the extendibility and international status and competitiveness of higher education.

The Virtual University

The differences between Conventional Universities (CUs) and Virtual Universities (VUs) can be summarized as follows. If the CUs have walls and thrive on in-house, institution-centred culture, the VUs have no walls and are open, flexible, externalized, masses-centred, multi-media based, innovative, digitalized clearing houses, in tandem with virtual or digitalized libraries, the internet, CD-ROMs, DVDs, online courses and related certifications. In short, they are mediated by e-learning technologies and are an inescapable reality. As such, what prospects and promise do the virtual support systems hold? Will the virtual university vision become a reality in a developing country such as Nigeria? This innovation is happening in a few developed countries and in most cases is a transnational initiative.

In Europe, one key strategy is the renewal of distance learning programmes through the internet. Consequently, the number of universities in Europe making extensive use of the internet is increasing, and more and more are easily entering into distance learning programmes. Furthermore, some European and American universities are embarking on ambitious programmes to incorporate new technologies in all aspects of their teaching and learning. A third strategy is cost effectiveness, especially the reduction of production costs, and this is of considerable interest to developing countries. For example, according to Murray Turnoff (1999) at the New Jersey Institute of Technology, setting up a virtual programme for 2, 000 students costs $1, 000.

The concepts of the virtual, flexible, e-university are at the project planning or experimentation stages in advanced countries such as the United States and those of the European Union (EU). In the case of the flexible university in the European Union, for example, there are eight ongoing projects: CANDLE, CUBER, LEDA, OR-WORLD, PEARL, UNIVERSAL, VOEU7 and WINDS7. Each has its own website and project completion dates between 2002–2004 (a few of these initiatives will be discussed later in this section) (EU 2001).

With higher education now part of the global market and knowledge transfer increasingly seen as the key driver of wealth creation, universities have to reinvent and or realign themselves. For example, in order to compete favourably in an increasingly commercial and international market, education institutions are collaborating in developing competitive curricula. They also face a major new challenge as knowledge providers for life-long learning. Consequently, higher institutions need more open technologies that meet user needs in terms of range, access and costs to make learning effective and cost-efficient. This will enable institutions to collaborate in producing, managing and delivering the curricula and skills required by future students.

In the European vision, for example, tomorrow's universities for lifelong learning will be very different from those of today, as they are increasingly serving a much wider client base. Curricula will be produced collaboratively from distributed educational resources, and flexibly managed and delivered to learners worldwide. The boundaries between academic education and vocational training will become increasingly blurred as learners access personalized and flexible learning services, available as and when they want them, as part of a continuum of lifelong learning. Students will no longer be confined to one curriculum, but will be able to build their own based on courses from multiple institutions.

The Learning Citizen and Virtual Institutions

Learning today is no longer confined to institutions such as schools, universities, companies or training centres. New technologies and tools offer learners greater flexibility, easier access to information and the opportunity to match learning to their specific needs, circumstances and learning profiles. The home is increasingly important in the learning environment for many citizens, including disadvantaged groups such as the unemployed or people with special needs, and those in remote and isolated locations. The challenge is to bring together educators and service providers to use the available technology and take on a new supportive, motivating and affordable way of learning that can benefit many groups in society.

Amongst others, the DOMITEL project has been delivering a range of courses directly to the home, thus allowing learners to interact with the tutor via a two-way video link. A series of prototypes was developed utilizing technologies such as cable television and ISDN. In Ireland, a 30-hour course was delivered live by cable from a purpose-built interactive classroom to sixty learners based in learning centres and their homes. In Portugal, a prototype interactive learning service delivered an IT course over cable TV, and in the Netherlands a distance-learning solution was developed for a speech therapy course for people with hearing implants.

The role of new IT-based approaches in enhancing and facilitating life-long learning for individuals is being addressed under the learning citizen action line. The research addresses intelligent, user-friendly solutions with the innovative integration of technologies. Projects address research into how people define their learning goals and manage the learning processes, while solutions are supportive and motivating. A holistic and multi-disciplinary approach is emphasized including a comprehensive evaluation of the appropriateness of the used technology and benefits for the user. When fully implemented, the work is expected to result in scalable solutions and European-level best practice guidelines and recommendations.

Among the projects looking at the learning citizen, there is EDCOMNET, which is developing a virtual learning community web portal for adult citizens. FELLOWS will develop and validate new distance-learning services for user groups who need access to education and training outside formal education settings. The main objective of HERO is to promote the rehabilitation of offenders, while HOPE aims to improve the learning process of socially excluded individuals such as young prisoners. NEMO will improve the lifelong learning process for deaf, mentally disordered and elderly people. METACAMPUS aims at fulfilling the life-long learning needs of European citizens by providing flexible access to services for personal development (European Union 2001).

Following on from this overview of current projects related to virtual universities lifelong learning, what are the implications for the universities? At the 1999 Sao Paulo Conference of University Administrators, it was stated that universities must: (1) collectively organize the exploitation of knowledge production, consortia of producers and consortia of consumers, and (2) devise a common strategy to address the problem of their relationships with telecommunication operators and IT service providers. This would reach an agreement on new learning processes, digitalizing knowledge production, common multimedia projects, ODL and lifelong learning projects. More importantly for developing countries, the level of development of basic telecommunication infrastructure and energy generation and supply is crucial. It simply means that no country can hope to join the virtual distance revolution if its telecommunications and electricity infrastructures are primitive or unreliable, or if universities and these vital service sectors do not share a common vision and fail to network as major partners in qualitative and mass education delivery.

Perspectives on Africa and Nigeria

So far in this chapter, the role of higher education institutions, especially universities, has been discussed in relation to the expected transformations in organization, teaching, learning, research and service to the global community. Also, conventional and ODL systems have been focused on with respect to the impact that ITs should make, considering various ongoing virtual learning framework projects, such as the virtual university, e-university and flexible university. However, whether or not ITs will reduce the gap in progress or development between the advanced and developing economies of the world or disparities among developing nations remains a central issue. Could universities in the south hope to leapfrog and join the IT revolution for educational advancement when social, political, economic and especially telecommunications and energy infrastructures remain primitive and unreliable? Will African ODL providers move beyond print, radio and residential talk and chalk modes of education and training in the next twenty-five years?

Nigeria has now taken up the challenge of re-establishing the National Open University of Nigeria, first opened in 1983 and suspended due to an inefficient postal service, an inadequate supply of qualified manpower to run the study centres, the poor reception of both visual and audio on certain programme frequencies, a very high cost of infrastructure, uncertain learner profiles, and fears of massive examination malpractices (Hamza 2000, 41–43). However, today the context of change needed for the success of the resuscitated National Open University of Nigeria seems to be more promising. In the words of Hamza (2000):

> There is so much expertise now in this (ITs) field not only in the advanced countries but here (in the private sector) in Nigeria. The Commonwealth of Learning is ever ready to support the efforts of Commonwealth developing countries to benefit fully from the new information and communication in

> developing their human potential through distance education. As a matter of fact, the time is coming very soon when the conventional face-to-face teaching method will become obsolete. Schools and classrooms will exist mostly as socializing enterprises.

Nevertheless, such new initiatives have to prove sceptics, informed critics and cynics wrong with the quality of their outputs and outcomes. Useful lessons could be drawn from the experiences of the British Open University as illustrated by its former vice-chancellor, Sir John Daniel, formerly Assistant Director-General (education) at UNESCO, and now Chief Executive of the Commonwealth of Learning (COL):

> When this new university (OU) was proposed in the late 1960s, the press and most of the academic and educational establishment in Britain ridiculed the idea. When they saw the output they changed their minds and today the Open University ranks 6th out of the 100 UK universities for the quality of its teaching. In various disciplines from Geology to Music, the majority of UK students studying in programmes with an excellent quality rating are with the Open University. (Daniel 2002, 19–24)

In the last ten years, especially since 1998, the situation of higher education in sub-Saharan Africa seems to be making a significant turnaround through the concerted effort of all stakeholders in sub-regional governments to face the stark realities of illiteracy, poverty, rising enrolment in tertiary education, inadequate infrastructures and funding of education, and the various multilateral and bilateral initiatives put in place.

The report of the June 2003 meeting of Higher Education Partners held in Paris gave much cause for hope. It was a serious follow up to the Conference on Higher Education held in 1998. Between that date and 2003, sub-Saharan Africa had reportedly seen progress through reforms such as improved access, improved relevance and quality, reduction in the impact of brain drain, a strengthened research capacity, greater access to new information and communication technologies and improved access of women to higher education. In terms of future prospects for higher education in the sub-region, the report is quite optimistic in view of the priority that African governments, through regional organizations such as NEPAD, are giving to teacher training and the creation of centres of excellence.

The relevant issues in the current concept of higher education and in particular open and distance modes of delivery are those of reform, which have been addressed:

- greater access or all-inclusiveness, especially for the unreached or disadvantaged
- relevance, especially in this learner need-driven initiative
- quality in the face of the challenges posed by time and space
- learner satisfaction in terms of appropriate competencies and adaptability
- research in line with the traditional mandate of universities and international acceptability, quality service and leadership.

The use of and access to IT in programme delivery is of paramount significance, as are the more traditional materials.

Certain results achieved by higher education systems in African countries can be listed as follows:

(1) Establishment of a university-wide data communication network connecting all academic buildings on the main campus with fibre optic cable.
(2) Full internet connectivity provided via a satellite link. Establishment of a virtual distance learning system using the fibre optic and wireless backbone and internet infrastructure.
(3) Establishment of a visual distance-learning system using the fibre optic and wireless backbone and internet infrastructure.
(4) Computerization of many aspects of the administrative system.
(5) Computer-based network services and management information system.
(6) Access to computing facilities to students and staff.
(7) University-based internet systems to support interactive regional study centres for distance learners.
(8) Improved opportunities to distance education, in particular through the African Virtual University and the Francophone Digital Campus.
(9) Promotion of research in sub-Sahara Africa, mainly through the reinforcement of regional and international networks.
(10) The prospect of the International Telecommunication Union implementing its recommendation to increase internet connectivity in sub-Saharan Africa to 1% by 2005, provide internet access for all secondary school pupils by 2000 and primary school pupils by 2011.

Certain highlights are of interest here and relate to achievements recorded by Nigeria in this regard. From 1999 to 2001, the Commonwealth of Learning UNESCSO/BREDA organized five training workshops and produced a guide (Shabani & Okebukola 2001, 13) on the development of materials for distance education. The training programme covered not only the development of print materials, but also audio and video-cassettes, CD-ROMs and online materials.

With regard to information and communication technology, the National Open University of Nigeria plans an initial student enrolment distributed according to location to eighteen national centres with prospected figures at 600, 000 students by 2007 (ibid., 11). Nigeria has also launched a virtual library project which offers services to more than 1.4 million students and 160, 000 academic staff (ibid., 17).

Several reform measures have characterized Nigeria's higher education since 2000 relating to ITs and virtual access. The first is the relaunch in 2003 and actual take off of the National Open University of Nigeria (NOUN). With an initial grant of M 4.5 billion, NOUN matriculated its pioneer students in early 2004. The relaunch was brought about by the phenomenal rise in demand for higher education and the frustrations of potential beneficiaries over non-admission to existing universities. The first key pre-relaunch planning activity to address the problem was the organization of a Workshop on Distance Education in Abuja, September 27–29, 2000, with the collaboration of the Commonwealth of Learning (COL) and UNESCO. Furthermore, a Plan of Action for a Decade of Distance Education in Nigeria (2001–2010) was developed at the National Workshop where the conference declared:

Abuja declaration 2001–2012

Abuja Declaration of the 2001–2012 Decade of Distance Education in Nigeria

In order to enhance education as a form of human resource development, and satisfy the exceptionally large demand for education by our huge and rapidly expanding population by which (still mainly rural, remote, under-represented and marginalized through resources location, economic and other reason[s]) we, the participants here assembled in Abuja this day the 29th September, 2000, representing the people of Nigeria herein referred to as Stakeholders solemnly resolve to adopt Distance Education as a desirable and inevitable mode for providing access to all and achieving equitable representation by taking the distance out of education. We therefore declare 2001–2010 AS THE DECADE OF DISTANCE EDUCATION IN NIGERIA.

Signed:

PROF. A.B. FAFUNWA
For and on behalf of all participants
29th September, 2000

Source: Dhanarajan (2000).

The action plan, closely anchored to the tertiary education tradition of teaching, research and service, took cognizance of the role of the university in meeting the goals and needs of target groups of the Universal Basic Education (UBE) Scheme, including teacher education.

NOUN is subject to the laws governing the establishment and operation of conventional universities, its programmes and resources; IT operations are also subject to accreditation by the National Universities Commission (NUC). The NUC offers both part-time and full-time courses in the following schools and centres: the School of Arts and Social Sciences, the School of Business and Human Resource Management, the School of Education, the School of Science and Technology, the Centre for Continuing Education and Work Place Training, the Regional Centre for Training and Development in Open and Distance Learning, as well as the Directorate of Learner Support Services. Study centres have been established in all six geopolitical zones of Nigeria. Resource centres are in Abuja, Bauchi, Calabar, Enugu, Kaduna and at the Women Development Centre in Abeokuta. Furthermore, several innovative courses offered at NOUN include a B.A. in Criminology and Security Studies, Peace Studies and Conflict in Resolution Law, a B.Sc in Tourism Studies, Cooperative Management, Hotel and Catering Management, Sciences and Information Technology for Teachers. In the School of Science and Technology, courses include B.Sc Nursing Science, Agriculture Extension Management, Computer Science and Data Management.

The University's Student Handbook states, *inter alia*:

> The Open University is an equal opportunity university … meeting the individual where he or she is and attending to his or her needs from there … The Open University is not a cheap or compromising avenue for obtaining a degree. It merely provides a quality cost effective, flexible avenue for doing so.

The second landmark IT-mediated reform strategy is the Nigerian Virtual Library project for universities and other institutions of higher education launched in 2003. This was facilitated by the UNESCO/Japan Funds in trust cooperation with a project budget of $113, 679 (including programme support costs). Two major workshops were held. The first was with the express purpose of including all stakeholders in Nigeria in the preparation of their own feasibility study/needs assessment. The second was to include key players from the active donor community in Nigeria in a consultative session prior to finalization of the feasibility study. Furthermore, particularly significant is the aim of the workshops to:

> tap into the ever-increasing indigenous knowledge and capacities present in Nigeria and engender ownership by the principal players from the beginning. This will also aid in building bridges between the key institutions involved in the virtual library in Nigeria …. (UNESCO 2003)

Based on the Implementation Status Report of February 28, 2003, a lot has been achieved in streamlining and harmonizing the roles and activities of the key actors, which are the National Universities Commission (NUC), the National Information Technology Development Agency (NITDA) and the National Library. Nigerian universities are also finalizing their action plans to implement the virtual library project as well as provide complementary IT centres/facilities for internet access to all students and staff.

The third landmark innovation was the successful launch in September 2003 of the Virtual Institutes of Higher Education Pedagogy

(VIHEP). This is all the more important as it targets all higher education teaching personnel who do not have a professional teaching qualification, as well as professionals who are expected to avail themselves of opportunities for continuous professional development. The objectives of the Virtual Institute (NUC 2003) are:

(1) To provide academic staff in tertiary institutions in Nigeria, especially universities, with internet-based training on modern methods of teaching and learning in higher education.
(2) To enhance the knowledge and skills of academic staff on such issues as teaching of large classes, effective utilization of (meagre) resources, modern methods of assessment and evaluation of student performance, basic guidance and counselling techniques, basic skills of curriculum development and techniques for writing grant-winning proposals.
(3) To share experiences among academic staff in Nigerian universities on best practices in university teaching and how to deal with academic vices such as examination malpractice, cultism and plagiarism.
(4) To try out draft training modules for the National Higher Education Pedagogic Centre.

The course is free for all participants and the various modules being offered online follow specific time schedules. The modules are of particular relevance for enhancing the quality of higher education delivery in Nigeria.

The modules, though related to the development of pedagogical skills, are independent for the purpose of participation in VII1ER, and hence participants will be certified module by module. Candidates who successfully complete a module will receive a certificate of completion within a week of the close of the institute for that module. While some staff may elect to participate in selected modules, others may enrol for all modules (NUC 2003).

Conclusion

We can safely conclude that the concept of new technologies falls within the contexts of the information and knowledge society and lifelong learning. Higher education institutions—universities, polytechnics and colleges of further education—are expected to assume greater roles and responsibilities in relation to national and community need-based education policy and delivery. While the lower (primary and secondary) levels of education systems in developing countries can be said to be too rigid due to their examination centeredness, higher education should offer more possibilities for developing a wide range of open, flexible delivery systems including, of course, distance education. Furthermore, in higher education, programme development, focused teaching, research development and service are the hallmarks of its activities.

For the purpose of this discussion we shall briefly examine the new roles and expected transformation that the second industrial revolution, IT, has brought to bear on higher education institutions. As Blanc (1999, 2) points out: "New technologies are challenging teaching and research methods, means of organization and internal functioning and even the definition of the university's mission and its role in society."

The context for Blanc's observation is the global awakening that inspired 151 university administrators or managers to meet in Sao Paola, Brazil in October 1996 to review the new roles, implications and challenges for the "University in the information society." Not only should universities now have to take stock and reposition, they should also be catalysts of top-bottom innovations that could transform school systems. Furthermore, the very organization of universities must change profoundly, taking into account both the direct impact of IT on the functioning of processes (such as the computerization of student management systems or the transformation of libraries) and their impact on the demands of the new knowledge and learning society.

This means that the role of each actor must change, such as the rector (vice chancellor) and his managerial team (more visionaries, the provision of more support services, more motivators); the deans of faculties and managers of university centres (more strategies, needs analysis, initiators of innovation and reorientation), and the department and programme heads occupied with the definition of objectives, the evaluation of impact, and the development of teachers and researchers. But perhaps of much greater significance for universities in such a new information society are: (1) the new technology-driven ways of learning, teaching, storing and retrieval, sharing and information, and (2) new learning processes. As Blanc (1999, 4) shows, the implications are far reaching.

From now on, the student will learn more and more by themselves through work exchange. The teacher will no longer transmit previously organized knowledge, but will have to teach students how to think and organize individual learning paths. The role of the university will be to facilitate these processes, to provide access to information, self-learning and to grant certification for training and research.

In the area of general and professional teaching, initial investment is shared by several institutions to permit wide diffusion, thereby making teaching less expensive and more accessible to a greater number of students. Even if Open and Distance Learning (ODL) can be diffused quickly, mixed forms (alternating in-class and distance education) will probably be the most common in the future. The challenges developing countries should brace themselves for are also highlighted by Blanc (1999). They are:

(1) Academic activities will be profoundly modified in terms of programme structure, content and processes, the role and knowledge of teachers, teaching support and documentation sources. The academic world is beginning to meet the IT revolution head on, but even those academics who accept these changes, as well as the most recalcitrant, will need the assistance of IT specialists capable of understanding and imagining their needs. Will universities know how to initiate a veritable policy of human and technological resource development?
(2) Research is already being profoundly transformed. Cooperation between researchers at distant institutions has become so easy that projects may be carried out in virtual worldwide laboratories efficiently and with improved quality control. Also, serious questions still need to be answered with regard to the ownership of research results and the future identity of universities involved in this diluting process. The university may also produce and distribute specific services intended for external users. This relates to the classic cultural or educational packages (CD-ROM) or web pages used in the same way as book or television programmes, as well as to professional support (e.g. agriculture business), databases (e.g. financial, legal), and industrial patents.
(3) Universities will increasingly find themselves a part of the knowledge market, competing with other more flexible and powerful institutions that are already specialized in communication and the processing, storing and diffusion of information. What role will the university play in this competitive world? With whom is it going to partner and at what level? This means that a thorough redefinition of the university's vision and mission (research, production, distribution and accreditation) will be needed.

It is against the backdrop of this fast-track culture of technologic innovation that the slow track culture of change within public or mainstream educational systems can be better appreciated. For, while the government may be the first to proclaim its political will to embrace desirable changes or break with tradition, it soon lags far behind the private sector in actualizing policy and keeping pace with and sustaining innovations. Simply stated, the public policy, educational world and the IT world are very different entities because, on the one hand, IT is interested in dynamic short-term activities, is fast-moving, global, business-oriented, an information carrier, and works for mass customers on global networks. The educational world, on the other hand is interested in long-term activities, is slow-moving and culturally sensitive, is split into many small units with local areas of development, is socially-oriented, has the main vocation of building up the individual, and has an essential role of knowledge creation and transmission.

Consequently, universities in the information society cannot be content with carrying on business as usual, but must integrate the character of the IT world into their philosophical and epistemological frameworks. Such a transformation will then make tertiary education more open, flexible, innovative, relevant, qualitative and open to all.

These significant differences between public and private initiatives and the application of IT innovations in education have also inspired the Canadian Commission for UNESCO (2001) to evolve common points of reference for "working together to transform higher education, " the main outcome of the UNESCO-sponsored World Conference on Higher Education held in Paris, October 5–8, 1998, to provide stakeholders representing 182 governments and 300 non-governmental organizations with the direction needed for the twenty-first century.

The proceedings focused on four major challenges relating to the relevance of higher education, its quality, management and financing and international cooperation. More significantly, it was recognized that the scientific and technological breakthroughs and inventions of the twentieth century owe a lot to the spectacular growth of higher education (in the developed world) and the resultant worldwide legion of trained scientific and technological personnel.

Specifically, the conference raised six questions crucial to the vision and mission of tertiary education:

(1) How does higher education contribute to sustainable human development?

(2) What is the role of higher education today in the creation and dissemination of knowledge?
(3) How can higher education support the move towards learning throughout life?
(4) How can higher education help to humanize globalization?
(5) What is the proper role of public funding for higher education?
(6) How can partnerships help in meeting the challenges facing higher education?

The meeting point of these questions and the IT revolution can be better appreciated within the context of both the traditional function of education and training, research and service to the community where service would be strengthened through the development of course programmes. The meeting point then becomes a function of what is done at the university or polytechnic and what the economic business or professional environment expects in terms of the employability or entrepreneurial potentials of tertiary level products.

The second question is related to the vision and mission to be met by higher education as an intellectual catalyst and producer of human and technological resources, enhancing learning and training in the information and knowledge society. However, the World Conference on Higher Education (WCHE 1998) agreed that technological advancement could not be taken as a broad solution to all our problems.

The information society offers no guarantee that knowledge will be shared and that individual and collective identities will be respected. It does not always allow for the development or transmission of knowledge that may reside in different cultural contexts. There are many risks inherent in imposing a uniform reading of the world, and basic values such as equity, justice, freedom and diversity need to be reaffirmed. Higher education is in an exceptional position, playing an active role in ensuring that knowledge-based societies remain committed to world peace and democracy.

Accordingly, the conference adopted certain guidelines for universities relating to the crucial role of new technologies which may remain at the service of higher education and enabling higher educational institutions to meet the following obligations:

(1) Take the lead in using new technologies to modernize activities and encourage mobility between countries, institutions and the world of work.

(2) Establish networks to engage in technology transfers and promote the pooling of experiences (and best practices) in the application of information technologies to education.
(3) Create new learning environments in particular distance education courses and virtual campuses where cultural identities are respected.
(4) Modify rather than reduce their numbers and adopt continuing education policies that allow them to update and upgrade their pedagogical skills in this new educational context.

It is clear that higher education in the information and knowledge society must transform horizontally and vertically in terms of space and time (satellite, virtual, dispersed campuses, libraries and classroom, respectively) and educational paradigms (learner or group-centred learning models, course packages and technologies print, audio video, internet). The open distance learning and virtual concepts are among the most popular and need some in-depth analysis.

Another key player in the reform drive to bridge the IT divide, the National Information Technology Development Agency (NITDA), has, since its creation in 2001, evolved a national IT policy in line with the World Summit on the Information Society (WSIS) Plan of Action. Its mission is to "make Nigeria an IT capable country in Africa and a key player in the Information Society by the year 2004, using IT as the engine for sustainable development and global competitiveness." The Agency is actively involved in promoting the use of IT, software development and capacity building across the sectors of human resources development (including education), infrastructure, governance, research and development, health, agriculture, urban and rural development, trade and commerce, arts, culture and tourism, national security and law enforcement, legislation, global strategies and policy implementation, and IT popularization and awareness.

The impacts of NITDA's activities have been significant through direct or assisted involvement in various IT projects. An example is the NITDA Education Tax Fund Centres of Excellence launched in April 2004 to stimulate the local production of technology against the chronic penchant for technology consumption, areas of interest system engineering, software engineering, database technologies, super computing architectures, open source software development, and communication and information engineering. Having completed an imperative needs assessment compared to similar institutions around the world, NITDA, with the support of the ETF, is now in the implementation stage (Ajayi 2004).

The school system cannot be isolated from activities at the tertiary level and has also been a focal point for reform in the area of information and communication technology. On January 18, 2002, the Federal Government of Nigeria inaugurated the National Implementation Committee Computers in Schools (CISP). The membership comprised representatives of national and sub-regional examination bodies, the National Commission for Colleges of Education (NCCE), the National Universities Commission, Federal Ministries of Education, Communication, Science and Technology and the Nigeria Educational Research and Development Council (NERDC). Some of the committee's terms of reference included:

(1) working out the modalities for the introduction of effective computer education in schools
(2) establishing and equipping resource centres in 37 locations, one in each state and the Federal Capital Territory
(3) identifying and training in the different categories of personnel required for the project
(4) involving strategies for linkages between school, the open and distance learning scheme and the virtual library (Ajayi 2004).

Although computer education in Nigerian schools has been a prevocational elective subject in the Junior Secondary Curriculum, plans are under way to make it a compulsory course in the school curriculum, especially given the impetus of School Net Africa (2004) that is campaigning to increase access to IT for millions of African learners.

References

Ajayi, G. O. 2004. Implementing the WSIS process in Nigeria: The National IT Policy Care Studies and Experiences, secondary education and training. Paris: UNESCO IIEP.

Blanc, G. 1999. *The University in the Information Society*. Paris: Columbus.

Borisade, A. 2002. "Address of the Honourable Minister of Education." *Education Today* 8 (2): 3.

Canadian Commission for UNESCO. 2001. "Working Together to Transform Higher Education." Discussion Kit on the World Conference on Higher Education. Canada.

Daniel, J. 2002. "Automobiles, bananas, courses, degrees …: An ABC of higher education and globalization." Opening address, First global forum on international quality assurance, accreditation and the cognition qualifications in higher education. Paris: UNESCO. 19–24. October 17–18.

Delors, J. 1986. Learning, the treasure within. Paris: UNESCO Publishing.

Dhanarajan, Garira. 2000. "Distance and Open Education: An Overview." *Education today* 8 (2): 9–13.

European Union. 2001. Education and Training Project Kit.

Hamza, Y. 2000. "Challenges and Prospects of Re-establishing the Open University of Nigeria." *Education Today* 8 (9): 41–43.

Jegede, O. 2000. "Evolving a National Policy on Distance Education. An Agenda for Implementation." *Education Today* 8 (2): 14–29.

Juma, M. N. 2000. "Case Study 2: The African Virtual University (AVU). Kenyatm University, Kenya." In *Issues in Education and Technology*, edited by Cream Wright, 52–76. London: Commonwealth Secretariat.

National Universities Commission. 2003. Virtual Institute for Higher Education Pedagogy (VIHEP). Abuja.

Shabani, J. and Okebukola, R. (eds.). 2001. "Guide to the Development of Materials for Distance Education (Trail d)." Lagos: UNESCO-BREDA.

Turnoff, M. 1999. The University in the Information Society. Report of the Conference on the University and the Information Society. October 23–25, 1998. Sao Paulo, Brazil.

UNESCO. 1998. World Conference on Higher Education. Paris: UNESCO Publishing.

—. 2002. "Proceedings of the First Global Forum on International Quality Assurance, Accreditation and Recognition of Qualification in Higher Education." Paris: UNESCO Publishing. October 17–18, 2000.

—. 2003. "Recent Developments and Future Prospects of Higher Education in sub-Saharan Africa in the 21st Century." Report of the meeting of the Higher education partners. Paris, June 23–25.

CHAPTER FIVE

PUBLIC SERVICE DELIVERY IN NIGERIA

A.O. ABISOYE

Introduction

Public services are essential for the fabric of democratic societies. Public bureaucracy provides a semblance of the government of the nation, in that it is the permanent administration on which a government relies for conducting of its activities. The need for services that no individual can or will pay for but that benefit all is one of the justifications for taxation. Public service delivery is the implementation of those services such as sewage and trash disposal, street cleaning, public education, public safety/security, health, water and sanitation, transport, communication, and emergency services among others. There has been some move towards the privatization of many of these essential services, thereby giving rise to questions of equity, justice and values which are fundamental to the democratic ethos. Democracy and bureaucracy are so interrelated to the extent that the quality of one determines the status of the other. Nonetheless, the concepts connote public trust, implying loyalty to the people by doing good things to help society.

Conceptual and Theoretical Issues—The Concept of Democracy

Democracy, as a concept, is riddled with questions. As for its empirical referent, it is a contested terrain. The process of unravelling it may start with a journey to its etymological roots. The Greek words *Demos* ["people"] and *Kratos* ["power" or "rule"] give an indication of the essence of democracy. *Demokratia* or democracy is therefore the empowerment of the people.

The concept of democracy is inseparable from the notion of power in the hands of the people. It connotes a system of political structures in which sovereignty belongs to the people. Democracy is a political regime in which all power derives its legitimacy from the people (Manent 2003).

In the view of John D. May, democracy is defined as the necessary correspondence between acts of governance and the wishes with respect to those acts of the persons who are affected (Oyadare 1994).
The constituent elements of a democratic system outlined by Pericles, the Athenian leader and Orator, include:

> Power does not rest with the few in a democracy, but with many;
> In law, as it touches individuals, all are equal;
> Man's advancement depends, not (on) mere rotation, but on his true worth;
> Nor does poverty dim (the citizen's) reputation or prevent him from assisting the state if he has the capacity;
> Liberty marks both our public politics and the feelings which touch our daily life together;
> Our private concourse is untroubled, our life in the state free from illegality (Asobie 1995, 2)

In essence, the main principles of democracy include rule of law, accountability, equality before the law, the mass participation of people in decision-making through the choices they make at the polls, predictability of tenure of political office holders, liberty and freedom of expression.

The models of democracy could reasonably be divided into two broad types: direct or participatory democracy (a system of decision making about public affairs in which citizens are directly involved) and liberal or representative democracy (a system of rules embracing elected "officers" who undertake to represent the interests and/or views of citizens within the framework of "the rule of law"). A representative, according to Rehfeld (2006), is someone who looks out for the substitutive interest of those who elected them. Another form of democracy, identified by Dalton et al. (2004), is Advocacy Democracy, in which citizens or public interest groups interact directly with governments and even participate directly in the policy formulation process, although actual decisions remain in official hands.

In whichever society it operates, democracy is a system of open government and public decision-making by the will of the majority or with the consent of the majority without prejudice to the rights of the minority (or minorities). Indeed, the peculiar value of democracy is thought to lie in the fact that, according to Barry (1992), it is the only form of government that can advance the interests of all the members of a politically organized community.

The Concept of Bureaucracy

The bureaucracy, as it is commonly referred to in the United States, or the civil service, is a permanent body of officials employed to implement the plans and decisions of government. Civil service, according to Augustus Adebayo, is the entire service of government which is divided into departments and in which civil servants work (Olagboye 2005). The Nigerian Civil Service consists of employees in Nigerian government agencies other than the military. Most employees are career civil servants in the Nigerian ministries, progressing based on qualifications and seniority.

The civil service has progressed beyond a mere "set of arrangements, procedures, and people for implementing and administering public policy" (Donovan, Morgan & Potholm 1986). The civil service now also plays a significant role in initiating new programmes and policies and has thus become an important policy maker, as well as a policy implementer (Olagboye 2005). Thus, the civil service in Nigeria not only assists in formulating public policies, it also very often creates policies.

The civil service is mainly organized around the federal ministries, headed by a minister appointed by the president. The ministries are responsible for various parastatals (government owned corporations) such as universities (education), the National Broadcasting Commission (information) and the Nigerian National Petroleum Corporation (petroleum). Other parastatals are the responsibility of the office of the presidency, such as the Independent National Electoral Commission, the Economic and Financial Crimes Commission, and the Federal Civil Service Commission. The service has six additional units which provide services to all departments on the civil service (Olagboye 2005): the Established & Record Office (E & RO), the Career Management Office (CMO), the Manpower Development Office (MDO), the Management Service Office (MSO), the Common Service Office (CSO) and the Bureau of Public Service Reforms (BPSR).

The main organ through which the executive discharges its constitutional and other responsibilities is the civil service. In this connection, Section 318 of the 1999 constitution defines the federal civil service as:

> Services of the federation in a civil capacity as staff of the office of the president, the vice president, a ministry or department of the government of the federation assigned with the responsibility for any business of the government of the federation

Similarly, the civil service of the state implies:

> service of the government of a state in a civil capacity as staff of the Governor, the Deputy Governor or a ministry or department of the government of the state assigned with the responsibility for any business of the government of the state.

In the opinion of Suleiman (2009), the public sector refers to all organizations that exist as part of government machinery for implementing policy decisions and delivering services that are of value to citizens. This is a mandatory institution under the Nigerian Constitution of 1999. Chapter VI of the Constitution, Executive Part I (D) and Part II (C), provides for a public service at the federal and state levels of government.

The public sector in Nigeria is made up of the following:

(i) The civil service, which is often referred to as the core service and is composed of line ministries and extra-ministerial agencies; and
(ii) The public bureaucracy, which is composed of the enlarged public service, including:
 (a) Service of the state and national assemblies
 (b) The Judiciary
 (c) The Armed Forces
 (d) The police and other security agencies
 (e) Paramilitary service (immigration, customs, prisons)
 (f) Parastatals and agencies including social services, educational institutions, research institutes, etc.

It is perhaps pertinent to note here that the chairpersons of local government and their supervisory councillors perform functions analogous to those of the federal and state executive council, irrespective of their local government areas.

Functions of the Civil Service

The specific responsibilities of the Nigerian civil service include:

(i) Assisting the government in the formation and implementation of public policies and programmes
(ii) Data collection, storage and input for public policy formulation by the government
(iii) Provision of continuity in public policy formulation and implementation on both short and long term bases for the good of the

nation irrespective of the political party or set of military officers in power

(iv) Maintenance and operation of an efficient and effective administrative machinery for the day-to-day discharge of government functions

(v) Preparation and implementation of the annual estimates/ budget of the government

(vi) Collection of government revenue and control of government expenditure to ensure the judicious application of public funds

(vii) Maintenance and operation of an efficient and effective personnel management system covering all personnel in government service

(viii) Assisting government in the promotion of national unity and integration

(ix) Provision of efficient and effective social services to the citizens of Nigeria (Olagboye 2005, 6–7).

Some of these functions may seem rather simple and routine but they are crucial in a developing economy like Nigeria, where continuity in governance and public policy is both desirable and essential. However, by the nature of its colonial design the bureaucracy since independence has remained virtually the same through the various regimes. This is because the bureaucrats have continued to serve a "regime" and not the public, as such. The sustainability of the current democratic dispensation would largely depend on the refocusing of the loyalty of the bureaucrats to service the people rather than being pawns in the hands of self-serving political actors.

Regardless of the system of government under focus, governments in most countries are structurally and constitutionally linked to the civil service. In Nigeria, where different forms of government have been experimented with, the structure and constitutional relationships between the government and the civil service have continued to endure. In Nigeria, being a federation, both the central government and the government of each federating state have a civil service. Suleiman (2009) posited that many civil servants found it easier to align themselves with the government of the day and participate in the treasury looting that has reduced Nigeria to an embarrassment among the countries of serious nations.

Theorizing Democracy and Bureaucracy

The Critical Elite Theory is hereby applied in explaining the two concepts (Bureaucracy and Democracy) under focus, especially in how they interact to affect the larger society. The theory states that one or more sets of powerful, controlling elites exist within all societies. Regardless of the nature of the government or the economy there is always an oligarchy, for the masses can and do not govern themselves. In essence, the functional elite perspective claims that as societies become more complex we need individuals with specialized skills to fill the important leadership posts.

However, the critical elite theory claims that power lies in the hands of a relatively small group of people who use it mostly for their own benefit. Among the social theorists usually placed in this category are Thorstein Veblen, C. Wright Mills, Ralph Miliband and G. William Domhoff (Kloby 2004). Although the elite are always a minority of the population, they control a large proportion of the available resources and are usually well-organized and quite cohesive. Power is centralized in the hands of the elite members, and the elites commonly employ all available means to protect and preserve their power and enhance it wherever possible. They share power with others only when it is in their self-interest to do so, and they never voluntarily surrender power.

To rule their society, elites employ a variety of techniques. These include dominating the economy, using police and military force, manipulating the educational system and the mass media, sanctioning or eliminating those who oppose them, and creating ideologies that legitimize their power and rule. Elites use their available means and position of power to advance their own interests or the interest of their agency. Scholars have put forward the idea that no matter what a political party says about how democratic and free it is, it will still be mainly influenced or controlled by a small group of elites, named the "iron law of oligarchy." It has often been said that all political parties are elitist, as in order for a party to survive it needs to have a leadership structure which will lead to a minority of people having a greater influence than the rest of the members.

Democracy and Bureaucracy, at least in their present forms in Nigeria, share many defining features of the Elite theory. Ojagbohunmi (1994, 166–167) recalls a period in history when the powers of the civil servants became great:

> Under General Gowon's administration (1966–1975), certain developments in the socio-economic milieu of Nigeria such as the creation of more states in 1967, the prosecution of the Civil War (1967–1970), the oil boom of the early 1970s and the concomitant expansion of government business and the post-war million naira re-construction programmes—all made considerable demands and impact on the civil service. Bureaucratic power grew tremendously as top civil servants exercised military leaders in exercising governmental power, outshining their ministers in the exercise of influence and power unrestricted influence on policy making. A small

> group of permanent secretaries popularly referred to as "Super Permanent Secretaries" emerged as partners of game.

Despite the various reforms aimed at reducing the influence of bureaucracy in the running of government, it is noteworthy that bureaucratic influence in both policy formulation and implementation remained very solid.

Evolution of Public Service in Nigeria

The public service in Nigeria is a colonial heritage of public administration. The Nigerian civil service has its origins in the era of the "scramble for Africa" and the "Partition of West Africa, " which culminated in the colonization of most of Africa. The Nigerian civil service could be thought of as first taking root in 1861 when the territory of Lagos was formally ceded to the British government as a purely colonial instrument designed to serve British colonial interest. In the words of the Directorate for Social Mobilization in its political education manual, the Nigerian civil service during the colonial period "made Nigerians obey the colonialists and worked to help British colonialists take away our crops, minerals and other products."

During that time, the upper echelon of the civil service was dominated by the Europeans on whom the executive, judicial and legislative powers were concentrated. The bureaucrats enjoyed certain privileges and became arrogant because they were ready instruments in the hands of the colonialists. They thus became isolated from the public. Oyugi (1988) summarizes the nature of the bureaucracy under the colonial era as follows:

> The colonial bureaucracy tended to arrogate into itself all political functions always acting to suppress organizations whose activities were manifestly political. The colonial bureaucracy was a "political organization" without a legitimate constituency. It was both unrepresentative and unresponsive—the two hallmarks of an undemocratic social system. It lacked respect for competitive politics. It acted politically but pretended to be apolitical.

It is not out of place to identify with the view of Oyedele (2006) that the Nigerian bureaucracy was not originally designed to work for the interests of Nigeria and its people, but rather to serve British colonial interests.

Succeeding constitutional reviews increased the stake of Nigerians at the helm of the public service until independence in 1960. Independence was supposed to catalyze the evolution of the civil service as a national institution, spearheading the rapid transformation of the nation and ensuring continuity in administration.

Various panels have studied and made recommendations for reforming the civil service, including the Morgan Commission of 1963, the Adebo Commission of 1971, the Udoji Commission of 1972–74 and the Dotun Philips Panel of 1985. The 1988 Civil Service Reorganization Decree, promulgated by the Babangida administration, had a major impact on the structure and efficiency of the civil service. The later report of the Ayida Panel made recommendations to reverse some of the past innovations and to return to the more efficient civil service of earlier years. The civil service has been undergoing gradual and systematic reforms and restructuring since the advent of the Fourth Republic on May 29, 1999. In August 2009 the head of the civil service, Stephen Osagiede Oronsaye, proposed reforms where permanent secretaries and directors would spend a maximum of eight years in office.

Critics of the various reform processes rated the outcomes of the various efforts as poor. For instance, Suleiman (2009) stated that although the Nigerian public service has undergone changes and transformation over the years, unfortunately successive reforms have not made significant impacts to re-engineer the public sector. Reforms were tailored towards achieving efficiency and effectiveness of the service because the belief of successive governments was that a thoroughbred public service was necessary for the effective delivery of public good. He alluded to the Udoji commission, which was to conduct a comprehensive review of the standard of service and compensation in the civil service and public corporations. Apart from the preoccupation with wages and salaries, the commission recommended a unified and integrated administrative structure, the elimination of waste, the removal of inefficient departments and the introduction of a result-oriented public sector that functioned on the basis of management by objective. Sadly, however, the goals of the reforms were not achieved. The commission is better known for the salary increases it gave to public sector workers.

In 2003, the federal government embarked on yet another reform of the public sector. This has produced a number of changes to the structure of the public service and its procedure, particularly the monetization of salaries and allowance. Nevertheless, the universal conclusion of scholars on the issue is that the various reforms had not achieved much.

Notable among the factors identified by scholars as being responsible for inefficiency of the public sector in Nigeria include:

(i) Poor capacity of the majority of civil servants, sometimes to the point of illiteracy
(ii) Outdated administrative machinery
(iii) Certificate forgery to gain entry and get promotions
(iv) Age falsification to remain in service beyond the statutory stipulated period/age
(v) Corruption
(vi) Nepotism
(vii) Policy reversals, and
(viii) Primordial considerations like ethnicity at the expense of merit.

Blending Democracy and Bureaucracy for the Good of the People

There is a general tendency to blame politicians for the poverty, underdevelopment and colossal tragedy of leadership that best describes Nigeria today. From military dictatorship to the "democratic" government, all appear to have conspired to reduce governance to the manipulation of public office to deceive and loot public funds for personal use. The only permanent feature of government, whether under military or civilian dispensation, is the civil service. This is why civil servants cannot escape their responsibilities for the rot that characterizes every aspect of the public sector in Nigeria.

Mosher (1982) argues that a civilization can devolve or evolve through the decisions and actions (or indecisions and inactions) of those public servants who are not elected but appointed. There is no gain in saying that the bulk of governmental decisions and actions are determined and influenced by the background, associations and values of educated (or not), unelected administrative officials. Representative democratic participation entails the delegation of authority to popularly elected officers, who then select and delegate powers to other officers. The unelected officers—un-removable administrators—are usually chosen merely on criteria of social class, general competence and special skills. The majority of public officers have specialized skills and competences that the elected officials do not usually possess, and it is obvious that this set of public officers makes decisions of great significance for all the people.

The growing incidence of insecurity, mounting problems of corruption, a declining standard of living, non-adherence to the rule of law, the recurring incidence of a faulty electoral process manifest in the form of electoral fraud and violence, and political godfatherism are among the numerous vices plaguing the current democratic process. There is therefore an imperative need to reappraise what constitutes the dividends of democracy and the roles of bureaucracy in the delivery to the teeming downtrodden mass of Nigerians.

Conclusion

A weak bureaucratic structure allows a situation wherein the public servants are kleptocrats with a brazen desire to loot the nation's treasury. Most of the political leaders have proved themselves to be anti-people, but the bureaucracy has a moral obligation to steer the nation in the right direction, even if the political leadership fails.

For instance, the effort to fight the scourge of corruption is far from conscientious, the anti-corruption agencies are cockeyed, the judicial plea bargaining is perceived as a tacit approval of corrupt practices, and it is difficult to win the battle against poverty if public funds keep disappearing into private pockets. Worse still, much of the looted funds is stashed in foreign bank accounts, thereby helping to further develop other economies. The result at the domestic front is a plethora of development woes typified by poor infrastructures (notably inadequate electricity and bad roads), substandard schools and universities, under-equipped hospitals leading to huge amount of money being spent on government officials, and medical care being sought abroad, rapid deindustrialization and mass youth unemployment.

A democracy that would engender development would be an all-inclusive one. That is, a kind of democracy where the majority of people has direct access to their elected representatives as well as a highly liberalized bureaucracy. Liberalizing the bureaucracy is attainable by making the Ombudsman functional and effective. Strategies of planning for the population without their active involvement may create a lot of stress for the people. Indeed, such an approach negates the most important element in the democratic process, which stipulates consultation with the people in designing that which is claimed to benefit them.

Liberalizing the bureaucracy may likely address the situation painted by Oyedele (2006):

> The situation in Nigeria today is that the bureaucracy has grown so large that it has become isolated from the people. It has become irresponsive to the needs of the people to the extent that it can no longer be influenced by public opinion. The citizens have little or no mechanism through which they can control and stop the arbitrary actions of bureaucrats.

Overall, the attainment of a democratic ethos can be greatly influenced by the nature of public service delivery. Much as there is an imperative need to elect people of proven integrity into government, there is also an overriding need for the public sector to meet their calling. The further restructuring of the public service sector may also be needful to ensure a shift from its perception of a public welfare service to a highly efficient and professionalized set up. Doing this will probably guarantee a reward for the populace for their enormous investment in democracy.

References

Adebayo, A. 1981. *Principles and Practice of Public Administration in Nigeria* (1989 ed.). Ibadan: Spectrum Books Ltd.

Asobie, A. 1995. "The African Riddle: What Democracy? Whose State! Which Africa?" Keynote Address Delivered at the 1995 Biennial Congress of the African Political Science Association held in Ibadan, Nigeria. August 21–25, 1995.

Barry, N. I. 1992. *An Introduction to Modern Political Theory*. London: Macmillan Educational Book Ltd. 260.

Dalton, R. J., Scarrow, S. E. & Cain, B. E. 2004. "Advanced Democracies and New Politics." *Journal of Democracy* 15 (1).

Kloby, J. 2004. *Inequality, Power, and Development, Issues in Political Sociology*. New York: Humanity Book.

Manent, P. 2003. "Modern Democracy as a System of Separation." *Journal of Democracy* 14 (1): 114–125.

Ojagbohunmi, G. 1994. "The Civil Service Reforms, Structural Adjustment and Transition to Democratic Rule Programme in Nigeria, 1986–1992." In *Democratization in Africa: Nigerian Perspective*, edited by Omo Omoniyi, Dirk Berg-Schlosser, Adesina Sambo & Ada Okwuosa, 165–183. Benin City: Hima & Hima Ltd. 1.

Oyadare, B. A. 1994. "The Nigeria Political Class: Threat to Post-Transition Democracy." In *Democratization in Africa: Nigeria Perspective*, edited by Omo Omoniyi, Dirk Berg-Schlossen, Adesina Sambo & Ada Okwuosa, 2: 202. Benin City: Hima & Hima Ltd.

Oyedele, S. O. 2006. "Bureaucracy and Democarcy." In *Challenges of Sustainable Democracy in Nigeria*, edited by Emmanuel O. Ojo, 89–94. Ibadan: John Archers (Publishers) Ltd.

Oyugi, W. O. 1998. "Bureaucracy and Democracy in Africa" In *Democratic Theory and Practice in Africa*, edited by Oyugi, W. O. & Odhiambo, E. S., 99–102. Kenya: University of Nairobi.

Relfield, A. 2006. "Towards a General Theory of Political Representative." *The Journal of Politics* 68 (1): 1–2.

Suleiman, S. 2009. "Nigeria: Why the Public Sector is inefficient." Thesis. Public Administration. Ahmadu Bello University, Zaria. Tuesday, April 28, 2009.

CHAPTER SIX

THE IMPORTANCE OF CAPTURE AND CULTURE FISHERIES TO DEVELOPMENT IN NIGERIA

M.D. ENAIKELE

Introduction

Development as a concept has witnessed a large number and variety of definitions and interpretations, and its popularization has seen it incorporated and applied in diverse academic disciplines. More often than not, the term "development" is used in an exclusively economic sense, which implies an increase in production and capital investments. Political scientists have also broadened the concept to mean the ability to enhance the capacity of political systems. At the same time, sociologists interpret the concept as essentially a process of change resulting from structural differentiation. This is why, to a large extent, development cannot be seen as a purely economic affair but rather as an overall social process dependent on the outcome of efforts to deal with the total environment (Rodney 1976).

There are numerous indices of development. These include growth in income and wealth generation, equitable distribution of income, decrease in infant mortality rates, increase in literacy rates and other indicators like poverty reduction and food security, etc. that add to quality of life. Food security is one of the major indices of development because food production and income generation are related to addressing the issue of poverty and development, as witnessed by the striking correlation between poverty and food shortage (The Netherlands technical Centre for Agriculture and Cooperation 1999). This link is fundamentally pronounced though many other factors may be involved. Almost half of the present world's population live on less than US $2 a day, and one billion on less than US $1, while 800 million do not have sufficient and regular supplies of food (ibid., 1). The Food and Agriculture Organisation State of Food Insecurity Report estimates that 799 million people in 98 developing nations are not getting enough food to live normal, healthy and active lives (FAO 2000). In Africa, the average food available is only 2, 700 calories per person per day, while in Western Europe and North America the average food available is more than 3, 500 calories per person per day.

Also, the proportion of the African population with inadequate access to food has increased to 33% from the 20% projected in 1989 (International Year for the Eradication of Poverty 1996). Consequently, the proportion of undernourished people has been uniformly high in sub-Saharan Africa where the present annual food shortage will increase to 400 million tonnes by 2025 (Paquote 1991). This shortage is larger than what could conceivably be filled with food aid. The solution, therefore, is to increase food production. The idea of reducing consumption per capita is not an option given its already low average. While increasing food production is an important option, the Food and Agriculture Organisation (FAO) cautioned that unless an urgent step is taken to prioritise food production for development, by the year 2010 sub-Saharan Africa will need US $28.7 billion to import food to supplement the regional food requirements (Technical Centre for Agriculture and Rural Cooperation 1995).

The campaign for food security as a strategy for addressing poverty and development was developed by the FAO during the food crisis of the mid-1970s, when the world food production rate dropped for the first time since the Second World War (FAO 2000).

Since then, emphasis has been shifted to food production and income generation because food production and economic access to food through income generation are profoundly linked with poverty alleviation, especially because food production is a major source of income for the rural poor and a prospect for food security and development

In Nigeria, where there is a recorded experience of food shortage, various successive governments have embarked on several national accelerated food-production related development programmes. These include the Rural Irrigation and River Basin Development Programme launched in 1973, the Agricultural Development Programme (ADP) in 1975, Operation Feed the Nation (OFN) in 1976, Green Revolution in 1980, the Directorate of Food Road and Rural Infrastructure (DFRRI) in 1986, the Strategic Grain Reserve Programme (SGRP) in 1988, the Artisanal and Inshore Fisheries Development Programme (AIFDP) in 1988, and, most recently, the adopted New Partnership for Africa Development (NEPAD) resolution on sustainable Fisheries and Aquaculture in 2005.

Also, the United Nations Development Programmes' (UNDP) strategy emphasises food production and income generation as the ultimate goals of addressing food security, poverty and development in

Nigeria (United Nations System in Nigeria Partnership 1995). This initiative rests on the optimistic view that to ensure food security, improved food production and economic access to food supply through income generation must form an integral part of the development strategy. Given the precarious nutritional circumstance under which most Nigerians live, coupled with hunger, there is an obvious need to evolve promising means of promoting food production through capture and culture fisheries in Nigeria. This is so because fish provides an estimated 40% of the total animal protein consumed by an average Nigerian. In some parts of the country, especially in Lagos, fish accounts for up to 80% of animal protein consumed (Areola 2007).

Despite these, the contribution of fisheries to development has consistently been underestimated both in national development and poverty reduction strategies, because it has often not been seen as a priority sector by policy makers. This is because when faced with resource allocation decisions, policy makers are often quick to prioritise the use of water bodies for human consumption, hydro-electric power, transportation and industrial use over capture and culture fisheries.

The poor policy priority given to capture and culture fisheries is incidentally linked with the poor attention given to agriculture because of the rising fortune of the petroleum sector (Udousung 2012). Food demand, and in particular the demand for fish, has continued to increase with the growing population and increase in per capita consumption.

This chapter attempts to articulate the importance of capture and culture fisheries to development in Nigeria. To properly situate this objective, the chapter adopts the Millennium Development Goals (MGDs) index to x-ray the strategic importance of fisheries to development. The reason for this is that fishing is one sector of the economy that can be identified as capable of achieving the MDGs.

The MDGs are eight international development goals officially established by the United Nations in 2000, following the adoption of the United Nations Millennium Declaration. All 193 United Nations member states agreed to achieve these goals by the year 2015. The goals are:

*Reducing extreme poverty and hunger
*Achieving universal primary education
*Promoting gender equality and women empowerment
*Reducing child mortality rates
*Improving maternal health
*Combating HIV/AIDS, malaria, and other diseases
*Ensuring environmental sustainability

*and developing a global partnership for development.

Nigeria is one of the 193 nations that endorsed the MDGs in 2000, but did not initiate any concrete policy or programme towards achieving them until 2004 when it adopted the National Economic Empowerment and Development Strategy (NEEDS) and the Local Government Economic Empowerment and Development Strategies (LEEDS). NEEDS and LEEDS seek to reorientate values, reduce poverty, create wealth and generate employment under the presidential initiative on fisheries management and development, amongst other initiatives. The ultimate goal is to make Nigeria self-sufficient in fishing in the short term, with a target annual production of two million metric tons by the year 2010 (Areola 2007).

Fish, being a “rich food for poor people, ” is well placed to make an important contribution to the MDGs. Since the last decade, capture and culture fisheries have in some cases been embedded within national poverty reduction strategy plans, becoming a key part of macro-economic growth. The renewed interest in the ways in which capture and culture fisheries can contribute to poverty alleviation, food security, income generation and female empowerment at household, community and national levels is very critical to development.

Physical, Demographic and Socio-economic description of Nigeria and its Fishing Resources

Nigeria is a comparatively large country with an area of 924, 000 square kilometres, spanning longitude 30°E to 16°E and latitude 4°N to 14°N, with a population of over 157 million people. Nigeria is blessed with a coastline of about 870 kilometres bordering the Atlantic Ocean and the Gulf of Guinea, a maritime area of 46, 000 kilometres^2 and about 3, 000 kilometres of inland water bodies (Usoro 2012). Nigeria is rich in lakes, reservoirs and wetlands and its major cities are situated along the coast, lakes and numerous rivers emptying into the Atlantic, the relatively wide continental shelf of which provides a diverse assemblage of fishery resources. The resources exploited from these water bodies include prawns, shrimps, crabs, oysters, pelagic and demersal fish species (Isiebor, Awosika & Smith 2013). Otitolaye opines that in 1996 the fish supply in Nigeria was 466, 053 tons, out of which 200, 171 tons were produced locally. Artisanal fisheries (that is, capture fisheries) provide more than 82% of the domestic fish supply, giving livelihoods to one million fishers (Otitolaye 1999).

Aquaculture (that is, culture fisheries) is also an economically viable enterprise in Nigeria, with some 2, 642 fish farms producing 85, 000 metric tons of fish, thereby making the country the largest aquaculture producer in Africa. This production is however still negligible when compared to the growing population (Chichi 2010). Yet, the fishing industries contribute not only to the animal protein intake for the population, but also directly or indirectly to livelihoods through jobs creation (Ajayi & Talabi 1984) and Oloruntuyi (1998) observe that of all the estimated total area of perennial water swamp and brackish water available in Nigeria, a considerable proportion possesses the desirable characteristics for aquaculture in terms of water supply, soil types, topography and access, etc. Out of about 0.8 million hectares of swampland in six coastal states (Ondo, Ogun, Bendel [now Edo and Delta], Rivers, Cross River and Lagos), it is estimated that about 27 hectares are being utilized for aquaculture. Besides the FAO/World Bank fishery report (FAO/World Bank Fishery Report 1982), Adikwu (1999) also observes that the potential for small- to large-scale fish farming exists all over the country. Among this are large river basins, impounded reservoirs (currently being used for drinking water supplies) and the vast brackish and marine water areas of the southern part of the country.

The Importance of Capture and Culture Fisheries to Development in Nigeria

The benefits of capture and culture fisheries to development relate to the reduction of extreme poverty through employment, income generation and food security; contribution to the goal of universal primary education, female empowerment, reduction of child mortality and improvement of maternal health, combatting HIV/AIDS, malaria and other diseases, ensuring environmental sustainability and developing a global partnership for development.

Reduction of Extreme Poverty

Fish contributes to development through the reduction of extreme poverty. Poverty is a dynamic phenomenon, and is extreme when it manifests in insufficient nutritional food consumption required for healthy living. More than four in every ten Nigerians live under conditions of extreme poverty of less than N 320 per-capital per month, barely providing a quarter of the nutritional requirement for healthy living. Yet, in Nigeria, fish provides about 40% of the dietary protein intake. In the coastal and riverine communities, it is as high as 80% (Areola 2007). It is a particularly important component of the diets of the "poor, " as it is often the most affordable form of animal protein and provides more minerals than the same quantity of meat. Fish is rich in iron, zinc, magnesium, phosphorous, calcium, vitamin A and vitamin C, and is a good source of iodine. Many of these vital nutrients are found in small amounts only, if at all, in staple foods such as maize, rice and cassava, which make up the bulk of people's diets in Nigeria (Bene, Macfadyen & Allison 2007).

Fisheries create employment and generate income, thereby contributing to poverty alleviation. In the same way, they could also contribute to development. Capture and culture fisheries provide jobs for intensive small-scale fishers and serve as a "safety net" for the poor, who would otherwise have to migrate to the urban centres for work. For example, capture and culture fisheries provide 6 to 9 million full- and part-time jobs and the income from fishing supports 30–45 million people. Of this number, many are women involved in fish processing and marketing (Hall 2005). Job creation in capture and culture fisheries serves as an engine for income generation and brings development to the people, especially at the grassroots level.

Contribution to the Goal of Universal Primary Education

The contribution of fisheries to development through education is indirect. Poverty is heavily linked with the Nigerian children's education because poverty and irregular income are the leading causes of low educational attainment. Basically, education assists in the reduction of poverty by increasing the value and efficiency of labour offered by the poor and by mitigating the health and nutritional consequences of poverty. Article 28, section 1 of the United Nations Convention on the Rights of the Child states that the "state party should recognise the rights of the child to universal basic education." But, in Nigeria, more than 20% of primary school-aged children and 80% of secondary school-aged children are not enrolled in school (World Bank/Federal Office of Statistics/National Planning Commission 2000).

Therefore, policies and programmes eradicating poverty and supporting capture and culture fisheries could indirectly impact on the educational attainment of an average Nigerian child, especially in the riverine communities where the majority are trapped in poverty.

Contribution to Gender Equality and Female Empowerment

The ways in which capture and culture fisheries can contribute to development at household, community and national levels is critical to gender equality and female empowerment through women's fishing-related livelihood activities. This is because the portfolios of the women's fishing related activities are essential for securing their families' improved livelihoods. Especially in the riverine communities where women are very active in capture and culture fisheries and also processing and marketing of fish resources (Alfred-Ockiya 2000), policies and programmes targeting female empowerment through fisheries development will profoundly impact on the women's income generating capacities (Kingdom, Alfred-Ockiya & Adeyemo 2008). This suggests that women will increasingly share in their families economic burdens, spending their income on themselves, their children's education and other areas.

> The involvement of women in sharing their families' economic burdens clearly explains the strength of their increasingly active participations in family decision-making, an important aspect of gender equality and female empowerment (Enaikele, Okekunle & Aluko 2010).

Reducing Child Mortality Rate

Poverty is associated with the Nigerian child health and mortality rates. The statistics on poverty in Nigeria are sufficient to suggest that a Nigerian child is more vulnerable to several preventive diseases like cerebrospinal meningitis, polio, malaria and yellow fever (Adebayo 2010). Children's health and mortality rates are good indicators of a healthy nation and development. In Nigeria, child mortality and malnutrition are very high. Recent studies have identified low birth weight as a leading factor in child mortality (McCormack 2008), but through capture and culture fisheries sufficient fatty acids can be obtained for both neurological development of the brains and bodies of infants, children, and pregnant and lactating women (World Fish Centre 2005).

Improving Maternal Health

In Nigeria, giving birth to a baby may be life threatening, especially where drug shortages and counterfeiting are present and per capital health spending is ridiculously low and does not focus on quality health delivery (Ayoboly 1997). Apart from poverty, limited access to medical treatment and poor protein-rich food are the primary causes for the high mortality rates among children and child-bearing women. Especially among children, malnutrition resulting from protein deficiency is serious enough to cause kwashiorkor, stunted growth and wasting (Connor 1991).

According to the opinion of experts, maternal health conditions can only be improved by a three-stage programme comprising: child spacing and care during pregnancy and childbirth; timely access to hospitals where complications can be treated; and sufficient protein-rich food, such as fish. Fish consumption during pregnancy and lactation reduces susceptibility to disease, improves the health status of women and reduces the risk of low birth weight, which is a key factor in both maternal and child mortality (Pelletier 1994).

Combating HIV/AIDS, Malaria and other Diseases

While the most obvious contributions of capture and culture fisheries are in terms of income generation, poverty alleviation and food security, they also help in combating HIV/AIDS, malaria and other diseases. Poverty and poor nutrition are closely linked to these. Poverty leads to reduced access to health services and exposes people to nutritional deficiencies, parasitic diseases, and increased susceptibility to infections (Stillwagon 1994). Food-insecure, underfeeding and ill individuals have weakened immune systems and are more vulnerable to HIV infection and the eventual development of AIDS (Drimie 2002). Also, malnutrition makes people more susceptible to endemic parasitic diseases such as malaria, schistosomiasis, sleeping sickness and intestinal parasites. These in turn exhaust the body's immune system and make people increasingly susceptible to infections connected to HIV. Malnutrition is a serious morbidity syndrome and disease complication that affects the functioning of the immune system and consequently impacts on survivability and quality of life (Haddad & Gillespie 2001). The daily intake of a balanced diet rich in both macro- and micro- nutrients is important in building the body's immunity to diseases and to thereby maintain good health.

What those fighting HIV/AIDS need are body building and nourishing food nutrients for repair and maintenance and sustaining a healthy weight. Fish is a food rich in both macro- and micro-nutrients, with good quality proteins and fats (macro), and vitamins and minerals (micro) necessary for repair and maintenance of the human body. On average, fish contains 16–28% high quality proteins and 0.25–25% essential vitamins, minerals such as calcium, phosphorus, iron, magnesium and vitamins including B-complex, vitamin A and D, and essential polyunsaturated fatty acids (World Fish Centre 2001). These nutrients are particularly essential for people with health problems such as HIV/AIDS, tuberculosis and malaria. Therefore, this fact relating to the importance of fish in combatting HIV/AIDS and malaria is extremely important for the socio-economic development of the country.

Ensuring Environmental Sustainability

In developing countries, especially Nigeria, fishery resources constitute a major component of natural resources. Capture fisheries are mostly exploited by trawler owners (industrial fishing) and the artisanal fishers. Artisanal fishery covers the operation of small-scale canoe fisheries operating in the coastal marine and inland waters. The fishers in this sector operate within a limited fishing range with small canoes of about 3–6 metres mostly powered by paddles (FAO 1994). The limited fishing range and lack of other tangible employment opportunities in the coastal communities confine them to fishing (Matthew 2000). Following this, the artisanal fishers have no option but to continue exploiting the available resources, resulting in overfishing. Much environmental damage in brackish and marine water environments through overfishing can be pinned on the activities of industrial fisheries.

The implication of overfishing, resulting from exploiting the available fish resources excessively, intensively and frequently, suggests the depletion of resources, otherwise known as the "tragedy of the commons" (Utomakili & Fabiyi 1993). Therefore, with a growing population, increasing fish production through culture fisheries has an important role in over dependence on capture fisheries and achieving protein increase, food security and environmental sustainability. The innovative concept of culture fisheries represents a break with the past, when fish from the natural stock (i.e. the wild) were considered the only supply source (Williams 1997). This is important because fish production can no longer be left only to nature, since the biophysical limit of natural production from the wild appears to have been reached, if not exceeded (John 1994).
Culture fisheries have an integral role to play with regard to the conservation and sustainable use of the wild as they can reduce pressure on capture fisheries and the environment. The need to move toward the development of capture fisheries through a sustainable and socially beneficial exploitation of resources has led to the concept of culture fisheries. The overall goal of this is to address the shortfalls in capture fisheries and to ensure that fish production is secured for the present and future generations and sustained at an optimum level to guarantee a continuous supply through natural production (Enaikele & Olutayo 2010).

The demand for fish obviously highlights the need for a parallel development of culture fisheries. Culture fisheries, therefore, are not a replacement for capture fisheries; at best, they represent a complementary or supplementary technology (International Centre for Living Aquatic Resources Management 1991). Hence, the sustainable exploitation of capture fishery resources requires preservation of the ecological and biophysical resources. This suggests fish exploitation that meets the needs of the present generation without compromising the future (ibid.).

Developing the Global Partnership for Development

Fish is one of the most traded agricultural commodities and a major export for many developing countries, largely because it offers opportunities for trade agreements which contribute to peace and development (World Fish Centre Fisheries and Millennium Development Goals Solutions for Africa World Fish Centre 2005). Fish is a global trade that strengthens partnerships between developing and developed countries. For example, an estimated 40% of world fish production enters international trade, with 2005 exports of US$ 77 billion representing a 40% increase over those of 2000. The main flow is from developing countries to developed nations, the former having 57% of the trade volume and 77% of its value (FAO Fisheries Statistics 2001). It is a good means of wealth creation, balancing the trade and foreign exchange for some developing countries and financing other food imports (Chichi 2010). In Africa, fish has turned from importation to a net exportation, with exports valued at US $2.7 billion annually (FAO FAOSTAT data 2004). In Nigeria, fisheries contribute about US $1 billion to the nation's Gross Domestic Product. The demand for fish and investment in commercial fish farming (i.e. culture fisheries) in Nigeria is rapidly expanding at 25–33% per year and 85, 000 metric tons of fish are produced in these farms, thereby making Nigeria the largest aquaculture producer in Africa. On the other hand, the capture fisheries account for a total landing of 504, 000 metric tons with an average N 200, 000 per ton, equalling N 100 billion (Chichi 2010).

Marine water makes it possible to engage in commercial fishing on the high seas. The fishing sector has, over the years, enjoyed continuous relevance in the volume of trade and fishing capacity, capable of impacting positively on national food security and development. This is because fishing trawlers operating in this sector provide social and economic opportunities and benefits that result in positive multiplication effects, such as job creation and supply of fish to boost food security.

Besides, through fisheries, countries have been able to form diplomatic collaborations and global partnerships for peace and development and tackle the problem of piracy and illegal fishing, imposing enormous risks to fishing trawlers and international trade on the high seas. Nigeria's Exclusive Economic Zone (EEZ) extends to a distance of 200 nautical miles (370 kilometres) from its coast. It includes the territorial waters, contiguous zone and the continental shelf where the Nigerian Navy and Customs Service dispatch their personnel to check territorial incursion, illegal fishing, piracy and smuggling. In an effort to check rising piracy and illegal fishing, the Nigerian Navy are collaborating with the navies of thirteen other countries—the USA, France, Spain, Belgium, Benin, Cameroon, Equatorial Guinea, Gabon, Ghana, Italy, Congo, Sao Tome and Principe and Togo. This diplomatic collaboration is part of the African Partnership Station (APS), formed to check the upsurge of illegal activities especially in the Gulf of Guinea. The USA's "SIMPSON" and France's "FRIGATE SIROCO" are security vessels presently patrolling Nigeria's territorial water and the Gulf of Guinea (Ruddle 2008).

Promotion of Culture and Tourism

The ways in which fisheries can contribute to the promotion of culture and tourism are critical to national development. The tourism industry has experienced increasing popularity in Nigeria, reaching a level of considerable significance in the nation's economy. Tourism facilitates an important avenue through which the state and federal government realize revenue for national development. The tourism industry also helps in boosting business in the operation of hostels, guest houses, resort centres, and in providing huge employment opportunities. For example, the Argugu International Fishing and Cultural Festival is contributing to the promotion of Nigeria's cultural heritage and tourism. In recent times, the festival has featured a highly diversified and multi-sponsored grand fishing competition, bare hand fishing demonstrations, an agricultural show, craft exhibitions, national wrestling and boxing tournaments, swimming competitions of different styles, a diving competition, canoe racing, wild duck catching, cultural entertainment, and traditional symphonies and instrumentalists.

The four-day Argugu fishing festival is presently the most widely attended in Nigeria, drawing tourists from all over the world. Despite these impacts, Nigeria still has large, untapped tourism potentials in fisheries as the industry has the capacity to drive the nation's socio-economic development.

Problems hindering the contribution of Fisheries to Development in Nigeria

Though Nigeria contributes about US $1 billion in fishery contributions to the nation's Gross Domestic Product through exports, the fish exported is mainly obtained by domestic fleets operating within the EEZ. But the activity of the foreign illegal industrial fleets in Nigeria's territorial waters is of much concern because of the over exploitation of fisheries. Since the domestic waters have already been overfished and are unable to sustain increased exploitation, further exploitation by these illegal industrial fleets has resulted in major economic and social woes for the country. Even where access to the EEZ is negotiated and granted by license, catches are under-reported and are rarely thoroughly monitored by government agencies. The monitoring and enforcement are combined responsibilities of the Federal Department of Fisheries (FDF), the Customs and Exercise Department and quarantine officials. The fact is that the inspectorate of the Federal Department of Fisheries, the Customs and Exercise Department or the quarantine department can be relied upon for effective monitoring and enforcement.

Also, additional revenue is lost by the government where various fees and taxes are avoided by these illegal fleet operators. This illegal fishing also threatens food security, livelihoods and potential employment for small-scale fishing communities. Since capture fisheries are in critical conditions, and have probably now exceeded their capacities to fulfil the demand for fish, this is exacerbated because the activities of industrial fisheries have major negative impacts on the marine ecosystems. This in turn can eventually be expected to have negative repercussions on development in Nigeria.

Although much environmental damage in marine environments can be pinned on industrial fisheries, another closely related and inseparable fact is that the potential contribution of fisheries to development is severely constrained by the current global reality of climate change. In Nigeria, the marine and brackish water provides fish products including crabs, skippers, oyster products, periwinkles, white and pink shrimps, palegic fish species (principally bonga), sardines and demersal species, notably croackers, barracuda, catfish, and snappers. With the rise in sea level induced by climate change, the fish resources will either be forced to change location or die off. What this suggests is that a rise in sea level will have implications for fish production to feed the growing population (Enaikele, Okekunle & Olutayo 2011).

Above all, government policy meant to contribute to poverty alleviation, rural transformation, reduce unemployment and improve food security rarely focuses serious attention on the development of fisheries because, when faced with resource allocation decisions, policy makers are often quick to prioritise the use of water bodies for human consumption, hydro-electric power, transportation and industrial use over capture and culture fisheries. The poor policy priority given to capture and culture fisheries is incidentally linked with the poor attention given to agriculture, because of the rising fortune of the petroleum sector (Udosung, Umoh & Ekanem 2012). Even where there are policy programmes, such programmes are rarely implemented well because of corruption and the non-participation of the people in their conception and implementation.

The Way Forward and Conclusion

Capture and culture fisheries have the capacity to drive the nation's socio-economic development. For fisheries to contribute to development, the FAO Code of Conduct for Responsible Fisheries needs to be adopted. This states that countries should ensure that fishers and fish farmers are involved in the policy conception and implementation of programmes that concern fisheries.

Besides this, the government should rigorously monitor and enforce policy and laws on the high seas to prevent illegal fishing taking its toll on available fishery stocks, food security and rural communities' livelihoods. Also, the government should come up with programmes and policies to encourage investment opportunities in capture and culture fisheries by embarking on fiscal policies such as granting credit and loan facilities and granting tax exemptions to key fishery operators.

References

Adebayo, C. 2010. *Health Care for All: Chasing an Ever-Elusive Mirage*. Progress of Nigerian Children. Lagos: UNICEF/FOS Publication. 9–10.

Adikwu, I. A. 1999. "Aquaculture in Nigeria: Prospects and Constraints." *Journal of Fisheries Technology* 1 (1): 16–25.

Ayayi, T. D. & Talabi, S. O. 1984. *The Potentials and Strategies for Optimum Utilization of the Fisheries Resources of Nigeria.* Lagos: Nigerian Institute for Oceanography and Marine Research.

Alfred, Ockiya J. F. 2000. "Socio-Economic Activities of Women in Artisanal Fisheries in the Niger Delta." *Aquafield* 1: 1–7.

Areola, F. O. 2007. "Fish Marketing and Export Potentials of Fish and Fisheries Products of Nigeria." Paper presented at the Educative and Informative Aquaculture Workshop and Aqua Exhibitions, Lagos, Nigeria.

Ayobolu, S. 1999. *Caught in the Poverty Trap*. Progress of Nigerian Children. Lagos: UNICEF/FOS Publication.

Bene, C. G., Macfadyen, A. & Allison, E. A. 2007. *Increasing the Contribution of Small Scale Fisheries to Poverty Alleviation and Food Security.* FAO Fisheries Technical Paper No. 481. FAO of the United Nations.

Chichi, Q. 2010. *Fisheries Contribute US $1 Billion to Nigeria's GDP.* http://www.allvoice.com/contribu-ted-news/62832 (accessed January 25, 2013).

Cornor, A. O. 1991. *Poverty in Africa. A Geographical Approach.* London: Belhaven Press.

Drimie, S. 2002. "The Impact of HIV/AIDS on Rural Households and Land Issues in South and Eastern Africa." A background paper prepared for the Food and Agriculture Organisation (FAO) Sub-regional Office for Southern and Eastern Africa, Pretoria. Human Science Research Council.

Enaikele, M.D.; Okekunle, A.A. and Aluko, T.K.O. 2010. Grassroot Women Empowerment and Participation in Fish Farming: A Survey of Women in Selected Communities in Lagos State, Nigeria. *Journal of Global Approach to Extension Practice* 6 (2): 58–63.

Enaikele, M. D. & Olutayo, A. O. 2010. "Explorative Analysis of the Effect of Inland Fisheries Decree on Sustainable Exploitation of Inland Fisheries in Lagos State, Nigeria." *Journal of Agricultural Extension and Rural Development* 2 (8): 154–160.

Enaikele, M. D., Okekunle, A. A. & Olutayo, A. O. 2011. "Climate Change and Global Warming: Mainstreaming the Implication for Poverty in Nigeria." *Journal of Applied Research* 3 (1): 1–8.

FAO. 1994. *A Catalogue of Small Scale Fishing Gear in Nigeria*. FAO Regional Office Accra and NIOMR. 11.

—. 2000. *State of Food Insecurity Report*. FAO of the United Nations, Rome, Italy. 1-20.

—. 2000. *Food Comes First*. FAO of the United Nations, Rome, Italy. 5.

—. 2001. *Commodities Fish Statistics*. FAO of the United Nations, Rome, Italy.

—. *FAOSTATdata,* 2004. http://faostat.fao.org/collections (accessed January 25, 2013).

FAO/WorldBank. 1982. Fishery Report: *A Report for the Federal Department of Fisheries of the Federal Ministry of Agriculture, Lagos Nigeria*. FAO of the United Nations, Rome Italy.

Federal Ministry of Information. 1991. *Towards Self Sufficient in Food: Know Nigeria Series No. 1*. Federal Ministry of Information, Lagos, Nigeria.

George, C. K. *The Challenges of Urbanization in Nigeria urban Centres: The Lagos Mega City Situation.* A Town Planning perspectives. Lagos: Libro-Gem Books.

Hall, S. *African Fisheries and Aquaculture and the Millennium Development Goals.* A Keynote Address in Proceedings of the NEPAD-Fish for All Summit. August 22–25, Abuja.

Haddad, L. & Gillespie, S. 2001. "Effective Food and Nutrition Policy Response for HIV/AIDS: What do we Know and What we need to Know." *Journal of International Development.* 13 (4): 437–511.

Isiebor, C. E., Awosika, L. & Smith, S. V. *Preliminary Water, Salt and Nutrient Budget for Lagos, Lagos, Nigeria* http://data.ecology.su.se/mnode/Africa/Lagos/la-gosbud.htm (accessed December 3, 2013).

International Centre for Living Aquatic Resources Management (ICLARM). 1991. *The Context of Small Scale Integrated Agriculture: Agricultural System in Africa.* A Case Study of Malawi, Manila, Philippine. International Centre for Living Aquatic Resources Management.

John, J. *Managing Redundance in Exploited Fisheries Series.* The World Bank. Washington DC, USA.

Kingdom, T. J. F., Alfred-Ockiya, J. F. & Adeyemo, A. O. 2008. "Women Involvement in Fisherie in the Lower Taylor Creek Area, Bayelsa State." *Journal of Agric Resource Policies*. 3 (3): 34–38.

Matthew, S. 2000. *Managing Artisanal Small Scale Fisheries in Developing Countries: The Need for a Complimentary Approach.* Use of Property Rights in Fisheries Management. Ed. Shotton, R. FAO of the United Nations. Rome. 295.

McCormack, M. C. "The Contribution of Low Birth Weight in Infant Mortality and Childhood Morbidity." *Eng. Journal of Medicine* 3 (12): 82–90.

Odita, S. *Excercse Obangami Turns Heat on Pirate* http://odili.net/news/source/2012/mar/8/9.htm (accessed January 25, 2013).

Okumadewa, F. 2001. *Poverty Eradication in Nigeria. A Four Point Demand*. The House Anniversary Lecture delivered at the University of Ibadan.

Oloruntuyi, O. O. 1998. Aquaculture and its implications for the Nigerian Environment: Sustainable Utilization of Aquatic/Wetland Resources. 9th/10th Annual Conference for the Nigerian Association for Aquatic Science held at the University of Agriculture, Abeokuta, Nigeria. Edited by Otubusin, S. O., Ezeri, G. N. O. and Ugwumba, O. A. 211–218.

Otitolaye, J. O. 1999. "Economic Analysis of Fisheries Production in Nigeria." *Journal of Fisheries Technology* 1 (1): 34–37.

Paquote, E. 1991. "The Role of Information for Rural Development Issues in ACP Countries: Review and Perspectives." Proceedings of an International Seminar held June 12–16 at Montpellier, France.

Pelletier, D. L. 1994. "The Relationship between Child anthropometry and Mortality in Developing Countries: Implication for Policy." *Progress and Future Research Journal of Nutrition* 124 (10S).

Rodney, W. 1996. *How Europe Underdeveloped Africa*. London: Bogle-L Venture.

Ruddle, K. 2008. "Reconsidering the Contribution of Fisheries to Society and Millennium Fisheries for Global Welfare and Environment." 5th World Fisheries Congress.

Spore. 1995. *Population and Food Supply: The Challenges for Africa*. Spore No. 57. Wageningen: The Netherland. Technical Centre for Agricultural and Rural Cooperation. Spore. 1991. *Poverty Reduction and Agricultural Supply: A Question of Access*. Spore No. 80. Wageningen: The Netherlands. Technical Centre for Agricultural and Rural Cooperation.

Stillwagon, E. 2002. "HIV/AIDS in Africa: Fertile, Terrain." *Journal of Development Studies* 38 (6): 1–22.

Udosung, I. J., Umoh, G. S. & Ekanem, J. T. "Impact of Macro-economic Policies on Capture Fishery in Nigeria (1970–2000)." *Journal of Business Administration* 2 (7): 101–103.

United Nations. 1996. Poverty and Development: An (IM) Balance Sheet. International Year for the Eradication of Poverty. United Nations Development of Public Information. DP1/1779-POV-96-04647-May USA, New York.

United Nations System in Nigeria. 1995. *Partnership.* A Quarterly News Magazine. Lagos, Nigeria. The United Nations Information Centre.

Usoro, M. E. 2003. *Cabotage Policy and International Maritime Politics: the Nigerian Coastal and Island Shipping*

http://www.paulusoro.com/publication.cabotage (accessed July 5, 2012).
Utomakili, J. B. & Fabiyi, Y. L. 1993. "Economic Analysis of Fish Farming Industries in Nigeria." *Journal of West African Fisheries* VI: 296–304.
Williams, M. "Aquaculture and Sustainable Food Security in the Developing World." In *Sustainable Aquaculture*, edited by Bardach, J. E., 15–45. New York: John Wiley and Son Inc.
World Bank/Federal Office of Statistics/National Planning Commission. 2000. *Poverty and Welfare in Nigeria.* Abuja: FOS/NPC Publication. 1–21.
World Fish Centre. 2005. *Fish and Food Security in Africa.* World Fish Centre, Penang, Malaysia.
World Fish Centre. 2005. *Fisheries and Millennium Development Goals: Solutions for Africa.* World Fish Centre. Penang, Malaysia.
World Fish Centre. 2013. *The Impact of Nutrition and Fish Supplementation on the Response to Anti Retroviral Therapy, Zambia.* www.fao.org/fishery/topic-/12318 (accessed January 25, 2013).

CHAPTER SEVEN

IDENTITY CONSTRUCTION AND NATIONALISM IN NORTH-CENTRAL NIGERIA

COMFORT ERIMA UGBEM

Introduction

Identity construction, reconstruction and politics have engaged the attention of academia and contemporary society in recent times. This is connected to the rise in identity consciousness and politics as well as the resurgence of identity-related conflicts in many countries across the world. World over, there appears to be a pull from the state towards ethnic/regional/ religious enclaves. As such, in many countries the "centre" appears to be losing its hold. Violent contestations have occurred in many countries such as Rwanda, Burundi, Yugoslavia and Sudan. Some scholars have attributed this trend to globalization and its attendant characteristic of erasing boundaries between nation-states, while others have attributed it to the aftermath of colonialism and the need for resource control (Elfert, Miguel & Posner 2010; Guess 2006; Itenkel 2005; Abubakar 2001; Ejobowah 2000).

Specifically, Obi (2001) traces the resurgence of identity construction to the nature of the re-invigorated drive by global neoliberal forces to integrate Nigeria into the world capitalist system. Identity is transformed into a mobilizing element not only for contesting access to the state and oil power within a context of conflicting and competing ethnicity, but also a modality for organizing social forces to resist annihilation, extraction and exclusion by the hegemonic coalition of the ethnic elite. Alubo (2006) links this to the pride of place the ethnicity project has occupied in recent times, while Jega (2000) links it to the introduction of the Structural Adjustment Programme introduced to developing countries like Nigeria by the World Bank. Though identity construction and politics are consistent aspects of the social reality of human existence, they are more salient among ethnic groups, especially in developing countries like Nigeria.

Identities have historically been significant in Nigeria, especially during and after colonial rule. After the creation of Nigeria through the amalgamation of Northern and Southern protectorates by the colonial masters, suspicion of a deliberate administrative divide and rule policy warranted the inventions of identity-based constructions pitting the northern and southern parts against each other (Suberu & Osaghae 2005; Kalu 2004; Jega 2000). During this period and the immediate post-independence era, though other ethnicities existed, only three ethnic groups were noticeable: the Hausa-Fulani, the Igbo and the Yoruba. Over the last four decades, various ethnic identities have emerged and are still emerging. A classic example is cited by Suberu & Osaghae (2005), where the Igbo redefined themselves as Ikwere after the civil war.

The post-colonial Nigerian state has grappled with the daunting challenge of the rising tide of identity mobilizations and contestations among emerging ethnicities. North-central Nigeria is one of the regions in which there is a recurrence of identity construction and reconstruction, identity related conflict and the emergence of new groups contesting their exclusion as redefining who they are in relation to the state. This region comprises ethnic groups that hitherto existed independently but were eventually subsumed under the caliphate and emirate system of the Hausa Fulani. The North Central geo-political zone (The Middle Belt Region) has witnessed numerous identity mobilizations and violent ethnic conflicts in the history of post-independence Nigeria (Alubo 2006; Ajene 2006; Best 2006; Thomas 2002). The United Middle Belt Congress (UMBC), a regional group, was created to contest the non-inclusion of minority ethnic groups of the Middle Belt in the Nigerian political structure (Best 2006; Agbu & Osaghae 1998; Ajene 2006). This region forged a united front to resist the Hausa-Fulani domination. At this time, the various Middle Belt linguistic groups saw one another as of one social identity. Lately, however, the Middle Belt has witnessed fierce identity contestations showing a considerable breakdown or suspension of the wholesome Middle Belt identity (Alubo 2006).

Many of the ethnic groups in the Middle Belt have engaged one another in violent identity conflict, for example Tiv/Alago, Tiv/Fulani, Tiv/Jukun, Ebira/Igala, Ebira/Bassa, Tiv /Igede, etc. (see the Internal Displacement Monitoring Centre [IDMC] Report 2008; Okafor 2007; Alubo 2006; Best 2006; Tenuche 2006; Alubo 2004; Ibrahim 2000). Furthermore, within the Middle Belt, numerous identities have evolved claiming to be "nations" and/or "races, " like Tiv, Idoma and Igede. One noteworthy trend is that even within these "nations" other groups have emerged, not with different names or languages but who have redefined their identities as different from the larger group and are even beginning to undermine the so-called "nationhood" of the ethnic groups.

This chapter focuses on identity construction dynamics and nationalism in north-central Nigeria. It is divided into three sections of identity construction in the historical perspective, nationalism and identity dynamics, and a conclusion.

Identity Construction from the Historical Perspective

The construction of identity is a social process that influences and is influenced by social interaction. It does not take place in a vacuum but within or between groups engulfed in the struggle over social, economic and power relations (Gandu 2001). Identity essentially emerges from the dialectic between the individual/group and the society. It encompasses the sum total of a peoples' sources of meaning, history, geography and experience over a space of time (Castels 2010). Once it is formed it is also maintained, reshaped and modified through interactive processes which are determined by the social structure (Luckman & Berger 1966).

The ethnic groups in contemporary North-Central Nigeria existed as independent ethnic/cultural groups until the introduction of Islam and the Fulani conquest of the Hausa area, the British colonial occupation and consequent creation of the Protectorate of Northern Nigeria in 1900. The Hausa occupied the Northern half of the Northern protectorate, while the Southern half was occupied by over a hundred other ethnic groups who had distinct cultural practices, language and identities. The Hausa existed in various groups and traced their origins to different progenitors.

For instance, the Kanuri in Borno trace their origin to one Sef, who named the whole of the empire after himself—*sefewa*, meaning the people of Sef. Other Hausas west of Bornu trace their origin to one Bayajida, who founded the state of Daura and from which grew the seven Hausa states of Daura, Zaria, Gobir, Kastina, Rano and Biram. The Hausa existed in different states until the jihad of 1804–8, which superimposed a central political and religious authority on the fragmented Hausa states through conquest and Islamization discourse, reconstructing the Hausa into one political linguistic unit and inscribed Islamic piety as one of the most important markers of Hausa identity (Onchonu 2008; Burdon 1904; Ruxton 1906).

An Emirate and caliphate structure was created with a Sultan at Sokoto as a spiritual/religious and political head, and the Fulani as Emirs over the Hausa states (that had been reorganized as Emirates) who reported to the Sultanate. The Hausa followed in the hierarchy and then the *talakawas*, who were the commoners and the foot soldiers of the caliphate. The jihad was more or less a homogenizing process for the

Hausa and Fulani in terms of culture and religion as well as political and social structure, and it inherently portrayed Hausa as synonymous with being Muslim. Furthermore, the Fulani adopted the language of the Hausa and improved upon their administrative structure, the *habe* (Ruxton 1906). The whole of the process led to the creation of the Hausa-Fulani composite group as well as identity and nomenclature that are popularly used to describe the northwestern ethnic groups in contemporary Nigeria. This was the socio-political structure that the British colonialist met and proceeded to impose on the other ethnic groups in the southern half of the Northern Protectorate.

Colonial occupation in northern Nigeria was a critical step in the reconstruction of the identity of the ethnic groups in the southern half of the Northern region from their indigenous forms (Dudley 1968). The British set up their trading concerns along the Niger in 1878 and eventually created the Royal Niger Company, with branches in many parts of northern Nigeria (Makar 1994). In 1899, the Protectorate of Northern Nigeria was created and the territories of the Royal Niger Company were consequently transferred to the colonial office, with Lord Lugard taking over affairs as the first commissioner of the Protectorate of Northern Nigeria. The creation of the Protectorate overtly brought all the ethnic groups within this area under the northern identity. Furthermore, within the Northern Protectorate, or the identity of "northern, " two major identities were created. The British integrated the Fulani and the Hausa into a wholesome dominant identity called the Hausa-Fulani, while all the other ethnic groups/socio-cultural groups in northern Nigeria were given a pagan identity. The British created a dominant identity for the Hausa-Fulani predicated on a supposedly factual assumption as to the origin of the Fulani.

> Thus it would seem that in quite ancient times the existence of different races within the belt of Negroland was established. There were evidently superior and inferior tribes; and without attempting to follow the question in detail, it is interesting, though not surprising, to observe that along the whole line of the fertile belt **the superior races,** modified by **intercourse with the white pressure from the north**, gradually established themselves in possession of the uplands bordering more nearly upon the desert and civilization, while the inferior races were driven back towards the then impenetrable regions of barbarism and equatorial Africa. This movement of all that was inferior towards the south is a fact of supreme importance to the subsequent history of the Negro belt. **Today I believe it will be found that there has been a still further recession southwards of the inferior races, and 9° north would perhaps be nearer to the limit of their northern extension. It is interesting to observe that**

> **Northern Nigeria stretches from 7° to 14°, thus including within its limits both classes of natives … It is also in this neighbourhood, about the sources of the Senegal, that the original home in Africa of the Fulani, who count as a partly white race, is placed.** The movement of this remarkable people in Africa within historic time has unquestionably been from west to east, but this does not preclude the theory of some more remote eastern origin which may have preceded their African immigration. **Whether Phoenician, Egyptian, Indian, or simply Arab, they are evidently a race distinct from the Negroid and other black types by which they have been surrounded, and notwithstanding the marked effect produced on some portions of their people by intermarriage with Negro women, they have kept the distinctive qualifications of their race through a known period of two thousand years. The Fulah of today is as distinct from the pure Negro as was the first Fulah of whom we have record. How long they may have existed in Africa before any record of them was made it is with our present knowledge impossible to say. The Hausa and the Songhay are other races which, though black, are absolutely distinct from the pure Negro type.** (Shaw 1905, 21–22)

Here, the Hausa and Fulani were portrayed as superior to the others who were Negroes. Though Negro refers to a racial classification in abstract terms, in this context it underscored the fact that the other ethnic groups were of a different race, inferior to that of the Hausa and Fulani. The data below further gives insight on the inferior/superior identities created for the Hausa-Fulani and the other ethnic groups:

> Hence every cause, natural and artificial alike, has combined to the one end, of establishing the superior races in the northern and the inferior races in the southern portions of the fertile belt. The result as we see it today is strikingly illustrated in British territory by a journey from the Niger mouth to Sokoto. The river in its windings makes a sectional cut of which the general direction is from north to south, and leaving the **nude savage of the coast to prowl in dusky nakedness** through the mangrove swamps of Southern Nigeria at its mouths, the traveller who enters the river sees the natives on the banks ever increasing in decency and dignity as the latitude recedes from the equator. (Shaw 1905, 22–23)

Here, the Hausa and the Fulani were regarded as superior races while the other ethnic groups to the southern half of the protectorate were regarded as inferior. This inferior/superior identity is further illustrated in the following:

> … as with climate and nature, so it is with man. From the light-coloured, straight-featured Fulani, one passes through many gradations to the typical

> Negro of the coast. The characters of the two types are as different as their looks. Ethnology teaches us the effect of environment on race and it is therefore easy to understand why the forest and swamp-dwellers of the south should be of a lower type than the inhabitants of the open northern plains. But history tells of the southward movement of superior races from the north, and it seems probable that this pressure has forced coastward inferior aboriginal plain-dwellers. Whatever be the cause, the important point to remember is the very great difference which exists, both in character and appearance, between the inhabitants of the northern plateau and the natives of the southern forests … England pictures West Africa as peopled by “niggers, " the type of negro whom it helped to degrade by the over-sea slave trade; for the Mohammedan states of Northern Nigeria this picture does not hold good. The offensive name of nigger is as applicable as it is objectionable to the dignified Hausa and Fulani. Not only did this tract escape this product of European civilization, but we have there an entirely different type, a higher race, one from which great things may be hoped in the future, and which will assuredly make its mark in the collection of races that constitute the British Empire …. (Bourdon 1904, 636–7)

While a superior identity was constructed for the Fulani, the other ethnic groups had their identities reconstructed from their indigenous forms to pagans. The Fulani were seen as being of indo-Germanic stock, which inherently meant they were at a higher stage of civilization, while the Hausa were likened to the Berber and the Coptic, still showing that they were of a higher civilization and therefore superior to the other ethnic groups. This racial identity portrayed the Hausa-Fulani as being in a state of higher civilization than the other ethnic groups, who were designated as pagans. These pagans were described as cannibals who wore no clothing, showing that compared to the Fulani they were at a lower stage in civilization.

The pagan identity, indicating barbarism, savagery, timidity, unsettlement, lack of cohesion, backwardness and primitiveness, was also an identity of a conquered people who were forced into their present environment by the Hausa-Fulani. The identity of pagan was used in all official colonial documents, and it was commonplace to find documents with titles such as Pagan Administration, Pagan Education, Pagan (raw) Memorandum on the treatment of, Expedition into Pagan territory … of, etc. The colonialist overtly fancied the Hausa Fulani culture and social structure and proceeded to impose this on the pagan tribes, who had to become *civilized* by leaving their own backward, barbaric, lower forms of culture and social structure in favour of a higher Hausa Fulani one.

The first reaction to the inferior identity imposed on the ethnic groups was the reconstruction of identity by the ethnic groups from the inferior barbaric light it had been portrayed in to their indigenous identities. This was manifested in various protests and resistances carried out by the various ethnic groups. Among the Tiv there was the *Iyambuan* movement which emerged to challenge the powers of the elders whom the youth believed had been bought over by the colonial powers. This movement emerged in the Tiv land in the 1930s to challenge the authorities and structures that the British had established. It was a cult which promised its adherents eternal life as well as immunity from the British. *Nyambuan* means “meat that has gone bad, ” and this was in reference to the barbaric identity as well as the colonial administrative arrangements. The movement emerged as a parallel institution to ridicule the political structure and especially the work of colonial agents and missionaries, exposing the perceived/real disorder of an alien-imposed rule cum identity.

Among the Idoma, various protests and altercations took place, as discussed in the previous section. The Igede revolted led by an Igede traditional physician named *Ogbiloko*, who had previously worked as a messenger with the colonialists and was uncomfortable with the inferior status and identity imposed on them by the British. He led the Igede in a revolt to protest the imposed identity. Most of the resistances put up by the ethnic groups were largely repressed. Besides these revolts the ethnic groups created sociocultural organizations to recreate and emphasize their distinct ethnic identities away from the barbaric and backward ones imposed on them. Hence, among the Tiv a progressive union, TPU, was created to, among other things, promote Tiv values and culture as well as agitate for a paramount Tiv chief.

Among the Idoma a Hope Rising Union was formed to create a sense of identity among the groups under this division. These two organizations agitated for the creation of the Tiv and the Idoma traditional councils in the Benue, recreating the identity of their ethnic groups away from the barbaric light in which the colonialists had portrayed them. These groups also sought to create a parallel institution such as the caliphate whereby they had a paramount ruler with other chiefs or kings, like that of the emirate and the caliphate system of the Hausa-Fulani. These groups had hitherto been described as unorganized and unsettled in comparison to the Fulani, but they changed these perceptions. Further, in the 1940s, realizing that those independent constructions of identity would not achieve the desired liberation, these ethnic groups created a middle belt identity, counter to the pagan identity imposed on them by the colonialist. This identity was a construction to protest their political alienation, socio-economic marginalisation and discrimination by the Hausa-Fulani cum British.

> The middle belt movement was … a political reaction of the non-Islamic groups of the middle belt area, to the colonial type of relationship and domination of their societies by a culturally different group, which had existed within the very political boundaries of the north as a unit of the Nigerian federation. The reaction took the form of achieving specific types of political identities in the middle belt area in order to produce support for the demands of the middle belt region. This was meant to separate the middle belt groups and Islamic federation in the context of their identities. (Logmans 1985, 11)

Contesting the imposition and dominance of the Hausa-Fulani identity, the middle belt identity was a reaction to the Hausa-Fulani identity as well as the pagan identity imposed on the pagan ethnic groups. Though seemingly homogenous, it comprised several multiple identities which had to be voluntarily/necessarily subsumed for it to thrive. According to Tarka (1958, 2):

> The Middle Belt … comprises of four national groups which include the Nupe group: comprising the Nupe proper, the Igbirras, Igalas, Idomas and the Gwaris; The Tiv: comprising of the Tiv proper, the Aragos and the Jukuns; The Birom Group, comprising the Birom proper, the Eggons, the Angas and the Ankwes; The Bachama group: comprising the Bachama proper, the Chamba and the Bolawas … These people shared a common culture, and a common destiny which was different from those of their enemies, the Hausa and Fulani group. They generally have common body structures, identical national marks, a similar habitat or abode, the same geographical problem, and the same customs and traditions as well as the same ways of worship … The middle belt people are bound together by strings of nature, by their common way of life, by traditions and intermarriage. They are they so called pagans or Kafiris or the Banza Bakwai (useless seven) … The Middle Belt people constitute an ethnic and religious minority group compared to the Hausa-Fulani Muslim who constitute two thirds of the total population of the entire North. (Proceedings of the Minorities Commission 1958, 2)

The Middle Belt identity, as with most reconstructed identities in relation to a collective, was resisted by the government of the Northern Region who saw it as the handiwork of Christian missionaries principally originating from outside the region, as other regions felt the north had a higher population and the pagan tribes were too weak to make such agitations.

The middle belt identity was considered a threat to the access and control of political space and valued resources at the centre, so efforts were made by the leadership of the northern region to frustrate the existence of that identity. This identity remained until the early days of independence when the ethnic groups in the middle belt began to redefine who they were in relation to one another and Nigeria as a whole.

Nationalism and Identity Dynamics

Following independence in 1960, many ethnic groups in Nigeria, especially among the minorities, began to reconstruct their identities in relation to the whole, and as such began to redefine their relationship to the whole of Nigeria. There were secession attempts by some ethnic groups. Isaac Boro declared the Niger-Delta Republic but were quashed. The Igbos also attempted secession with the declaration of the Biafra Nigerian Republic, leading to a three-year civil war that was eventually brought to an end in 1967. The result of this was the division of the country into twelve regions, with the Northern Region divided into six states in 1967: Northwestern, Kano, North Eastern, North-Central, Kwara and Benue-Plateau State. With the creation of states, ethnic groups became more conscious of their distinctiveness and as such began to pull out of the middle belt agenda towards the accentuation of distinct ethnic identities. Instead of allaying the fears of the minorities, the creation of states sparked agitations from the minority ethnic groups.

Instead of creating a middle belt state to serve as a home to the entire pagan ethnic group, the middle belt was fragmented into three states. This caused a major breakdown in the middle belt identity, and several identities emerged. First was a dichotomization within each state as majorities and minorities emerged. This majority was designated in terms of numbers and determined access to resources, opportunities and rights within the state, and as such many of the ethnic groups began to engage one another in violent and nonviolent conflict. Apart from majority minority issues, indigenship, settlership visitorship and strangership emerged. Ethnic groups who had wholesomely created the middle belt identity began to recreate their identities as more distinct ethnicities. These reconstructions assumed violent dimensions as some ethnic groups declared others as *persona non grata*, resulting in the hunting down and physical elimination of such groups. Maier (2001) captures this in the following:

> Since independence, the Middle belt has been a scene of frequent flare-ups. The Nigerian and international media describe the frequent clashes as religious but in fact they stem from minority ethnic groups attempts to wrench themselves free from what they see as domination by the Hausa-Fulani establishment. Other eruptions involve disputes between neighbouring ethnic groups over land and access to political offices. The

> people of a given area often claim they are indigenes and their enemies are the strangers or settlers seeking to upset the mythical natural order of things. (Maier 2001, 194)

The reconstruction of identities inherently created an "us/them" dichotomy among people who were hitherto of the same social identity. As such, concepts of settler, stranger and visitor emerged with regards to social existence, sources of livelihood, access to factors of production as well as recognition within one's place of abode. This was also manifest in non-violent identity contests regarding other groups in derogatory terms. The data below, based a research work on the social relations of identity construction among ethnic groups in Benue state, attests to this. According to a Tiv:

> The Idoma does not like the Tiv man also the Etulo and the Jukun. The Tiv man is not wanted in any place in Nigeria. Looking back at the killings in Taraba, Nassarawa, Plateau and Wurukum and the destruction and killing in Zaki biam. (Tiv female/IDI/12 September 2011)

Yet another Idoma affirmed that:

> The Tiv are very wicked and domineering. The Igede used to be very close but now they seem not to accept us. The Jukuns; I am afraid of the Jukuns because we believe they are mermaids and witches and wizards. While the Etulo, we are not that close so I don't have anything to say about them. (Idoma female/IDI/October 2011)

Another Tiv said:

> The Jukuns and Idoma are troublesome and I cannot marry them. The Jukuns also practice witchcraft. The Idoma have no regard for widows. Anyway, I will not marry another tribe apart from Tiv because they [other tribes] are lazy. (Tiv female/IDI/12 September 2011)

An Idoma respondent says:

> The Tiv people refer to us as a tree, an object that you beat and it stands still. (Idoma male/IDI/15th October 2011)

While an Igede asserts that:

> Other ethnic groups refer to us as their servants and they do not want to give us their daughters in marriage yet they marry our girls. (Igede male/IDI/ 12th September 2011)

Perceptions, differences, judgements and boundaries which were hitherto subsumed/de-emphasised to pave way for the existence of a Middle Belt identity began to be mobilized to redefine who they were in relation to the collective. A possibility also exists that these differences were not perceived at the time of the creation and emphasis of the Middle Belt identity, but as it failed to achieve access to the centre as well as valued resources in the society, various ethnic groups began to create/recreate boundaries and differences to create a platform of access to the centre, emphasizing the otherness of the other.

Conclusion

Today, North-Central Nigeria continues as a centre for identity construction and reconstruction as well as conflict, which are also inevitable aspects of identity construction. Today, many other identities have emerged and are competing for attention within Nigeria, making it difficult for the centre to hold. As such, allegiance to the Nigerian state is weakened while stronger allegiance exists with regards to the ethnic groups. As such, ethnicity is a huge movement in North-Central Nigeria which threatens the very existence of the Nigerian state as a whole. Though the Nigerian state exists in principle, the sense of belonging and participation which constitute nationhood exists among the various parts like the middle belt that make up the whole.

References

Abubakar, D. 2001. "Ethnic Identity, Democratization and the Future of the African State: Lessons from Nigeria." *Journal of African Issues, Ethnicity and Recent Democratic Experiments in Africa* 29 (112): 31–36.

Agbaje, J. 2005. "The Place of Yoruba Proverbs in the Understanding of Yoruba Philosophy and Education." *International Journal of African and African American Studies* 1 (5): 48–54.

Alubo, O. 2006. *Ethnic Conflicts and Citizenship Crises in the Central Region.* Ibadan: Spectrum Books Nigeria.

—. 2004. "Citizenship and Nation Making in Nigeria: New Challenges and Contestations." *Identity Culture and Politics* 5 (1 & 2).

—. 2009. "Citizenship and Identity Politics." A paper presented at the conference on citizenship and identity politics in Nigeria at CLEEN foundation Lagos, Nigeria.

Berger, P. & Luckmann, T. 1966. *The Social Construction of Reality: a Treatise in the Sociology of Knowledge*. New York: Doubleday and Company.

Dudley, B. 1968. "*Parties and Politics in Northern Nigeria.*" London: Frank Cass and Co Ltd.

Dwyer, D. & Minnegal, M. 1999. "Re-reading Relationships: Changing Constructions of Identity among Kubo of Papua New Guinea." *Ethnology* 38 (1): 59–80.

Ejobowah, B. 2000. "Who Owns the Oil: the Politics of Ethnicity in the Niger Delta." *Africa Today* 47 (1): 29–47.

Elfert, B., Miguel, E. & Posner, M. 2010. "Political Competition and Ethnic Identification in Africa." *American Journal of Political Science* 54 (2): 494–510.

Gandu, K. 2001. *Researching Social Identity: Theoretical and Epistemological Problems.* Zaria Historical Research.

Grande, A. 2000. "American Indian Geographies of Identity and Power at the Cross Roads of Idige'na and Mestizaje." *Harvard Educational Review* 70: 467–498.

Guess, T. 2006. "The Social Construction of Whiteness. Racism by Intent, Racism by Consequences." *Critical Sociology* 32 (4).

Hembe, G. N. 2003. *J. S. Tarka: The Dilemma of Africa Minority Politics in Nigeria.* Makurdi: Aboki Publishers.

Ikelegbe, A. 2005. "State, Ethnic Militias and Conflict in Nigeria." *Canadian Journal of African Studies* 39 (3): 490–416.

Itenkel, M. 2005. "Academic Identity and Autonomy in a Changing Policy Environment." *Higher Education* 49 (1&2): 155–176.

Jenkins, J. 1994. "Rethinking Ethnicity: Identity Categorization and Power." *Ethnic and Racial Studies* 17 (12): 192–223.

Kalu, A. 2004. "Constitutionalism in Nigeria; a Conceptual Analysis of Ethnicity and Policies." *West African Reviews* 6: 1–30.

Lugard, F. 1904. "Northern Nigeria." *The Geographical Journal* 12 (4): 1–27.

Maines, D. 2000. "The Social Construction of Meaning, Charting Futures for Sociology: Culture and Meaning." *American Sociological Association* 29 (4): 577–584.

Makar, T. 1994. *The History of Political Change among the Tiv in the 19th and 20th Centuries.* Enugu: Forth Dimension Publishing Co. Ltd.

Obi, C. 2001. *The Changing Forms of Identity Politics in Nigeria under the Economic Adjustment: the Case of the Oil Minorities of the Niger Delta*. Nordic African Institute Uppsala.

Ochonu, M. 2008. "Colonialism within Colonialism: the Hausa-Caliphate imaginary and the British Colonial Administration of the Nigerian Middle Belt." *African Studies Quarterly* 10 (2–3): 96–127.

Ode, M. 2003. "The History of the Igede People of North Central Nigeria." *Agba News magazine* 1: 1–5.

Okafor, E. 2007. "Sociological Implications of Communal and Ethno-religious Clashes in the New Democratic Nigeria." *Kamla- Raj Sudan Tribes* 5 (1): 35–45.

Olutayo, A. 2012. "'Verstehen, ' Everyday Sociology and Development: Incorporating African Indigenous Knowledge." *Critical Sociology* 38 (5): 1–10.

Omobowale, O. & Olutayo, O. 2009. "Social Capital and Human Development in Nigeria, the Case of Lalupon Community, Ibadan, Oyo State." *African Identities* 7 (1): 71–82.

Omobowale, O. 2008. "Clentelism and Social Structure: an Analysis of Patronage in Yoruba Social Thought." *African Spectrum* 43 (2): 203–224.

Orr, C. 1911. "The Hausa Race." *Journal of the Royal African Society* 7 (27): 278–283.

Ritzer, G. 2008. *Sociological Theory.* Mcgraw-Hill Companies.

Ruxton, H. 1904. "Notes on the Tribes of the Muri Province." *Journal of The Royal African Society* 7 (28): 374–386.

Scholte, A. 1996. "The Geography of Collective Identities in a Globalizing World." *Review of International Political Economy* 3 (4): 565–607.

Shaw, F. 1904. *A Tropical Dependency.* London: James Nisbet and Co. Ltd.

Skeldon, R. & Jower, J. 1995. "Discourse on Migration and Ethnic Identity; Interviews with Professionals in Hong Kong." *Transactions of the Institute of British Geographers* 20 (3): 342–356.

Storr. 2009. "Decalage: a Thematic Interpretation of Cultural Differences in African Diaspora." *Journal of Black Studies* 39 (5): 665–668.

Suberu, R. & Osaghe, E. 2005. *History of Identities, Violence, and Stability in Nigeria.* Centre for Research on Inequality, Human Security and Ethnicity, Crise, University of Oxford United Kingdom Internal Displacement Monitoring Centre Report 2008.

Archival Sources

Armstrong, R. 1955. The Idoma Speaking Peoples of the Niger Benue Confluence. *Ethno Graphic Survey of Africa.* Ed. Forde. London: International African Institute.

Benue-Plateau State: Some Facts and Figures.
Charles, O. 1965. *The Making of Northern Nigeria*. London: Frank Cass and co. Ltd.
NAK, SNP, 17/34252 *Northern Province Annual Reports* 1918.
NAK, SNP, 17/34252 *Northern Province Annual Reports* 1928.
CSO/26/2. File No.12874 *Benue Province Annual Report* 1927.
CSO/26/2. File No.12874 *Benue Province Annual Report* 1928.
CSO/26/2. File No.12874 *Benue Province Annual Report* 1931.
CSO/26/2. File No.12874 *Benue Province Annual Report* 1932.
CSO/26/2. File No. 12874 *Benue Province Annual Report* 1933.
Meek, C. 1925. *Northern Tribes of Nigeria: an Anthropological Account of the Northern Provinces of Nigeria Together With the 1921 Decimal Census.* London: Oxford University Press.
Memorandum on the Treatment of Pagans (Raw) 1921.
Munshi Expedition 1906.
Njelele Patrol 1928.
Pagan Administration, 1924.
Proceedings of the Minorities Commission 1958.
Record of Proceedings of the Education Department Conference 1927.
Reports of the Willinks minorities commission 1959.
Abraham, R. 1933. *The Idoma People*. London: Crown Agents.

Unpublished Thesis

Okpe, O. 1994. "The Idoma and Minority Group Politics in Northern Nigeria 1944–1960. A Study in the Aspect of the National Question." Thesis. History. University of Jos.
Odey, M. 1980. "The Political History of the Igede from the Pre-colonial Era to 1923." Project. History. University of Jos.

CHAPTER EIGHT

INTERNATIONAL MIGRATION AND DEVELOPMENT IN NIGERIA

OLAYINKA AKANLE

Introduction

Nigeria today confronts a huge development challenge as clearly demonstrated in the high levels of poverty, insecurity, corruption, terrorism, crime and general low quality of life in the country. In fact, Nigeria is better known for these problems than for any major positive strides it has made. This is why it has been argued that, against the paradox of its huge resource endowment, the country remains among the most problematic development cases for the twentieth and twenty-first centuries (Akanle 2013a; 2013b; Akanle & Olutayo 2011; 2012a). This is because its under-development characteristics are a puzzle and represent a substantial historical paradox. Nigeria can be summarily regarded as a "troubled" and "confused" giant of Africa. Nigeria's poverty burden is in the threshold of 70–90%, and while the land is very suitable for agriculture, food production is comatose, creating food insecurity.

Hence, although Nigeria is among the largest exporters of oil and has a population of almost 200 million, crude oil has proved to be a curse as it has led to wanton corruption and fixation at the level of a mono-product economy. Even though Nigeria returned to democracy in 1999 with high hopes and expectations from the citizens that quality of life would improve and poverty would become history, this has yet to be the case as corruption and poor governance have further made development impossible. Even poverty eradication programmes like NAPEP (the National Poverty Eradication Programme), that are supposed to make poverty history, are bedevilled with corruption and poor programme conception and implementation (Akanle 2009a; 2009b; 2009c).

Nigeria has witnessed extraordinary and unprecedented policies and institutional reforms since its return to democracy. Yet these reforms have led more to corruption, unemployment, political high-handedness and poverty. Generally, the quality of life indicators and signals of development pre and post democratization have been largely negative, and this has led to the conception that the Nigerian democracy is nothing but mediocre (Civil Liberties Organization [CLO] 2003). International migration thus becomes a coping and survival mechanism in the face of growing and excruciating poverty and youth neglect within precarious developmental milieu, and does not necessarily stop at the individual migrant level encompassing families, communities and nationalities (World Bank 2011; Adepoju 2010). Individual actions at the level of African social relations only become meaningful and understandable when considered in relation to the significant others. Nigerians' and Africans' actions impact the significant others just as those of the significant others affect individual actions.

When Nigerians migrate it is for the individual migrant's benefit, just as it is for the community's and groups'. This becomes understandable against the background of the African community and family life orientation that only appreciates the individual's actions against the background of family. If migration rewards and outcomes benefit development in Nigeria and Africa, family/community level relations must be well comprehended. In other words, if migration is for development (M4D), kinship implications must be well comprehended and appropriated (Akanle 2012; Akanle & Olutayo 2012b; Akanle 2011; Akanle & Olutayo 2009). Regrettably, most extant studies on the interface of migration and development in developing nations and Nigeria particularly have not sufficiently appreciated kinship nuances and forces in understanding the implications of international migration. To fill the lacunae, this chapter explores the interface of international migration and development in Nigeria. Issues engaged in this chapter include causes of contemporary international in Nigeria, remittances, return migration and kinship.

Causes of Contemporary International Migration, Remittances and Return in Nigeria

Migration, especially internationally to the north, comes with a lot of positive financial consequences even when it could "constitute a huge structural burden on the host countries especially of the North" (Akanle 2009, 181d). The new-found interest and attraction in the interface of migration and development is largely due to the fact that gains from northward migration from the developing nations have enormous positive advantages for the underdeveloped world of the south. Hence, while many receiving countries have come to see migration dispassionately, as a veritable replacement for young and aging populations, they have also retooled migration policies to not unnecessarily forbid migration but to make it more selective. For example, rapidly aging workforces have forced such countries as Japan, Sweden, Norway, Moldova, Cape Verde, the UK and other parts of the European Union to factor increased immigration into their labour policies (Migration Policy Institute 2009), while a few European nations with reversed population growth have adopted pro-migration policies just as many developing nations encourage emigration for perceived migration gains. Most developing nations also see migration gains through remittances from their nationals (migrants) abroad. The only measure of migration gains for many such nations is the amount of money their migrants send home, and this is very substantial for many nations in Latin America and even sub-Saharan Africa.

Remittances today are the most popular outcome of international migration. Most Africans migrate northward based on observable consequences of remittances sent by initial international migrants from their local communities. While this is the position in most developing societies including Latin America and the Caribbean, Adu-Okoree & Onoma (2012) recently found that when sub-Saharan Africans, particularly Ghanaians, migrate they remit back to their families and hometowns, playing an important role in rural development. Adu-Okoree & Onoma (2012) found that as a result of this, community people acquired farmland, bought vehicles and built houses[2] which they would otherwise not have been able to do. Generally, nationally and internationally, interest in remittances accentuated as Foreign Direct Assistance (FDA), Foreign Direct Investments (FDIs) and grants dwindled as a result of financial crises, ethnic strife, internal and external terrorism, kidnapping, crime, political instability, governance irresponsibility, and conflicts (Akanle & Olutayo 2009).

> Nigeria remains firmly rooted among the top recipients of remittances in the world, and is the largest in sub-Saharan Africa. As documented in the World Bank "Outlook for Remittance Flows 2012–14" report. Nigerians in the Diaspora sent remittances totalling N 1.727 trillion ($11 billion) home in 2011, the highest in Africa, and the seventh largest in the world (World Bank "Outlook for Remittance Flows 2012–2014 (Report).

Some other recipients of large amounts of remittances include Pakistan, Bangladesh, Vietnam, Egypt and Lebanon. Remittances today are best considered as the most stable resource in the world and the developing

[2] These are common measures of development in most African societies.

nations must devise strategies to leverage on them for development. While global prices for natural resources fluctuate and are sometimes unsustainable, remittance flow is direct and has proven to be regular and directly deployable for development without any value addition in terms of processing. In other words, while many developing nations lack the technical capacities to process primary materials for development, this is not necessary for remittances, making them simple and useable for even the least technically endowed nations in Africa and the rest of the developing world for development. Hence, according to the World Bank's Migration and Development data, although it is projected that the global economic outlook will slow down due to the negative consequences on employment, among migrant workers, especially even in high-income countries, remittances will increase by 2014 to an estimated $515 billion. An estimated $441 billion of this will be to developing countries. It was further estimated that remittances flows to developing countries will total $351 billion in 2011, and remittances globally will be about $406 billion.

Regardless of the volume, increase and simplicity of remittances, it may not necessarily automatically lead to development against the background of migrants' and kin lifestyles (Africa Recruit 2003; Osili 2004). Worldviews and orientations of migrants and kin are other factors that may negatively impact development potentials and outcomes of development, and these have been major banes of M4D in Africa and identical societies. The nature (whether regular or irregular), purpose and reason for migration, the process of migration financing, and how migrants raised the funds for migration all affect the eventual use of remittances. For instance, many migrants borrowed funds from families, friends and even communities. Many also sell their property and those of their kin. Interestingly, all those who contribute to initial fund raising for migration expect higher returns on their migration investments (Nwajiuba 2005) and this will affect remittance deployment outcomes eventually. Hernandez-Coss & Bun (2006) and the World Bank (2005) documented common uses of migrants' remittances in Nigeria, demonstrating that migrants usually send the first remittance batch for (1) loan repayments, (2) family up-keep, (3) social security, (4) financing of kin's education, (5) return on family investments, (6) special occasions like funerals, weddings, pilgrimages etc., and (7) business development and sustainability.

The most common destination countries among Nigerian migrants are the United States, the UK and Canada. Playing the numbers game in migration studies is not easy as watertight figures are rarely available, but we can use reliable estimates. For instance, it is estimated that almost 5 million Nigerians are in the USA, with an estimated 90, 000 in the UK, and about 500, 000 hold dual citizenship. Estimations have put the figures of "illegal/undocumented immigrants" at between 800, 000 and 3 million (Ogbebulu 2008; United Nations 2009). According to Datta et al. (2006), the immediate causes of Nigerian migrations range from the individual, household to macro-structural. Migrations in Nigeria are mainly due to poverty, economic problems, modernization, comatose industrialization, unemployment, government ineptitude, lack of social welfare, competitive air fare, faster travel, and easy exchange of information that facilitate desirable livelihoods in other countries. Gravil (1985), Ekeh (1989), Long (2005) and Van Den Bersselaar (2005) have added more nuanced socio-cultural causes, relating cases of when migrants are seen as successful, having achieved their desires against the odds.

Return is the critical flipside of emigration and is perceived as the climax of migration for sustainable development. Labour in the context of migration is a migratory resource and is expected to have its ultimate rest in the place of origin. Through migration, human efforts and economic activities are converted to labour across regions. Home land and community/nation of origin is supposedly the ultimate destination in the final analysis, especially given the socio-cultural milieu within which Africans and Nigerians migrate. Among the Yoruba of southwestern Nigeria, for instance, a migrant is not expected to die while migrating or to die abroad, as this is considered shameful and the peak of failure. A Yoruba proverb says "*ile labo si mi oko, ajo ko le dun ko da bi ile, a o ko ere oko dele*" ["home is the place of ultimate rest after work/travel, it does not matter how enjoyable living abroad is, it cannot be as enjoyable as home, we shall return home with our successes abroad"] (this is a prayer usually said in the course of migration).

Against this important socio-cultural background, while it would be ordinarily expected that migrants will return after a period abroad due to age, level of success and affection for their homes, few actually do, and the returnees' contributions and/or potentials to contribute to national development are still not clear in real terms. For instance, the return ratio of Nigeria is negative, showing that most who migrated abroad actually do not return. According to data from the United Nations (UN) in 2009, the Average Annual Net Migration for the country was 60.0/thousands. Unfortunately, within the framework of migrants' return options for development, it is believed that when migrants return home they can contribute to national development in a number of more direct and impactful ways. If migrants are to return to contribute to national development, as seen in the cases of India and China, as against the diaspora option as seen in the cases of Mexico and Latin America generally, return must be managed and sufficiently comprehended as an essential element, and a comprehensive approach and broader framework must be adopted to efficiently understand migration issues (International Organisation for Migrations [IOM] and European Union [EU] 2006). Moreover, the place and influence of kinship must be prioritized.

Methodology

The study that led to this chapter was carried out in Lagos State Nigeria. Lagos state was created on May 27, 1967 (Lagos State Government Center for Rural Development 2006). The total area of the state is 358.861 hectares or 3.577 km, ^{2} comprising only 0.4% of Nigeria. Ironically, Lagos state is arguably the most economically booming in Nigeria. The reason for this is that, regardless of its land mass disadvantage, the state has a unique history of being the capital of Nigeria until 1991 and has one of the best seaports in Africa, just as it is the most popular state in the country. It also contains the busiest international airport in Nigeria, Murtala Muhammed Airport. Hence, Lagos state is among the fastest growing in the world and Africa's leading emerging megacity. More importantly, the state has the highest number of international returnees in Nigeria, distantly followed by capital city Abuja (the Federal Capital Territory). Also, many residents of Lagos state are either local or international migrants or potential migrants at any point in time.

This study is purely qualitative and based on data collection methods and the triangulation of in-depth interviews (66 IDIs), twelve life histories and Focus Group Discussions (14 FGDs). The study populations were international migrants who lived abroad for a minimum of five years but returned to Nigeria, living there for a minimum of two years. Data analysis was carried out through ethnographic summaries aided by software for qualitative data analysis. This chapter engages with the total issues in the full migration cycle, i.e. pre-emigration, departure and return.

Findings and Discussion

Data revealed that returnees still valued kinship identification and relations with their origins, manifested in their kinship tracing and local kinship identity preference. This is also why some continue to relate with their kin and maintained that they would go any length to do so, as observed through supporting kinship identity constructions, re-constructions and maintenance. They appreciated their kin as important parts of existence. A female returnee puts the situation insightfully during

Life History (LH) capturing, talking about African kinship, relationship informality, extended families and support systems as African social welfare structures, and comparing them with how she lived in Europe and America:

> I don't know anybody on my father's side (because he travelled at a very young age). My cousins and all that kind of things (real kinship and practical family relationships) just started when I came to take time to know some of them. I met all of them at my mother's 70th birthday party. I saw, for instance, the way they interacted with each other. They know each other, they just don't know us (herself and her siblings who were most of the time abroad) and so what family is here and what family is abroad are highly different. Abroad, at 18 years old, you are independent and it is everyone for himself. But in Nigeria when you are in really big, big, big, big trouble, you can't come and call the family. There are many situations here where family members gather and try and sort things out while in Europe, for example, it is not common at all!

This shows the development usefulness of the returnees' kinship system as African states attempt to leverage on M4D. This continued valuation must however be understood against the backdrop of multi-sited socialization processes at home and abroad, as already demonstrated by Trager (2001), Reynolds (2002) and Jones (2008). It is important to note that unlike Uduku (2002), who suggests that returnees permanently return through the immediate re-establishment of contact with kin and get jobs or stay in private businesses, it was found that returnees are often still in transit and must be uncritically conceived as permanent returnees, even when they display such disposition overtly. Returnees' permanent returns are still largely conditional on the governance environment, state of infrastructures and capacity for re-emigration. These determining conditions are very important as they could either be enablers or threats to returnees' goals, and the reasons for return and eventual usefulness as drivers of growth and development.

For instance, when a particular returnee was confronted with future migration plans, determinants and a course to test for the permanence of their return during their life history, she submitted that she could go anywhere, easily and at any time, particularly due to her career and well-being. She is a "global person with a base in Nigeria but the world is out there to conquer." Regardless of the situation, however, even though she sees herself as a returnee and has accepted Nigeria as her home and base and the family heritage as the main reason for return, she still goes overseas frequently and always holds a flight return ticket to London against negative occurrences that could jeopardize her well-being and interests. Such eventualities prevent her from becoming "broke, " providing security against being prevented from modern foreign infrastructures, lacking in her home country yet needed for her career, social life and intention to relax away from chaotic Nigeria. According to her:

> I have been back and forth to London. I have a return ticket because I don't want to get sick[3] here. I got pretty sick last year and I had to run back for a month. I go to London at least once a year.

This finding is in line with those of Uduku (2002), Straubhaar (2000), Ite (2002) and Mayr & Peri (2008), according to which returnees usually have investments abroad and only return for economic and development purposes. If these purposes are threatened, return would understandably be transient, even if the original and long-term intention of return is permanence.

Influencers of initial emigrations are also very important in understanding the histories and dynamics of migrations, particularly return and the likelihood of returnees' eventual contributions to development. In this regard, earlier family emigrations actually influenced returnees' emigrations in the first instance, observed to be mostly linked with knowledge sharing about an "enviable" life abroad that determines chain migration. This influence was consistent among returnees. According to one during IDI, returnees "envied" earlier emigrants, and earlier migrants' attitudes to their emigration decision were essentially positive:

> Things were good. He (kinsman) travelled and did not return until three years later. When he came, he actually had a wife and children there and had already become a citizen.

Locating these trajectories within Weberian Social Action Theory could be insightful. Humans are social actors in the sense that they engage in actions which become meaningful when significant others (actors) are involved. Stimuli are released that inform actions and reactions. Meanings are attached to these stimuli (respect and desired types of life abroad) subjectively by actors who are rational, and these subjective meanings and interpretations are contingent upon values and a generalized group ethos. The outcomes of these subjective meanings' attachments and motives determine the eventual actions, reactions and ultimate outcomes of actions. In this regard, returnees relate within definite kinship networks as

---

[3] "Sick" here includes medical, financial and social ailments

designed by their groups. Their orientations, values and general existences are defined and described as meaningful, successful or otherwise by the valued significant others based on the outcomes of actions. Once people as actors relate through migrations and support within kinship networks, and such relationships and actions are valued due to outcomes, those who migrate thus become "icons, " according to Togunde & Osagie (2009). The icons of progress are those who blaze a trail, find the network paths and are forerunners valued in the network due to the outcomes of their actions, considered beneficial to the networks.

The initial "signals" that earlier migrants (as migratory forerunners) send home in terms of remittances and general support information become the stimuli that families attach meaning to. Due to the subjective meaning attachments and interpretations, it is thus expected that a predetermined, valued and expected course of action is taken, which is emigration. Consistently with Weberian action theory, kin groups' expectations and migration norms, as understood by returnees through the internalization of group norms and values, influence their return and the nature of their contribution to the family and the nation, to some extent. The flow of supports is therefore mutual. According to a female returnee:

> I was sending suitcases of clothes to my siblings. I felt in African tradition when you travel you never come empty-handed. Whatever little gift I give were just social things like CDs, DVDs, a discman, fashion items that were in vogue so they could have access to them. But whatever gift I give to my mother, she always says I should stop wasting money although she would finally appreciate it.

Another reported giving support to their family through survival needs like feeding, school fees, rent, festivities and general family upkeep. It was noted that most returnees gave these supports to aid kin survival and reduce stress, because these were the expectations from home. Common opinions of this group of returnees were, as captured by male returnees:

> My dad really tried for me. The contribution he made towards my traveling was really great even when I was there, he really was of help. I also always supported him. I always asked him whatever he needed because I did not want him to lack anything. Sometimes during the ileya festival I bought rams and also bought clothes for my junior ones so that I could make them happy.

Kin also give some support to returnees. Data gathered and analyzed were very insightful during FGDs, and a common thread in discussion was:

> It is advice basically. We give advice. We tell him how to spend his money. To build houses, businesses and how to do the business.

Another commonly mentioned support from kin to returnees was provision of temporary accommodation. A lot of the returnees preferred to return to family apartments before moving to their own accommodation. Support is generally related to security, survival strategies and information sharing. The kin usually guide the returnees on how to live, especially during the early part of return. A man in a FGD session also observed:

> We supported him; guided him and people came around him and gave him any assistance that could make him happy.

Flows of supports are therefore, in a way, expected and are lubricants for the maintenance of the kinship networks of returnees as they engage in actions that are subjectively meaningful. The nature, positivity and/or negativity of mobilization and appropriation of kinship networks resources somewhat affect the eventual nature and process of relationships among kin and returnees. While some kin disappointed returnees as they readjusted to the Nigerian environment and put limits on the development contribution of returnees, some people in the returnees' social networks performed more positively. This impacted on the ultimate nature of relationships that developed and subsisted between returnees and kin as well as between returnees and the social networks, especially their friends. This is consistent with the findings of Aguilar (2009), Mason (2008), Mason & Tipper (2008) and Finch (2008).

Concluding statements

From the analysis of primary and secondary data gathered for this study and chapter, it could be observed that Nigerians are among the most migratory in the world, and their main countries of destination are the United States, the United Kingdom and Canada. Other destinations of choice include Spain, France and the Scandinavian countries. Hence, Nigerian migrants send substantial remittances to Nigeria, the rate of which is among the highest in the world and Africa. Remittances remain the major migration contribution to Nigerian development. Aside from money, there are other remittances to Nigeria in the form of gifts, migration advices and prestige afforded to kin and migrants. Just as migrants give support and remittances to their families, families also give support to migrants in the form of initial migration funds, and guidance and contribution to the reintegration process upon return. An important issue is that kin are the major gatekeepers of migrants' contribution to national development. Remittances, for instance, pass through families, and their eventual use is sometimes independent of the migrants' intentions.

Also, whether migrants will contribute to national development or not depends on the nature of information given to them by the family. Generally, the attitudes of kin to migrants' contributions to national development ultimately determine migrants' eventual actions. When such attitudes are negative, migrants' propensity to contribute will also be negative, and vice versa. If kin are not supportive and pester migrants for support, this could also stop them from returning home or outrightly discourage them from contributing to national development, even through the diaspora option. This is important as migrants still value and respect their kinship networks, although the sustainability of such networks also depends on their instrumentality and dynamics, especially relative to other subsisting social networks. Kinship and social networks are thus liable to reconstructions depending on instrumentalities with migration and support frameworks. It is noteworthy that return is not automatically permanent. Migrants return to the country with the possibility of re-emigration if return projections and expectations are threatened, since returnees are calculative and rational.

Against these backdrops, it is possible to observe gaps in the general conceptions of the government, and the annexation of returnees and Diaspora for Development (D4D). International migrants still value and annex kinship capitals. Support and remittances to and from kin are important capitals facilitating migrations. In surviving abroad and returning, peculiar expectations are placed on returnees, and in some instances the expectations are potent obligations guided by informal but efficacious rules. Although the findings of this study might not have rendered the "Diaspora for national development" of the government useless, they have given insights into how to re-conceptualize and improve the notion of diaspora annexation for development. There is a need for robust policy and practice re-conceptualization and retooling, given the findings of this study. There is also a need for a nexus between political zeal and appreciation of important social mechanics if international migration capitals are to be well and positively annexed for sustainable development. National-, group- and individual-level efforts are therefore recommended. Government policies for development targeting international migrants, especially returnees, should therefore leverage kin group norms of supports within the domain of migration history and outcomes for development potentialities.

The National/state socio-economic and political environments

Fig. 1. Return and support orientations and behaviour change model

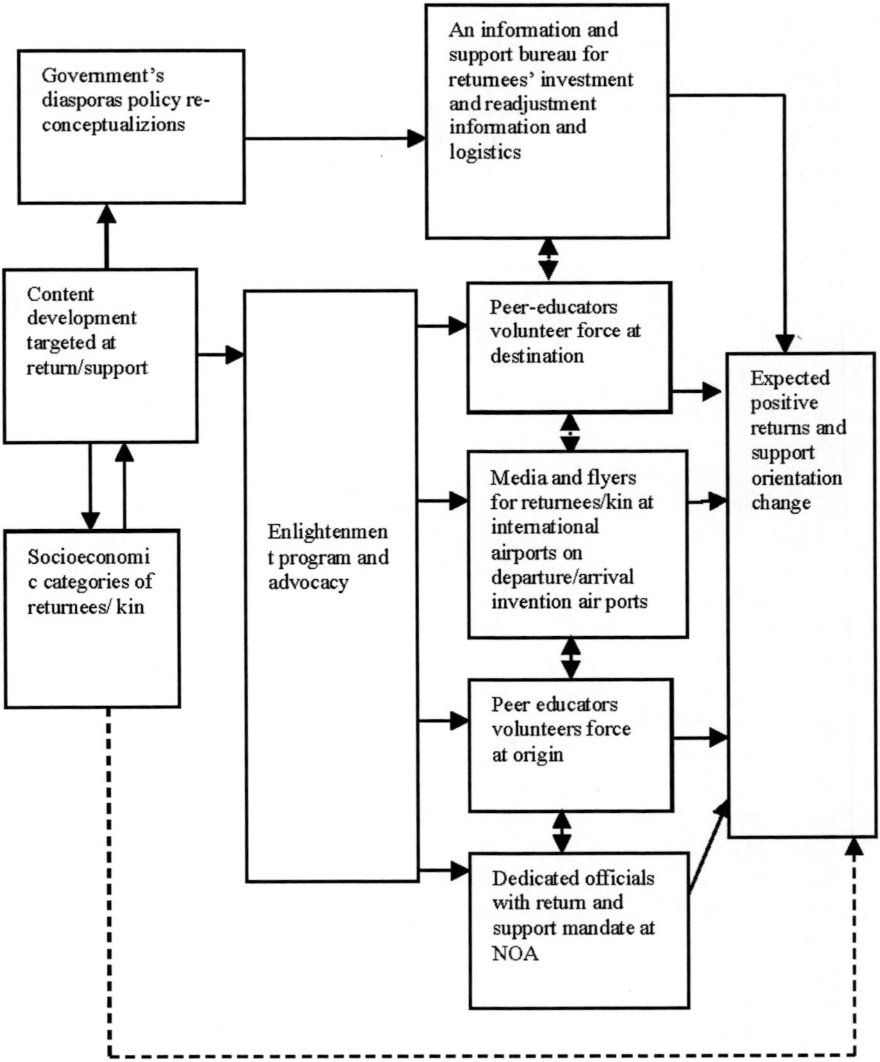

Source: Akanle, 2013a

Fig. 1 above gives a return and support orientation and behaviour change model to generally capture issues that could make international migration, especially return, useful in driving development positively. The model shows the need for content development that would target return migrations and support. This content development should however pay attention to the socioeconomic categories of returnees and their kin groups. This factor is so crucial that two-way traffic is noted and can indirectly impact the extent of success of expected orientation change. The content development should make direct inputs and have direct impact on government orientation and diaspora policy reconceptualizations. The contents developed should be well packaged for enlightenment programmes and advocacies.

Enlightenment and advocacy should be driven for maximum impacts through Peer Educators Volunteer Force (PEVF) at the destination countries and origin, and print and electronic media and flyers for returnees and kin at international airports upon departure and arrival. Dedicated officials with return and support mandates at the National Orientation Agency should also be involved. It should be noted that these agents and advocacies are to interact and exchange activity information. They are therefore not mutually exclusive but highly inclusive. In re-conceptualizing government orientation and diaspora policies, an Information and Support Bureau (ISB) should be established to provide logistics and necessary information for returnees, making the government and society more accessible to returnees and ultimately endear them to their origin and galvanize interest to contribute to its development.

The bureau is also to relate with the other agents on the enlightenment programme and advocacy to share information and strategies for coordination and inputs. If this strategy and framework are well adopted, the outcomes could be as expected with positive returns and support orientation change. It is, however, noteworthy that all strategies and expected outcomes significantly depend on the events with the larger national or state socioeconomic and political systems. This dependence is critical because all other events are directly impacted by the macro regimes. The macro setting includes the political, social, economic, cultural and general infrastructures which study categories have or do not have access to, and this could determine response to return and support and overall contributions to development efforts in real terms. A comprehensive and coordinated will and activities therefore become key among stakeholders, with the state, the groups and the individuals being of value.

This component is so crucial and could be very efficacious in driving the diaspora's and returnees' contributions to development, and positively drive returnees and Direct Foreign Investment (FDIs) into the country. This is because once information is readily available, interconnected and accessible like this, information and investment processes become less cumbersome and very transparent. An online information system could be launched in this regard through which returnees and others who are interested could access investment and other information. The experience of Mali becomes very useful and encouraging in this regard. On August 10, 2007, Mali launched an online information system to simplify and speed up access to unclassified government information and investment operations in the country. This resulted in concrete positive measures observed in market constructions, infrastructural enhancements, proactive public services, institutional business and investment supports, and rights protection among other development values accruable from the user-friendly information system.[4]

In line with the findings in this chapter, there is a need for Nigeria to borrow from the experiences of India, China, Israel, Japan, Korea, Ireland and others in the mature diaspora categories who have successfully appropriated their development capacities, as succinctly put by Ite (2002). According to Babawale (2008), in the case of India its booming economy rests on the support provided by returnees in such key sectors as information technology and services. The result of India's aggressive "diaspora for development" drive became manifest in the early 1990s after heavy investments in socio-economic, political and infrastructural developments that could attract the diaspora and other foreign investments. India's economy is booming with huge GDP capitalization and an enviable annual growth rate, driven by the Indian diaspora as they returned to the country in their thousands with the required capacities and orientations (ibid.).

Currently, Indian economy is fast growing and already ranks among the top ten in terms of purchasing power, just as it looks good to emerge the third largest in the world, due to overtake most Western economies in a couple of decades (ibid.). The government should have a plan instituted with a focus on building infrastructures that could make life comfortable for those returning. These infrastructures should be in

---

[4] See http://mali.investway.info (accessed December 18, 2009). For background information on the policy, see "Mali, Investing to Build: A Good Risk for your Investments," (2006), Minister of Promotion of Investments and small and Medium Enterprises, Bamako.

both the rural areas and the urban centres to make them accessible to all returnees. With such facilities as good roads, uninterrupted electricity, standard schools, stable democracies, reduced crime rates and stable economic policies, the returning diaspora would find the country conducive enough for permanent settling, with little impetus for re-emigration.

References

Adepoju, A. 2010. "Introduction: Rethinking the dynamics of migration within, from and to Africa." *International Migration: Within, to and from Africa in a Globalized World.* Ed. Adepoju, A. Ghana: Sub-Saharan Publishers.

Adu-Okoree, B. I. & Onoma, A. O. 2012. "Migrant Remittances: A Driving Force in Rural Development." *International Journal of Sociology and Anthropology* 4 (5): 172–178.

Africa Recruit. 2003. *African Diaspora: Survey on Remittance and Skills.* December.

Aguilar, F. 2009. "Labour Migration and Ties of Relatedness: Diasporic Houses and Investments in Memory in a Rural Philippine Village." Thesis.

Akanle, O. 2013a. *Kinship Networks and International Migration in Nigeria.* Newcastle: Cambridge Scholars Publishing.

—. 2013b. "The Development Exceptionality of Nigeria: The Context of Political and Social Currents." *Africa Today.* 59 (3): 31–48.

—. 2009a. "An Assessment of Legislative Inputs in Governance in Nigeria (1999–2008)." In *A Decade of Redemocratisation in Nigeria (1999–2009)*, edited by Ogundiya, I. A., Olutayo, O. A. & Amzat, 81–94. J. Sokoto: Usmanu Dan Fodiyyo University.

—. 2009b. "Electoral Legitimacy in Nigeria: Controversies and Prospects." In *A Decade of Redemocratisation in Nigeria (1999–2009)*, edited by Ogundiya, I. A., Olutayo, O. A. & Amzat, 111–126. J. Sokoto: Usmanu Dan Fodiyyo University.

—. 2009c. "Caught in the Morass: Road Map for Civil Society Organisations in 'Democratic' Nigeria." In *State and Civil Society Relations in Nigeria*, edited by Olutayo, O. A., Ogundiya, I. A. & Amzat, 221–239. J. Hope Publications Limited.

—. 2009d. "Immigration Cultism and the Nigerian Migrants: Tidal Dynamism in the Age of Globalization." In *Globalisation and Transnational Migrations: African and Africa in the contemporary*

Global System, edited by Adebayo, A. G. & Adesina, O. C., 181–200. Newcastle: Cambridge Scholars Publishing.

—. 2012. "Kinship Support Orientations and Class Dynamics of Nigerian International Migrants." *International Review of Modern Sociology* 38 (1): 131–153.

Akanle, O. & Olutayo, A. O. 2009. "Emancipating Remittance Discourse: A Look at Extra-financial Remittance in Nigeria." *Global Development Studies. International Development Options* 5 (3–4): 189–212.

—. 2012a. "Ethnography of Kinship Constructions among International Returnees in Nigeria: Proverbs as the Horses of Words." *Journal of Anthropological Research* 68 (2): 249–272.

—. 2012b. "Methodological Pathways to Kinship Networks and International Return Migration." *International Journal of Sociology and Anthropology* 4 (10): 296–302.

—. 2011. "Kinship Socio-Economics of Nigerian International Migrants." *Diaspora Studies* 4 (2): 105–124.

—. 2011. "Kinship Construction Variability among Nigerian International Migrants: The Context of Contemporary Diaspora." *Human Affairs* 21 (4): 470–480.

Babawale, T. 2008. *Africa and African Diaspora Relations: Challenges, opportunities and prospects*. Oxford: Malthouse Press Limited. CBAAC Occasional Monographs.

Civil Liberties Organisation. 2003. "A Mediocre Democracy: the Federal Government, Nigerians say First Years of Civil Governance was Business-as-Usual." *Report of a Democracy Perception Survey*. September.

Datta, K., Mcllwaine, G., Evans, Y., Herbert, J., May, J. & Wills, J. 2006. *Work and Survival Strategies among Low-paid Migrants in London.* U.K: Economic and Social Research Council/Queen Mary University of London.

Ekeh, P. P. 1989. "The Scope of Culture in Nigeria." In *Nigeria Since Independence: The First 25 Years*, edited by Ekeh, P. P. & Asiwaju, G.

Federal Ministry of Education (FME). 2005. Nigerian Education Sector Diagnosis: a Framework for Re-engineering the Education Sector. Federal Ministry of Education, Education Sector Analysis Unit, Nigeria.

Finch, J. 2008. "Naming Names: Kinship, Individuality and Personal Names." *Sociology* 42 (4): 709–725.

Gravil, R. 1985. "The Nigerian Aliens Expulsion Order of 1983." *Africans Affairs* 84 (337): 523–537.

Hernandez-Coss, R. & Bun, C. E. 2006. *The UK-Nigeria Remittance Corridor: Challenges of Embracing Formal Transfer Systems in a Dual Financial Environment.* London: Department for International Development (DfID).

International Organization for Migration (IOM) and European Union (EU). 2006. *"Coping with Return": an Overview of Methodology Development and Exchange of Best Practices on Voluntary Return Assistance in the Enlarged European Union with Particular Emphasis on Vulnerable Asylum Seekers*. Netherlands: IOM.

Ite, U. E. 2002. "Turning Brain Drain to Brain Gain: Personal Reflections on Using the Diaspora Option." *Africa Issues* 30 (1): 76–80.

Jones, J. L. 2008. "Spirituality and Academic Discourse: Building a Yoruba Studies Programme at a Research in one Institution." *Global African Spirituality, Social Capital and Self Reliance in Africa.*

Lagos State Government Centre for Rural Development. 2006. *Review and Update of Baseline Survey of Socio-economic Infrastructure in Lagos State.* Lagos: CERUD.

Long, J. 2005. "Rural-urban Migration and Socio-economic Mobility in Victorian Britain." *The Journal of Economic History* 65 (1): 1–35.

Mason, J. 2008. "Tangible Affinities and the Real Life Fascination of Kinship." *Sociology* 42 (1): 29–45.

Mason, J. & Tipper, B. 2008. "Being Related: how Children Define and Create Kinship." *Childhood* 15 (4): 441–460.

Mayr, K. & Peri, G. 2008. *Return Migration and the Brain Drain-Brain Gain Debate*. USA: The Center for Comparative Immigration Studies.

Migration Policy Institute. 2009. *Top 10 Migration Issues of 2008: Demography and Migration Flows, do Shrinking Populations mean more Migrants?* USA: Washington D.C.

Mines, R. & de Janvry, A. 1982. "Migration to the United States and Mexican Rural Development: A Case Study." *American Journal of Agricultural Economics* 64 (3): 444–454.

Nwajiuba, C. 2005. "International Migration and Livelihoods in Southeastern Nigeria." *Global Migration Perspectives* 50.

Ogbebulu, B. 2008. "The Contribution of Diaspora to Poverty Reduction and Development in Nigeria." *Nigerian Muse*.

Osili, U. O. 2004. "Migrants and Housing Investments: Theories and Evidence from Nigeria." *Economic and Cultural Change* 52 (4): 821–849.

Reynolds, R. R. 2002. "An African Brain Drain: Igbo Decisions to Immigrate into the US." *Review of African Political Economy* 92: 273–284.

Straubhaar, T. 2000. *International Mobility of the Highly Skilled: Brain Drain, Brain Gain of Brain Exchange.* Germany: Hamburg Institute of international Economics.

The World Bank. 2011. *Migration and Remittances Fact book.* Second Edition. Washington DC: The World Bank.

Togunde, D. R. & Osagie, S. O. 2009. "Icons of Progress: Returnees' Effects on Decisions by Nigerians to Migrate to the US." *International Journal of Modern Sociology* 35 (1): 115–135.

Trager, L. 2001. *Yoruba Hometowns: Community, Identity, and Development in Nigeria.* Ibadan: Spectrum Books Limited.

Uduku, O. 2002. "The Socio-economic Basis of a Diaspora Community: *Igbo bu ike.*" *Review of African Political Economy* 92: 301–311.

United Nations. 2009. *International Migration 2009.* New York: United Nations Department of Economic and Social Affairs. Population Division.

Van Den Baseelar, D. 2005. "Imagining Home: Migration and the Igbo Village in Colonial Nigeria." *The Journal of African History* 46: 51–73.

World Bank, 2005. BRCA Team Interviews in Abuja and Lagos. Nigeria office: World Bank.

CHAPTER NINE

TRANSNATIONAL SIMULTANEITY: AN EMERGING AFRICAN PERSPECTIVE OF THE CROSS-BORDER LIFESTYLE

ADEBUSUYI ADENIRAN

Introduction

Within the West African sub-region, notable communities of shuttle traders and occupational migrant groups of varying ethnic origins exist. Amongst such groups are the Ejigbo-Yoruba (Nigerian) migrants who, for instance, have had a long-distance experience of trans-border relations with the Ivorian society. Trans-border interactions, for purposes of trade and work, have become the most widespread pattern of mobility, especially since the colonial era. Meanwhile, they have not been dominated by males, as mobility used to be in parts of West Africa, particularly during the pre-colonial period, often a resulting factor of inter-ethnic strife and wars. The colonial and post-colonial migration of labour has equally encouraged a considerable number of women seeking opportunities for improvement in their existence, for instance in rewarding employment or enabling business ventures. Essentially, related cross-border engagements of the women have reflected the newly acquired "freedom of movement, " hitherto improbable within the pre-colonial setting (Adeniran 2012, 78–80; Afolayan 2004; Asiwaju 1996).

While the impact of cross-border migrants on trade and related socio-economic endeavours often improves as soon as they become potently entrenched in the host economy, their role as trade facilitators for exports and imports to and from their home country can only be effective if they remain in regular contact and are aware of developments influencing trade (Manning 2005; Bauder 2006). In the meantime, the problem of economic immobility, which the immigrants usually predicate their relocation upon, often resurfaces on the social plane when the vagaries of transnationalism present limits by way of undue foreclosures of their emancipatory propensities. As such, any emanating attempt at identity repositioning by the immigrants within the host society is bound to impact on their usual day-to-day experiences.

It is, perhaps, with this realisation that the Economic Community of West African States (ECOWAS) has found it expedient to transform its earlier intent of "ECOWAS of States" to "ECOWAS of People." Within the prism of this new expectation, it is useful to assess what is actually happening to the people directly rather than through the state.

Aims and Objectives of the research

The primary aim of this study is to present the practice of "transnational simultaneity" as an emergent African pattern of cross-border lifestyle. Other objectives include:

(i) To explore the evolutionary trend of cross-border interaction in West Africa
(ii) To examine the process of identity construction by Nigerian immigrants in Cote d'Ivoire
(iii) To explain the specific impacts of simultaneous attachment to two nations by Nigerian immigrants in Cote d'Ivoire
(iv) To analyse the practice of transnational simultaneity as a framework for attaining the goal of a borderless West African sub-region.

Theoretical and Methodological Considerations for the Study

The study's specificities are ingrained in the dictates of Charles Tilly's "Urban Sociological Postulate" (1996), in which the nature and pattern of migration to urban centres are interpreted by connoting related processes such as evolving social networks; that is, the notion of the "transnational social field."

Contrary to the assumptions of minimizing distances and multiplying opportunities repeatedly, individuals are keen on establishing regular migration between two widely separated locations, and concentrating their migratory practices within such a bipolar configuration. Chain migration in this respect is, of course, the arrangement whereby social ties persist between people of a particular origin and destination of migration, with people at the point of destination sending back information about new opportunities, recruiting new migrants and helping them to relocate. This form of cross-border interaction reflects the nature of prevalent practice by Ejigbo-Yoruba (Nigerian) migrants along the Nigerian-Ivorian migratory corridor.

In spite of subsisting colonial, cultural and geographical impediments between Nigeria and Cote d'Ivoire, the Ejigbo-Yoruba migrants have been able to sustain an existing chain of migration between the two countries over time and space, though a supposed sister nation of Ghana and two other West African countries, Togo and Benin Republic, have to be crossed.

Being an essentially reflexive exploratory study, relevant qualitative data collection techniques (non-participant observation, in-depth interviews [IDIs], focus group discussions [FGDs] and a case study) were utilised in generating primary data from the two study locations of Ejigbo, Nigeria and Abidjan, Cote d'Ivoire. This was done to provide the study with useful first-hand information on the nature of cross-border networking and mode of constructing the "self" within the transnational social space. Content analysis and ethnographic summaries were engaged in the process of data coding and analysis.

In Abidjan, only Ejigbo-Yoruba immigrants who have stayed for a minimum of five years in Cote d'Ivoire were engaged in the study, and in Ejigbo only Ejigbo-Yoruba returnees of a minimum of five years stay in Nigeria were involved. A pilot study preceded each of the main surveys in the two study locations to pre-test the potentiality of the research instruments and, indeed, get accustomed to the study locations.

Conceptual Framework for the Study

In order to determine the specific role(s) of the "transnational social field" in the cross-border process, especially in the bid to construct a network identity for the Ejigbo-Yoruba immigrants within the Ivorian social space, it is pertinent to have a concise definition of the subsisting concept. Such a definition, however, depicts a framework that potently links identity integration within the host society to opportunities presented by the transnational network culture, and which clearly identifies the determinants of such a process (see Fig. 1 below).

Fig. 1. Pictorial Overview of the Conceptual Framework

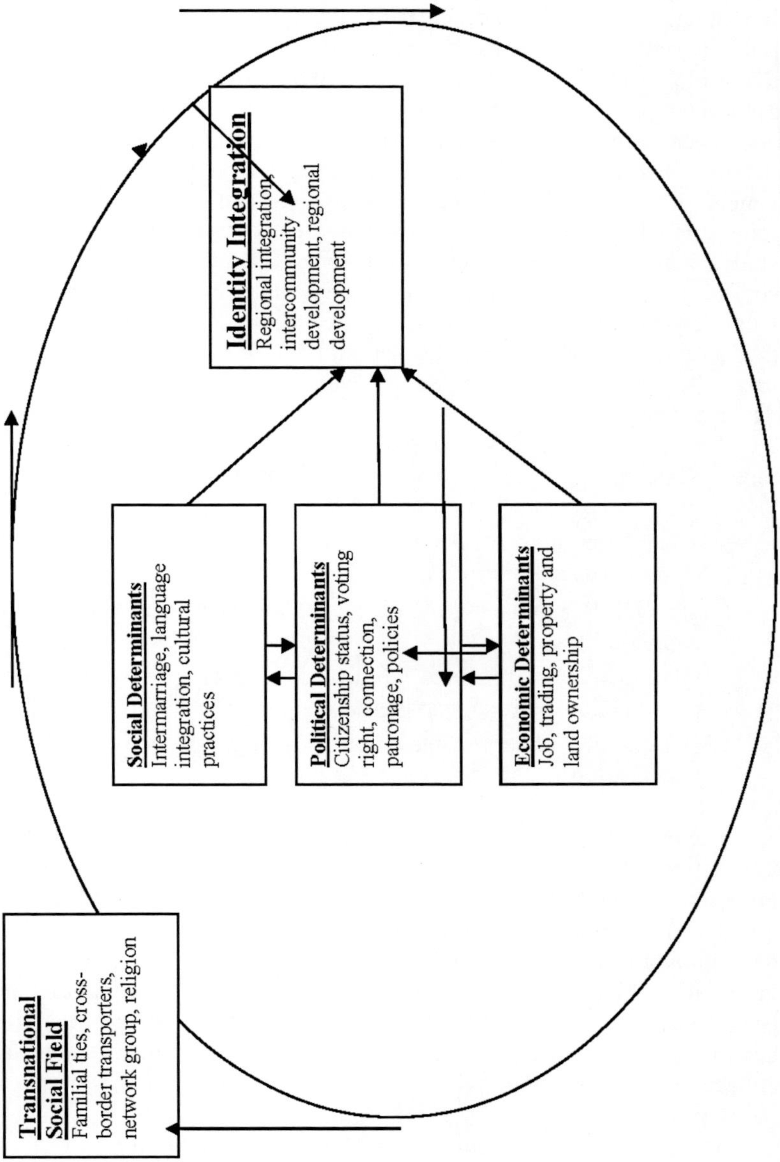

Source: Author's Conception, 2012

In this study, identity integration is defined as the process of image moulding in which the individual (or the collective) interest(s) at stake plays a significant role in depicting who an individual is (that is, the dispositional attribute), and why the individual is as such (that is, the underlying precursors of the dispositional attribute). Routinely, time, space and other people, in combination with the subsisting interests, are equal determinants of the process of identity integration. Proceeding from this general definition, which prioritizes individuals and institutions within the transnational network space, Fig. 1 above explains a feasible conceptual analysis model for the process of identity integration within the host society. That is, a model which is applicable in understanding such tangible determinants that could enhance network members' efforts to present a tenable network identity within the transnational network space, and also impact the process of larger regional integration and development.

The conceptual analysis consists of one primary networking axis and three distinct network identity determinants. That is:

(i) The "transnational social field" (or the cross-border network): the "primary networking axis"
(ii) Social determinants (intermarriage, language integration, cultural practices)
(iii) Political determinants (citizenship status, voting right, connection, patronage, policies)
(iv) Economic determinants (job, trading, property and land ownership).

The unilateral primary networking axis is described by vagaries of the transnational social field; that is, factors facilitating an enhanced level of migratory capability—familial ties, cross-border transporters, network group and religious outfits. The network identity determinants are often defined by a broader social, political and economic context of formal and informal regulations and cultures. While the primary networking axis provides an imperative platform for the adequate functioning of identified determinants, related determinants functionally impact one another, and collectively enable the process of identity integration within the transnational space.

At this juncture, two components of the conceptual framework call for specific emphasis. First, transnational networking is basically an interactive process, emanating from exchanges across the borders. This unfolds through the unwritten rules, traditions, beliefs and extant interests at stake (both individual and group). Second, identity integration, courtesy of the transnational social field, entails the replacement of individual identities with the network identity, which has remained sustainable over time and space.

Historical reflections on cross-border interactions in West Africa

The arrival of European colonialism at the twilight of the nineteenth century did redefine the frameworks for cross-cultural and cross-border relations in parts of the West African sub-region. Hitherto, various societies had existed as kingdoms and empires without any clearly defined borders. Nevertheless, nomadic herding and trading across the Sahara had caused significant human mobility and migration across parts of pre-colonial West Africa. As such, incidences of unregulated movements of individuals were necessitated.

The policies and workings of the colonial administration in West Africa did result in the geo-political delineation of borders, largely along the Francophone-Anglophone divide. The political economy of the colonial administration also encouraged unbridled internal migration within the emergent nation-states. A justification in this respect was the colonial manpower need in mineral extraction, agricultural production and public administration. Meanwhile, cross-border interactions, especially along the Francophone-Anglophone dichotomy, were unduly discouraged. Yet, ironically, such colonial creation could not stop the people from sustaining their pre-colonial socio-cultural and economic interactive frameworks after colonial rule. The established, pre-colonial modes of cross-border interaction had outwitted such contemporary tendencies (Adeniran 2009, 3676).

Despite this exigent set back in cross-border interactions amongst the people of West Africa, as facilitated by extant colonial interests, a lasting development is the fact that boundaries between the peoples of the same or different cultures (ethnic group) in different countries were routinely adjudged by to be artificial. Thus, many migrants from areas immediately across borders usually consider such movement as taking place within the same socio-cultural space rather than between two different nations (Okobiah 1989).

The process of migrant networking

Chain relations have tended to predetermine the pattern of assistance obtainable within the network interactions. The achievements of earlier migrants and the entrance of Ejigbo-Yoruba indigenes into cross-border transport business, and their extant willingness to transport people and goods on credit between the two points, have all helped the growth and sustenance of the familial pattern of the network:

> … the lifestyle of Abidjan people (Ejigbo-Yoruba immigrants) encouraged me to go initially … no home-based individual could spend the way they used to do then …. (IDI, male, returnee, 78 years, Ejigbo, August 18, 2010)

When people at home saw the progress that some of the migrants were making they were naturally encouraged to become part of the network process. For instance, most of the Ivorian-styled buildings constructed in Ejigbo by the Ejigbo-Yoruba immigrants based in Cote d'Ivoire did serve as sources of encouragement for the indigenes to dream of Cote d'Ivoire, especially in the 1950s. By implication, they enabled the growth of the migratory network along the Nigerian-Ivorian corridor. It is interesting to understand that most personal or communal projects became a reality through the cooperation between the immigrants and their relatives back home; for instance, the establishment of The French Language Centre in Ejigbo in 1969, which serves as a social network platform for potential migrants to Cote d'Ivoire. While the immigrants provided the funds, their relatives monitored the projects.

Aside from building on the existing level of trust, some of the relatives back home were either helped to set up businesses or migrate to Cote d'Ivoire to begin new lives. One of the major summations of the transnational social field becomes tenable here—that the pre-migratory social relations pattern between the migrants and their relatives at home are sustained for the growth of the network in particular, and the development of individuals at large (Observation, Ejigbo, June 2, 2010; IDI, female, returnee, 72 years, Ejigbo, August 8, 2010).

According to a male case profile, he has been encouraged to assist individuals of Ejigbo-Yoruba descent to migrate and settle in Cote d'Ivoire because he benefitted from the existing network structure between Ejigbo and Abidjan. He claimed that when he was tired of Nigeria after his secondary education, he had to beg a driving crew to get him to Cote d'Ivoire free of charge:

> … this is why I cannot reject anyone that desires to come here (Cote d'Ivoire) through me … many friends, many family members have come here through me. (Case profile, male, 55 years, cross-border transporter, Abidjan, June 20, 2010)

This network functionary affirms that it has been his "personal principle" to assist individuals to migrate to Cote d'Ivoire from Nigeria, even when it is not convenient. By implication, this gesture has facilitated the growth and sustenance of a prevalent "familial pattern" of the network function.

The pattern of migrants' identity construction

As a matter of routine, an average Ejigbo-Yoruba migrant in Cote d'Ivoire kept alive two distinct identities within the adopted social space. That is, a Nigerian identity, which is the original Ejigbo-Yoruba cleavage, and an Ivorian identity, which is a disposition that is essentially in the Ivorian social space. While the Nigerian identity depicts traits and attributes that are basically Nigerian (that is of Ejigbo-Yoruba), the Ivorian identity entails traits and peculiarities that are essentially Ivorian (that is of cosmopolitan Abidjan). Such an identity cleavage has, however, undoubtedly emanated from the larger network functioning.

The prevalent situation (and the interest at stake) usually determines the mode of related identity deployment in the process of interaction. While the need for a productive socio-economic integration into the host society has been the impetus for related identification with Ivorian culture, the need for a convenient reintegration into the Nigerian society thereafter has been the underlying factor for the continued attachment to Nigerian peculiarities. The following IDI submission has been quite appropriate in driving home this affirmation:

> … during selling and other business transactions, I do as if I am part of Ivorian society … among ourselves and whenever I visit Nigeria I relate like a typical Nigerian. (IDI, female, trader, 52 years, Semisel-Abidjan, June 21, 2010)

Though most of the Ejigbo-Yoruba in Cote d'Ivoire believe in Nigeria, they seemed to have been compelled to live and identify with specificities that are of the Ivorian society for obvious socio-economic consideration. One could observe that you would seldom find any mature Ejigbo-Yoruba indigene in Cote d'Ivoire without a building, or a business project, either completed or ongoing, in Nigeria. In fact, participation in such projects is seen as evidence that one has not been "lost" completely to the Ivorian society, and indeed serves as a means of re-oiling the wheel of pre-migratory social relations with relatives back home (Observations, Ejigbo May 4–9, 2010; Abidjan, June 20–July 2, 2010).

Besides, most of the Ejigbo-Yoruba immigrants would have ordinarily preferred to exist in Nigeria if relevant opportunities at the level of socio-economic participation had been available. In spite of attaining a considerable measure of their transnational goals, most Ejigbo-Yoruba immigrants still felt attached to Nigeria. This view has been buttressed further by the submission of the following male FGD participant:

> … I love Nigeria … I equally love Cote d'Ivoire … See what God has given me in this country … I have learnt to be like the people over the years. (FGD, male, entrepreneur, 56 years, Treichville-Abidjan, July 1, 2010)

Really, all I could see around him were riches and accomplishment. Though this male FGD participant is not educated, he functions as a "big time" contractor to the Ivorian national government, a feat that would have been seldom feasible in Nigeria considering his background. In realising his socio-economic goals he is at "home" with the Ivorian social space. Simultaneously, he is not prepared to neglect his "original" attachment to Nigeria, which is largely denominated by subsisting kinship interconnectedness. In this light, the notion of "methodological nationalism, " that recognises the potency of the limits of national borders in determining patterns of socio-economic interaction within a given "social space, " would become obliterated and pave the way for the emergence of a "transnational social space, " in which "national borders" no longer serve as impediments to interactions or functioning beyond geo-political boundaries.

Various observations made at a burial party (in Nigeria) for the father of a male Ejigbo-Yoruba immigrant in Macory-Abidjan did reveal that ceremonies among the people here do take after the usual styles and procedures in Nigeria. When I inquired of the reason for this, I was informed that they did not want to forget home (Nigeria). In fact, the arrangement of the street (not the party) was as if it was in Nigeria (Observations/Interactions, Macory-Abidjan, June 22, 2010).

I was to overhear a middle age woman cracking a joke at the gathering: "… leave my brother alone; unfortunately for him he has his passport on his cheeks."

The submission above laid credence to a prevalent "identity dualism" that most of the Ejigbo-Yoruba tend to imbibe in the transnational process. The middle age woman was jokingly affirming the Nigerianess in her "brother" as indicated by the tribal marks on his face, though he was flagrantly tending to claim to be "more Ivorian than the indigenes" while interacting within the public space. Such Ivorian cleavages were glaring in his dressing pattern, gesticulation and discussions (nearly all he was talking about were Ivorian issues and concerns) (Observations/ Interactions, Macory-Abidjan, June 22, 2010).

In most instances, the economic interests of individuals have been the precursors of such intent and practice amongst the immigrants. The situational contextualization of the "self" is seen to be contingent upon the "extant interests" at stake and the "social space" within which the related disposition is unfolding (FGD, female, over 40, Abidjan, June 26, 2010).

Transnational simultaneity—an emergent framework for a borderless ECOWAS sub-region

The process of simultaneous identification with two societies by the Ejigbo-Yoruba migrants within the Nigerian-Ivorian corridor seems to be presenting a positive framework for the realisation of the much-desired socio-economic integration of the West African sub-region. Amongst the relatively older returnee-indigenes of the Ejigbo community in Nigeria (that is, from 70 years and above), their retirement or relocation from Cote d'Ivoire has not prevented them from going back to the country intermittently, especially by road, despite the tediousness and exhaustive nature of such trips. Why? One, their existence is still largely tied to Cote d'Ivoire. They go there to collect rent on their houses, shops and other business ventures (often managed by their Ivorian spouses or children or relatives whom they took there). Some even go there to collect their retirement benefits and/or pensions from the Ivorian government (Observations, Ejigbo, May 19, 2010; Abidjan, June 21–July 2, 2010).

Two, to visit their Ivorian friends whom they must have met in the course of their sojourn in Cote d'Ivoire, especially those who, one way or another, facilitated the path of their existence while there, for instance in the process of acquiring Ivorian right of stay or citizenship, getting jobs and/or contracts, securing lands and/or property, marrying indigenes and, of course, acquiring local spiritual power (Observations, Ejigbo, June 19, 2010; Abidjan, June 21–July 2, 2010).

> … I am on my way to collect rent on my house and shops in Abobo-Abidjan (Cote d'Ivoire); to do my monthly pension verification and to visit my old friend at Bouake to renew my gbetugbetu (traditional spiritual power) which he gave me while we were working together. (IDI, male, returnee, 86 years, Ejigbo, June 18, 2010)

Regarding the IDI above, it is conspicuous that the respondent, as applicable to some other returnees, still has reasons for sustaining his relationship with the Ivorian society, from economic to family and, interestingly, spiritual considerations. One end product of these relationship patterns is the enhancement of the integration bond across the region, though in a rather inverse form.

Naming monuments and streets in some parts of Ejigbo, Nigeria and Abidjan, Cote d'Ivoire equally attests to the claim of regional integrative propensity, courtesy of the ongoing transnational processes along the Nigerian-Ivorian corridor. Oba Abidjan Street is a major street in Ejigbo. Furthermore, it comprises mainly properties of Cote d'Ivoire-based indigenes, and the most revered and respected Oba-Yoruba (Yoruba King) in Cote d'Ivoire, the late Chief Emmanuel Alabi, has his house and burial site here. It radiates a "high-class setting, " and savours the subsisting interconnectedness and identification of Ejigbo-Yoruba with the Ivorian society. Notably, an obtainable way of life in Cote d'Ivoire is replicated on this street, including the retail of goods imported solely from Cote d'Ivoire. In Cote d'Ivoire, one of the major streets in downtown Abidjan, Temidire, has been named in honour of the Ejigbo-Yoruba migrant group. Actually, the name is a Yoruba word. Equally, an obtainable way of life in Nigeria is replicated on this street, including the sale of goods imported solely from Nigeria.

The nature of the Ejigbo-Yoruba's interactions with the Ivorian society has potently made both Ejigbo and Abidjan communities become somewhat interdependent over the years. At the level of transaction, the CFA Franc has been popular legal tender in Ejigbo, and of course exchanged with the Nigerian Naira in most households in the town. Reciprocally, this is the situation with the Nigerian Naira against the CFA Franc in most Yoruba households in Abidjan, Cote d'Ivoire, often populated by the Ejigbo-Yoruba. Essentially, as many Ivorian commodities are sold in Ejigbo so are identifiable local Nigerian commodities/items are sold in Abidjan. Though as a group they tend to replicate most of the things done back in Abidjan, there still exists a remarkable departure from the ideal. The Ivorian society has actually impacted on them. As a consequence a new outlook, definitely not wholly Ivorian or wholly Nigerian (possibly, ECOWAS), has emerged. The speaking pattern of the people has been largely distorted; whenever they speak Yoruba, colloquial Abidjan French usually reflects it, and vice versa (Observations, Ejigbo, June 19, 2010; Abidjan, June 21–July 2, 2010).

Concluding comments

Since the Ejigbo-Yoruba immigrants are usually desirous of attaining formidable socio-economic acceptance within the host society (that is, Cote d'Ivoire), and to be in touch with families at home (in Nigeria), this study affirms that the resultant implication of such interactive pattern is the production of a people engaged in a kind of "transnational subsistence dualism" (that is, "transnational simultaneity"). This means that integration for socio-economic gains within the host society and re-integration into the home country thereafter are the main impetuses for the prevalent dualist disposition. As they tend to identify with the host's institutional peculiarities, so they tend to identify with their cultural affinity from home. As such, the projectable identity of individuals at a specific point in time would be factored by the subsisting social space within which related interactions are taking place and extant interests are at stake. Essentially, therefore, an epistemological framework for understanding the way a transnational migrants' community constructs its identity in relation to "home" and "host" communities has been presented.

Recommendations

(i) Greater attention should be given to contextualising the preference of Ejigbo-Yoruba for migrating to Cote d'Ivoire, despite prevalent colonial and contemporary impediments like language and related cultural specificities. Perhaps such a pattern of mobility could be utilised in explaining the possibility of a borderless West African sub-region.

(ii) A network identity to integrate network migrants into the socio-economic workings of the host community while facilitating the sustenance of the pre-migratory relations with the home front should be made sustainable.

(iii) Besides fostering regional integration, ongoing simultaneous attachment to Cote d'Ivoire and Nigeria by the Ejigbo-Yoruba migrants should be utilised in enabling inter-community development in West Africa.

(iv) The practice of "transnational simultaneity" by the Ejigbo-Yoruba should be engaged as a veritable platform for realising the goal of a borderless West African sub-region.

References

Adeniran, A. I. 2009. "Yoruba Wars of the 19th Century." In *The International Encyclopaedia of Revolution and Protest: 1500 to the Present*, edited by Ness, I., 3676–3678. Oxford: Wiley-Blackwell.

—. 2012. "Social Networking and Identity Integration within the ECOWAS Framework by Ejigbo-Yoruba in Cote d'Ivoire." Diss. University of Ibadan.

Afolayan, A. A. 2004. "Circulatory Migration in West Africa: a Case Study of Ejigbo in South Western Nigeria." Paris: *L'Harmattan*. 17–16.

Asiwaju, A. I. 1992. *West African History: the Significance for the Consolidation of ECOWAS*. Paper presented at the National Seminar on Research Priorities and Integration in ECOWAS. Nigerian Institute of International Affairs, Lagos, Nigeria. February.

Bauder, H. 2006. *Labour Movement: how Migration Regulates Labour Markets*. New York: New York University Press.

Manning, P. 2005. *Migration in World History*. New York and London: Routledge.

Okobiah, O. S. 1989. Population in History (National and International). Population Education Monographs. Lagos: NERDC. 13.

Tilly, C. 1996. "What Good is Urban History?" *Journal of Urban History* 22 (6): 702–719.

CHAPTER TEN

THE OIL CURSE AND THE NIGERIAN DEVELOPMENT DILEMMA

AUGUSTINE OKHOBO DOKPESI

Introduction: General Orientation

> Naturally, the people of Oloibiri would have been elated with the news that heralded the sighting of oil in their domain, even as the expectations of improved communal lifestyles heightened with the new vista and tremendous opportunities opening up to them. Surprisingly, those early hopes are today only reserved to become heaps of hopelessness, despair, regrets, hunger and deprivation. Oloibiri with all its former gaiety has today become a cow milked by its shepherd and left to survive on its own. It is just one of the many communities in the Niger Delta region whose present conditions have remained lamentable.
> (Premo 2005, 17).

Although the first oil in the Oloibiri community was struck in 1956, the oil industry became strategic to the Nigerian economy from 1972, when it contributed 54.4% of revenue to the Federation Account (CBN 1997). From a modest production figure of 5, 100 barrels per day (bpd) in 1958, oil production has risen to today's production quota of 2.6 million bpd. This phenomenal rise in oil wells and volume of production generated excitement on the part of host communities that their development challenges would soon be a thing of the past. However, while the revenue base of the government was expanding the expectations of the host communities diminished through neglect in the midst of the massive exploration and exploitation of oil and gas. Today, Oloibiri has no electricity or portable water. While the environmental problems of the oil industry generate a lack of incentive for farmers and fishermen, the attractiveness of the petro-dollar creates a lack of interest in these professions, especially among the youth. This generates an agrarian crisis as youths are no longer motivated towards these occupations, while those already in the business are discouraged by the continuous negative environmental impacts and lack of capital for expansion. These occupational disorientations and dislocations have worsened the rate of poverty and underdevelopment in the region.

In the larger scope, by virtue of its wealth potentials, oil ought to be a veritable source of human and societal development in Nigeria. Ironically, the manner in which it is harnessed and utilized has made it a curse. Therefore, understanding the present political economy of Nigeria requires an understanding of how oil politics plays out in the relations between social, political and ethnic groups in Nigeria. The conspiracy between the State's philosophy of fiscal sociology, anchored on a mono-product economy that solely depends on oil revenues, politically shared among the component units, and the self-centredness of the ruling class has generated poverty and underdevelopment in Nigeria. The struggles among members of this class for resource allocation underscore the struggles between these groups. This perhaps made Auty (2005, 32) assert that "resource-rich countries engender factional or predatory States." Auty further noted that the potential for economic distortion and collapse is more on the side of mineral resources than agriculture because the former is highly capital intensive and involves much foreign capital while at the same time employs a small workforce. Inputs are imported because of their specialized nature. The only benefits of mineral resources to the economy are royalties and tax payments.

Scholars have equally argued that increase in natural resource income does not necessarily translate to economic growth because of the interference of contending forces interested in the resource pie. In some cases, the conflict resulting from an aggravated predatory behaviour between groups generates counter-productive forces against economic growth (Yakub, quoted in Ogbonna 2012, 36). However, in spite of the tenability of these arguments, it must be emphasized that the relationship between resource abundance and development is understood within the context of leadership. The extent and manner in which leadership harnesses and utilizes available resources and the accruable revenues determine the state of a society in terms of growth and development. Dokpesi (2006) argues that although population and resources constitute the wealth of a nation, both cannot lead to development if there is no system of coordination effectively channelling them for development purposes.

Conceptual and Theoretical Issues: Sectoral Contributions to the Nigerian Economy

Oil has been providing more revenue to the common national pulse than the non-oil sectors in recent times, except for the period before 1972 when agriculture was still the mainstay of the Nigerian economy, as shown in Table 10.1 below:

Table 10.1. The contributions of oil revenue to the Federation Account

Year	Oil Revenue		Non-Oil Revenue		Total Federally collected Revenue
	Amount (Million Naira)	Percent	Amount (Million Naira)	Percent	
1970	166.6	26.3	467.4	73.7	634.0
1972	764.3	54.4	640.8	45.6	1, 405.1
1974	3, 724.0	82.1	813.4	17.6	4, 537.4
1976	5, 365.2	79.3	1, 400.7	20.7	6, 765.9
1978	4, 555.8	61.8	2, 815.2	38.2	7, 371.0
1980	12, 353.3	81.1	2, 880.2	18.9	15, 233.5
1982	7, 814.9	68.3	3, 618.8	31.7	11, 433.7
1984	8, 269.2	73.5	2, 984.1	26.5	11, 253.3
1986	8, 107.3	64.4	4, 488.5	35.6	12, 595.8
1988	19, 831.7	71.9	7, 765.0	28.1	27, 596.7
1990	71, 887.1	73.3	26, 215.3	26.7	98, 102.4
1992	164, 078.1	86.2	26, 375.1	13.8	190, 453.2
1994	160, 192.4	79.3	41, 718.4	20.7	201, 910.8
1996	369, 190.0	71.0	151, 000.0	29.0	520, 190.0
1998	324, 311.2	70.0	139, 297.6	30.0	463, 608.8
2000	1, 591, 675.8	83.5	314, 483.9	16.5	1, 906, 159.7
2002	1, 230, 851.2	71.0	500, 985.3	29.0	1, 731, 837.5
2004	3, 354, 800.00	85.6	565, 700.00	14.4	3, 920, 500.0
2006	5, 287, 566.90	88.6	677, 535.00	11.4	5, 965, 101.9
2008	6, 530, 630.10	73.9	1, 335, 960.00	26.1	7, 866, 590.1
2010	5, 396, 091.1	83.1	1, 907, 580.50	16.9	7, 303, 671.6

Source: Central Bank of Nigeria (CBN) Summary of Federal Government Finances, 1961–2010

Moreover, the total Federation Account revenue in 2011 was ₦9, 987.63 billion, for which oil contributed a staggering ₦8, 848.62 billion (88.60%), while non-oil sectors provided ₦1, 139.01 billion (11.40%). The improvement in total revenue was attributed to increased oil receipts occasioned by the rise in the price of crude oil on the global market (NPC 2012). Furthermore, the proven oil reserves of Nigeria improved from 0.184 in 1958 to its current 36 billion barrels. Furthermore, scholars have noted that Nigeria is even richer in gas than oil, and the gas reserves which were put at 2.260 billion Cubic Feet in 1958 have risen to 187 Trillion Cubic Feet (TCF) (Ogbonna & Ebimobewei 2012).

These facts and figures present a case of an economy wholly dependent on oil as a mono-product, and thus explain the pressure on the Niger Delta natural environment for the oil resources and the eventual adverse effect on the lives of the people. The strategic relevance of oil revenues to the Federation Account shows why there are too many contending interests in the allocation of federal revenues, that there is an over politicization of the revenue allocation formula, and why there is excessive dependence on oil revenue, by all the federating units, as the major source of government revenue.

Fiscal Federalism and the Politics of Revenue Allocation in Nigeria

Although the determination of the appropriate formula for the sharing of the federally collectible revenue has always been a flashpoint of inter-group politics and crisis in the Nigerian state (UNDP 2006), the interplay became intense in the post-oil boom era. Two factors account for this. In the first place, Nigeria degenerated into a mono-economic state relying almost wholly on oil revenue at the inception of the oil boom. Secondly, virtually every tier of government in Nigeria relies heavily on subvention from the Federation Account, for which oil accounts for no less than 70%. Such over reliance on oil revenue generates politics in revenue allocation.

The foundation for true federalism was laid in pre-independence Nigeria as a series of recommendations by government commissions led to the granting of greater fiscal autonomy to the regions. For instance, the Phillipson Commission, set up in 1946 to determine the appropriate framework for revenue sharing, recommended the principles of derivation and progress. However, according to Nnoli (1995), implementation was problematic for two reasons. First, there were accusations and counter-accusations by the regions of wrongful allocation of revenue. While the North argued that money due it had gone to the East, the East and West expressed dissatisfaction that the North received an unfairly large allocation. Second, even though the Commission had made its recommendation, each region still held on to its egocentric perception of what constituted an appropriate revenue formula. While the North demanded a distribution based on population, the West presented a case for derivation and the East pleaded for the principle of need. Despite this problem, however, the derivation principle benefited these regions as it was based on 50% (Teriba 1966; Phillips 1975; Oyevbare 1978). The subsequent commissions after Phillipson built on this. For instance, while both the Hicks-Phillipson Commission of 1951 and the Raisman Commission of 1958 recommended 50%, the Chicks Commission recommended 100% rent to the region of origin (Ibegwuru 2002). This was an era in which the Nigerian economy was agriculturally buoyant with cash crops derived mainly from the three dominant ethnic groups in Nigeria, i.e. groundnut from the North, cocoa from the West and palm oil from the East.

The idea of the Derivation Principle is that states should get from the Federation Account an amount proportionate to their individual contribution. "This principle was attacked because it makes rich states richer since the more developed states will contribute more to the Federation Account, starving needy states of development funds" (Salami 2011, 40). By 1957, the application of the principle of derivation had, according to Adedeji (1969, 254) "poisoned inter-governmental relationships and had exacerbated inter-regional rivalry and conflict. Perhaps more than any other single factor, it had hampered the development of a sense of national unity or common citizenship in Nigeria" (cited in Nnoli 1995). "It was into this weak federal system that commercial oil production was inserted" (Watts 2005, 59).

Perhaps based on this crisis, Gowon's military administration introduced a system of revenue allocation based on equal weighting of the principles of population and equality of states. This indeed marked the beginning of the erosion of true federalism in Nigeria. For the observers of Nigeria's federalism, Gowon's move may not have been based on just and benevolent grounds as it seemed to have realized the northern position on the revenue sharing formula. This happened at a time in which the "northerners sustained a fragile hegemony over a highly charged multi-ethnic polity" (Watts 2005, 59). It indeed succeeded in introducing a new dimension to the struggle for revenue allocation and the attendant laziness among federating units in Nigeria occasioned by the quick and easy wealth potentials of the emergent export product. In spite of its criticisms, the Derivation Principle was meant to reward hard work, create positive competition among political units and discourage laziness in the spirit of justice and fair play.

The enactment of Decree 9 of 1971, according to Nnoli (1995), anticipated the boom in oil revenues, and hence gave the federal government the sole right to rent and collect royalties from off-shore oil production. This consequently created the enabling conditions for the eventual centralization of oil revenue. The centralization was deliberate as a state controlled development strategy based on what Watts called Petro-capitalism. There was an urgent need to create unity among the regions torn apart especially by inter-regional struggles, mainly among the major ethnic groups, for resource allocation. As Watts (2005) rightly observed, oil kept Nigerians together by purchasing a kind of consent among the ethnic majorities. However, this measure, which ought to have served as an ad hoc means of providing an immediate and temporal response to our common fears and problems, seems to have become a permanent tool for realizing individual and group interests. This is buttressed by the fact that successive governments in Nigeria built on Gowon's legacy.

In the period between 1976 and 1979, for instance, the Federal Military Government created a dichotomy between onshore and offshore oil proceeds, with 100% of the offshore proceeds going directly into the Distributable Pool Account. Even the share of the onshore proceeds accruing to the Distributable Pool Account was raised to 80%. Between 1982 and 1992, derivation attracted a paltry 1.5% of oil proceeds, and this was tentatively increased to 3% from 1993 to 1998 as a palliative measure to stem the rising tempo of militant agitations, pending the determination of an appropriate derivation formula by the Constitutional Conference instituted to address crucial issues in the Nigerian polity within this period. On the recommendation of this conference, the derivation principle was raised to 13%. However, the delay in the implementation of this new allocation package generated a series of intergovernmental crises at the inception of the democratic regime in 1999, thus bringing the governors of the oil-rich region into closer alliance with the "resource control" agitators, and into conflict with the federal government (UNDP 2006).

While this revenue politics has provided a point of agreement for the majority of groups whose respective state governments rely heavily on oil revenue, it has also created a point of disagreement between the ethnic minorities in the Delta region and the Nigerian state. According to the UNDP Niger Delta Human Development Report (2006, 38), this state of affairs:

> Found expression at the National Political Reform Conference held in 2005. The Conference recommended an upward review of the derivation

> percentage to 17 per cent, but this was unacceptable to the Niger Delta delegates, who insisted on a minimum of 25 percent with a phased review to 50 per cent. Other delegates did not agree, leading to the collapse of the Conference and further polarization along oil-producing/non-oil-producing lines.

Jike (2002, 13) sees this development as part of the politics of inter-group dynamics within the Nigerian state. According to him:

> As the revenue from agriculture dropped and was overshadowed by the quick and big money that accompanied the discovery of oil among several ethnic minority homelands in the Niger Delta, the dominant ethnic groups who also controlled the levers of political power at the federal level altered the existing rule on revenue allocation.

This suggests that the pattern of politics of revenue allocation, which hitherto was majority versus majority ethnic groups, changed to that of minority versus majority ethnic groups. Oil wealth has, in recent times, become a major tool for political domination and class formation in Nigeria. Since the period of oil boom coincided with the domination of the military in Nigerian politics, it created an enabling environment for the ascendancy of the military bourgeois class (Adekanye 1993). Such ascendancy, coupled with its authoritarian dispositions, brought fundamental and frequent alterations to the revenue allocation formula which especially affected the principle of derivation (Gboyega 1996).

Oil Revenue and Development Challenges in Nigeria

For many years to come, the oil and gas industry in Nigeria will continue to play a vital role in the economy of the country because of its enormous wealth potentials. Nigeria relies on oil and gas so much that without the income accruing from it the government may not be able to execute public expenditure and survive as a nation (Ogbonna & Ebimobewe 2012). Paradoxically, this wealth, which ought to be used for socio-economic and infrastructural transformation of the country, has indeed induced a series of development challenges for leadership in Nigeria. Some of these challenges include the following.

Fiscal centralism

The Federal Government (FG) generates and collects the majority of the revenues in Nigeria. The Petroleum Decree of 1969, the Land Use Act Decree of 1978, the Exclusive Economic Zone Act of 1990 and the Oil

Pipeline Act of 1960 gave the legal right of ownership and control of natural resources to the FG. For instance, the Exclusive Economic Zone Act, cap 116, laws of Federation 1990, vests the exclusive right of exploration of natural resources in the sub-sea, sub-soil and superjacent waters in the exclusive economic zone in the FG of Nigeria. Apart from its excessive power to generate revenues through royalty, taxes, etc., the FG equally retains the majority of the revenues it generates. Between 1980 and 2008, for instance, the FG collected about 93.9% of the total government revenues (Adeleke 2011). In terms of revenue sharing among the tiers of government, the FG gets the highest share, as shown in the table below:

Table 10.2. Federation Account Allocation (2008–2011)

Item	2008	2009	2010	2011
FGN Share of Federation Account	2339.23	1923.21	2456.67	2792.51
VAT	58.25	67.44	81.05	93.52
FG Share (Subtotal)	2397.48	1990.65	2537.72	2886.03
State Share of FA	1455.77	1132	1246.06	1489.8
VAT	194.17	224.83	270.17	311.76
State Share (Subtotal)	1649.94	1356.83	1516.23	1801.56
Local Government of FA	1208.51	761.8	960.66	1148.57
VAT	135.92	157.37	189.12	217.89
Local Govt. Share (Subtotal)	1344.43	919.17	1149.78	1366.46
13% Derivation	534.42	1215.19	567.8	663.96
Grand Total	**5926.272**	**5481.84**	**5771.53**	**6718.01**

Source: National Planning Commission (NPC) (2012)

This is so because the Revenue Mobilization Allocation and Fiscal Commission (RMAFC) gives the lion's share of 52.68% to the FG, while the state and local governments collect 26.72% and 20.60% respectively (NPC 2012). This is at variance with the Nigerian colonial fiscal autonomy legacy which gave to the regions a relative measure of autonomy in revenue generation and retention. The implication is a situation in which the FG, which was hitherto relatively weak (Barkan et al. 2001), now became strong in terms of revenue generation and retention. The larger the FG's share, the bigger the "national cake" and the more the contending interests among groups and individuals with respect to its sharing. This may be related to why Watts argues that:

> Centralized oil revenues flowing into weak institutions and a charged, volatile federal system produced an undisciplined, corrupt and flabby oil-led development that was to fragment, pulverize, disintegrate and discredit the state and its forms of governance. (Watts 2005, 61)

What results from this is a situation of leadership anomie in which the supposed leaders struggle to realize personal and primordial interests as central at the expense of the common good of all.

Corruption

One of the consequences of the stupendous wealth that the oil industry generated for Nigeria following the oil boom of the 1970s was the intensification of corruption. As Yakub (2008) noted, the oil boom led to the expansion of the public sector and the deterioration in financial discipline and accountability. A similar situation occurred in Angola following the increase in oil revenues in the mid-1980s. According to Auty (2005), in Angola, oil prosperity led to the emergence of a predatory state in which government officials and the urban elite preyed on the commonwealth through several means including public sector subsidies that conferred a large fraction of the oil rent on the wealthy through personal allowances. In a related development, the 2010 World Bank report asserted that in Nigeria 80% of the oil revenue benefitted only 1% of the population (Ogbonna 2012). Iyare (2008) observed that between June 1999 and May 2007, for instance, the three tiers of government in Nigeria were allocated the sum of N 16.4447 trillion. Much of this money was said to have found its way into private pockets and this explains why the levels of poverty and income inequality increased within this period.

Within the same period, national budget implementation never went beyond 35%, and the N 1.9 trillion spent on the power sector never revived it. N 100 billion was wasted on a presidential jet, N 450 billion was spent, within the first 4 years, on roads without concrete evidence of their existence, and N 140 billion was wasted on petroleum refineries which never worked. In 2001 alone, more than N 23 billion was lost to financial fraud in 10 federal ministries. All this happened in the midst of the watchdog activities of the EFCC and the ICPC, the anti-corruption organs of the government. The Nigerian elite are said to have mismanaged a total sum of $500 billion within five decades of independence and this explains why there are worsening cases of infrastructural decay and human underdevelopment in the midst of plenty.

Value Attachment to Political Office-holding

In Nigeria today, the easiest way to get rich is to become a politician, as it provides an opportunity to get close to cutting the "national pie" prepared by the oil-wealth. Apart from the massive corruption in government by public officers, the huge pay which political office-holders receive in terms of bogus salaries and allowances has provided an attraction for holding political office in Nigeria. According to Balogun (2011), whereas the 2010 federal budget allocated N 156 billion to the National Assembly (NA), the 2011 budget reduced this to N 111.23 billion. Even with such a reduction, it thus implies that the almost one million civil servants in government establishments in Nigeria will have to manage with N 41.49 billion, while the 560 member parliament will have to manage with N 111.23 billion in the 2011 fiscal year. The cost of governance in Nigeria is quite expensive when this is added to what chief executives of each tier of government, their legion of aides and party faithful collect monthly as salaries and allowances. This is part of the dilemma of development in Nigeria as public officers are more interested in personal gains than their abnegation to development.

Laziness of Leadership

One of the differences between the agrarian economy and the petroleum economy is that the latter attracts less effort and more money compared to the former. Following the stupendous wealth the oil revenues generated for Nigeria beginning from the oil-boom era and its eventual centralization, agriculture was de-emphasized. For instance: "Malaysia got her first palm seedlings from Nigeria in the early 1960s when oil palm produce was already a major export of Nigeria. In the 1990s Malaysia's export of palm oil produce earned more than what Nigeria earned from oil exports" (Soludo 2006, 10). Petro-dollars create laziness for the operators of the machineries of governance across the tiers of government as each eagerly awaits what oil will contribute to the Federation Account (FA) and what it is due from such contributions as the basis for budgetary decisions. The psychology behind this is rightly captured in Kapucinksi's assertion that:

> Oil creates the illusion of a completely changed life, a life without work, life for free ... the concept of oil expresses perfectly the eternal human dream of wealth achieved through lucky accident. (Kapucinksi 1982, 35)

This psychology of dependence kills initiatives with respect to sourcing and developing other sources of revenue in Nigeria. Some states such as Niger, Sokoto, Bauchi and Borno depend on oil revenue so much that it accounts for more than 90% of the states' revenue in some years (Danjuma 1994). Available data shows that "20 of the 36 States are faced with visible traits of unstable and unfavourable financial standing, based on the high percentage of their wage bills in relation to the total revenue accruable" (NPC 2012, 89). Table 10.3 below shows how much some of these distressed states depend on federal allocations in spite of their abundant resources.

Although all states in Nigeria depend on the Federation Account Allocation (FAA), to which oil revenue accounts for around 80%, some are so dependent that any oil related crisis is likely to affect their annual fiscal budgetary allocations. Whereas, for instance, Taraba state budgeted N 73.9 billion for the 2012 fiscal year, 88% of this is estimated to come from the Federation Account allocation, while the remaining 12% is expected to be generated from internal revenues and perhaps other sources. Taraba state falls into the category of 20 of the 36 states in Nigeria which are either in a critical or completely distressed state of finance because they spend either 30%–48% or 50% and above of their total revenues on wage bills. In 2011, for instance, Kano state was said to have expended 126% of its revenue on personnel costs (NPC 2012). Paradoxically, these states are individually endowed with numerous resource potentials, most of which are as yet untapped. The quick and easy wealth which petroleum generates has created laziness undermining interest in solid mineral development in Nigeria. This creates the dilemma of a mono-product economy in the midst of multifarious natural resources: "This weak drive for internally generated revenue by the three tiers of government is not conducive for economic growth and prosperity" (Adeleke 2011, 31).

Table 10.3. States' Budgetary Dependence on Federation Account Allocation

S/N	States	2012 Budget (in N Billion)	Estimated 2012 Federation Account Allocations (in N Billion)	Estimated 2012 Internal Revenue (in N Billion)	Financial State	Untapped Resources
1	**Kaduna**	154.3	90 (58.3%)	64.3 (41.7%)	Critical State	Kaolin, Gold, Dolomite, Talc, Iron ore, Bennonite, Gemstones, Kainite Feldspar, Bismuth, Columbite, etc.
2	**Ondo**	156	78 (50%)	78 (50%)	Critical State	Benonite, Bitumen, Silica, Kaolin, etc.
3	**Ebonyi**	86.896	45(51.8%)	41.9 (48.3%)	Critical State	Silver, Salt, lead, Zinc, Limestone, Fluorite, etc.
4	**Yobe**	77.550	63.4 (81.7%)	14.2 (18.3%)	Critical State	Gypsum, Diatomite, etc.
5	**Kogi**	126	63.4 (55.6%)	56 (44.4%)	Critical State	Coal, Dolomite, Gold, Talc, Iron ore, Gemstones, Kaolin, Feldspar, Limestone, etc.
6	**Taraba**	73.9	65 (88%)	8.9 (12%)	Critical State	Coal, Gypsum, Silver, Gemstones, Baryte, Fluorite, etc
7	**Enugu**	76.3	62.2 (81.5%)	14.1 (18.5%)	Critical State	Coal, Iron ore, etc.
8	**Adamawa**	87.9	67.8 (77.1%)	20.1 (22.9%)	Critical State	Kaolin, Gypsum, Coal, etc.

9	**Borno**	149	86.2 (57.9%)	62.8 (42.1%)	Critical State	Diatomite, Gypsum, Benonite, Feldspar, etc.
10	**Benue**	112.78	74.8 (66.3%)	37.9 (33.7%)	Critical State	Coal, Fluorspar, Salt, Baryte, Limestone, etc.
11	**Plateau**	122	65.6 (53.7%)	56.4 (46.3%)	Critical State	Coal, Salt, Gemstones, Lead, Zinc, Kaolin, Baryte, Columbite, fluorite,
12	**Ekiti**	88.8	49.2 (554%)	39.6 (44.6%)	Critical State	Talc, Mica, Tantalite, Kaolin, etc.
13	**Katsina**	118.77	97.2 (82%)	21.6 (18.2%)	Completely Distressed	Fire clay, Gold, Manganese, Kaolin etc.
14	**Niger**	90.3	79.2 (88%)	11.1 (12.3%)	Completely Distressed	Dolomite, Gold, Talc, Gemstones, Kainite, Lithium etc
15	**Sokoto**	100.7	79.2 (79.2%)	21.5 (21%)	Completely Distressed	Fire clay, Gold, Gypsum, Phosphate, Limestone, etc.
16	**Kano**	220	129.2 (58.7%)	90.8 (41.3%)	Completely Distressed	Gold, Silver, Silica, Columbite, etc.

At independence, when oil was not yet the mainstay of the Nigerian economy, the solid minerals sector was already contributing not less than 1% to GDP. However, fifty years later, the industry could only contribute about 0.3% to the GDP. In the 1960s, for instance, coal was the source of the entire energy requirement for the country's industrial sector. Comparatively, in 2009 alone, mining contributed about 9% to South Africa's GDP. Nigeria has proven reserves of 34 solid minerals in commercial quantities. Its proven reserves of coal, for instance, stand at 639 million tons and this is capable of earning $6 billion yearly, or of generating electricity worth 7, 000MW for a period of thirty years, while its large deposits of talc have the potential for generating about $3 billion yearly. It has the second largest reserves of tantalite in the world, the largest deposits of Iron Ore in Africa and deposits of Limestone, Kaolin and Gypsum large enough to meet the cement requirement of the African continent for twenty years. However, the grossly underdeveloped statuses of these industries have in part contributed to the worsening condition of unemployment, generating insufficient funds for capital projects among the tiers of government, and creating a situation in which we are compelled to import minerals that we could produce domestically, such as Barites, Salt and Iron Ore (El-Rufai 2012).

States tend to be weak financially as they are unable to harness the resources of this industry because of "the fiscal and legislative relationships between them and the federal government" (Ndu 2003, 9, quoted in Ebegbulem 2011). The FG is given the legal right over resource exploitation, revenue creation and retention. The states which ought to either clamour for freedom to exploit the resources in their domains or for the FG to create the enabling ground for the full exploitation of these resources do not seem to bother. Instead, they seem to be more interested in a review of the revenue allocation formula as well as the politics of who owns the oil blocs in the continental shelf. This is a case of a lazy child who makes trouble over the father's so-called wealth, and does not want to assert their economic and financial independence. Babangida Aliu Muazu, in one of his public lectures, argued that:

> We must remember that the idea of common nationality implies that the resources of the nation should be considered as a common patrimony for the common good of all the citizens. We need to examine our revenue sharing arrangement to balance derivation with need requirements to guarantee the economic and political health of the nation. (Ojiabor & Onogu 2012, 62).

It is easy to understand the context in which Muazu erects his argument. He is a serving governor of Niger state whose budgetary decisions are dependent on the volume of the contributions of oil to the Federation Account. His group, the Northern Governors' Forum, has always argued that "all oil blocs outside 200 kilometres of the continental shelf should be shared as a common wealth, rather than allowing a few states to share the proceeds" (Eme & Anyadike 2012, 55). This underscores the psychology of resource dependence, and is a case of a greedy neighbour who likes to share the resources from their neighbour's land while at the same time keeping the exploitation of their own resources intact, perhaps for a rainy day.

Although in the 1970s both Nigeria and Indonesia experienced oil booms, the leaders of these countries did not make the same policy choice. While the Nigerian leadership was confused and did not know what to do with the oil wealth, and hence was paying the salaries of workers in a neighbouring country, the Indonesian leadership, according to Soludo (2006), invested wisely in the manufacturing sector of the economy. Consequently, while Indonesia's manufacturing sector increased its contribution to export earnings by 40%, Nigeria has not gone beyond the pre-oil boom era. Table 10.4 below compares Nigeria with some African countries in terms of average manufacturing exports by GDP percentage:

Table 10.4. African Countries' Average Manufacturing Exports by GDP Percentage

COUNTRIES	1980–1989	1990–1999	2000–2006
Benin	0.5	1.5	1.3
Cameroon	1.3	1.5	0.9
Cote d'Ivoire	3.4	6.3	7.8
Egypt	2.4	2.3	2.1
Gabon	2.8	1.4	4.0
Gambia	0.4	1.6	0.6
Ghana	0.3	3.1	4.5
Kenya	2.0	4.6	3.5
Madagascar	0.8	3.1	6.3
Mali	0.1	1.4	8.8
Mauritius	25.2	28.5	26.1
Morocco	6.0	10.0	14.0
Nigeria	0.0	0.6	0.7
Senegal	3.5	7.2	7.5
South Africa	4.4	9.1	13.2

Togo	2.5	4.0	13.7
Tunisia	11.7	21.6	25.0

Source: World Bank 2008 Report Quoted in National Planning Commission (NPC) (2011)

In spite of its wealth potentials, which ought to have been harnessed and channelled towards the development of the manufacturing sector of the economy, Nigeria recorded an abysmal performance in the periods under reference compared to other African countries with less potential. The manufacturing sector remains weak due to poor incentives arising from the decay of public infrastructure, which increases high cost of production, weak technological supports and low levels of innovation, leading to the production of low quality products and non-competitiveness. Moreover, the burden of taxes and levies is weighing heavily on the survival of the sector, especially the problem of multiple taxation (NPC 2010; 2011). Too much emphasis on oil and gas and less on other sectors like manufacturing will not only sustain a mono-product economic culture but also lead to a situation of sustained underdevelopment. The economy may experience an increase in GDP growth rate because of growth in oil and gas activities, and this may not have much impact on unemployment and poverty.

Concluding Remarks

In spite of its human and natural resources, Nigeria's potentials remain largely untapped and mismanaged. According to Soludo (2006), a substantial part of Nigeria's productive resources remains idle, waiting to be mobilized. A reasonable percentage of the able and qualified labour force is either unemployed or under-employed. With over 100 tertiary institutions producing more than 200, 000 graduates yearly, the basic human capital for progress is there. Moreover, only 40% of the arable land in Nigeria is under cultivation, with 60% lying fallow. Therefore, the lacuna in the relationship between resource mobilization and development lies in effective leadership. The Nigeria Vision 2020 Programme (2009) observed that political leaders at all levels of governance have not been able to successfully harness Nigeria's resources to build a sustainable economy, reduce poverty and provide the basic social infrastructures its population needs to live meaningful lives. This presents a paradox of a nation that is stupendously rich but poor in almost all ramifications.

As a mono-economic state, Nigeria experiences worsening cases of human and infrastructural decay even as the oil revenue rises consistently.

In 1985, for instance, 34.7 million people, representing 46.3% of a total population of 75 million Nigerians, were poor. In 1996 this figure increased to 67.1 million (65.6%) out of a population of 102.3 million. Incidentally, this was a period in which the total federally collectible revenues rose from slightly above N 15 billion to over N 523 billion. The recent NBS report (2010) reveals that 112.47 million (69%) Nigerians are poor in spite of the fact that the government revenue increased to over N 7.3trillion from over N 523billion in 1996 (NBS 2012).

Therefore, revenue decentralization is necessary not only in terms of giving the states a reasonable autonomy to explore resources in their respective domains but also to retain revenues while they pay certain royalties to the federal purse. As Egbulem (2011, 218) argues: "financial subordination makes a mockery of federalism. The states must not permanently remain dependent on the federal government for allocations." Apart from generating competition among states for resource exploitation, and hence driving away leadership laziness, the benefits of resource autonomy are, *inter alia*: increase in revenue; increase in GDP; employment generation; poverty reduction; and economic diversification. For Nigeria to have sustained growth, the wealth expected to be generated through expansion in natural resource exploitation should be channelled towards the development of the manufacturing sector of the economy for greater job opportunities, creating sustainable human development. However, the ability of the government to realize this is a function of its political will to harness resources and diversify the economy.

References

Adekanye, B. J. 1993. *Military Occupation and Social Stratification.* Inaugural Lecture. University of Ibadan, Ibadan.

Adeleke, S. 2011. "Taxation, Revenue Allocation and Fiscal Federalism in Nigeria: Issues, Challenges and Policy Options." *Economic Annals* LVI (189): 27–50.

Auty, R. M. 2005. "Natural Resource and Civil. Strife: A Two-stage Process." In *The Geopolitics of Resource Wars: Resource Dependence, Governance & Violence Frank Case*, edited by Billion, P. L., 29–49. London.

Balogun, O. 2011. "Nigeria: 2011 Budget Confirms the saying 'A Man on the Edge of a Precipice does not think'." www.marxist.com/nigeria-2011-budget–man-onedge-of-pre-cipice.htm.

Barkan, J. D., Gboyega, A. & Steven, M. 2001. "State and Local Governance in Nigeria." Public Sector and Capacity Building Program, Africa Region. World Bank.

Central Bank of Nigeria (CBN). 1997. *Annual Report and Statement of Accounts.* Abuja: CBN.

—. *Annual Report and Statement of Accounts.* Abuja: CBN.

Danjuma, T. Y. 1994. "Revenue Sharing and the Political Economy of Nigeria Federalism." In *Federalism and Nation Building in Nigeria: The Challenge of the 21st Century*, edited by Elaigwu, D., Lagams, I. & Galadians, P., 82–115. Abuja: National Council of Intergovt. Relations.

Dokpesi, A. O. 2006. *Political Sociology: a Brief Introduction.* Benin-City: Perfect Touch.

Ebegbulem, J. C. 2011. "Federalism and the Politics of Resource Control in Nigeria: A Critical Analysis of the Niger Delta Crisis." *International Journal of Humanities and Social Science* 1 (12): 218–229.

El-Rufai, N. A. 2011. "Unlocking the Potential in Solid Minerals" www.nigeriavillagesquare.com/index.php?option=com_content&view=article&id=18&Itemid=38.

Eme, O. I. & Anyadike, N. 2012. "The North and Political Economy of Revenue Allocation in Nigeria." *Kuwait Chapter of Arabia Journal of Business and Management Review* 1 (8): 54–75.

Gboyega, A. 1996. *Corruption and Democratization in Nigeria*. Lagos: Fredrich Ebert Foundation.

Ibegwuru, C. I. 2002. "Niger Delta Development Commission, the Niger Delta Perspective." *Human Rights Defenders* 5 (2): 130–139.

Ikporukpo, C. O. 2000. "Petroleum, Fiscal Federalism and Environmental Justice in Nigeria." Paper presented at the IFRA Seminar Series, U.I. July 2000.

Jike, U. I. 2002. "Ethnic Militia and the Spectre of Social Disorganization and Disunion in Contemporary Nigeria." In *Ethnic Militia and Youth Rebelliousness in Contemporary*, edited by Jike, V. I. Nigeria: A Book of Readings.

Kapucinksi, R. 1982. *Shah of Shahs*. New York: Vintage.

National Planning Commission (NPC). 2010. The First National Implementation Plan for NV20: 2020 (2010–2013). (Sectoral Plans and Programmes). Abuja: NPC. Vol.11

—. 2012. 2011 Annual Performance Report of the Nigerian Economy. The Presidency, NPC.

Nnoli, O. 1995. *Ethnicity and Development in Nigeria*. London: Ashgate Publishing Ltd.

Ogbonna, G. N. 2012. "Petroleum Income and the Nigerian Economy: Empirical Evidence." *Arabian Journal of Business Management Review* (OMAN Chapter) 1 (9): 33–59.

Ogbonna, G. N. & Ebimobewei, A. 2012. "Impact of Petroleum Revenue and the Economy of Nigeria." *Current Research Journal of Economic Theory* 4 (2): 11–17.

Ojiebor, O. & Onogu, S. 2012. "N 346.4 billion Debts Cripple States." *The Nation*, Thursday March 15.

Oyevbare, S. E. 1978. "The Politics of Revenue Allocation." In *Soldiers and Oil. The Political Transformation of Nigeria*, edited by Panter K. Brick, 224–249. London: Fankcass.

Phillips, A. O. 1975. "Revenue Allocation in Nigeria, 1970–80." *Nigerian Journal of Economic and Social Studies* 17: 1–28.

Teriba, O. 1966. "Nigerian Revenue Allocation Experience 1952–1965: a Study of Inter Governmental Fiscal and Financial Relations." *Nigerian Journal of Economic and Social Studies* 8: 361–382.

Premo, D. 2005. "Niger Delta Sitting on a Time Bomb." *National Standard* 1 (9).

Soludo, C. C. 2006. *Can Nigeria be the China of Africa?* Lagos: Adgozo Ltd.

United Nation Development Programme. 2006. *Niger Delta Human Development Report*. Abuja: UNDP.

Watts, M. 2005. "'Resource Course.' Governmentality, Oil & Power in the Niger Delta, Nigeria." In *The Geopolitics of Resource Wars: Resource Dependence, Governance & Violence*, edited by Billion, P. L. London: Frank Case.

Yakub, M. U. 2008. "The Impact of Oil on Nigerian Economy: The Boom and Bust Cycle." Central Bank Nigeria, Abuja.

CHAPTER ELEVEN

WHO ARE STREET BEGGARS, AND WHAT IS OUR RESPONSIBILITY TO A DENUDED CITIZENRY?

'TUNJI ADEWUYI

Introduction

Street begging is the practice of open solicitation for assistance with money, food and clothing from anonymous wayfarers through pleas, flagrant deceit, or exposure of deformities, and is a critical component of Nigeria's urban interactions and distractions (Mensah 1977, 1984; Cohen 1969). Over thirty million (or about one fifth) Nigerians make a living from full- and part-time overt and covert parasitism, with the generic and largest chunk of street begging stiffly anchored on the institutional orders of social stratification and strengthened by religious imperatives. With this bind firmly attached to the onslaught of modern innovations, and societal and policy disposition to the problem remaining blasé and undecided, street begging may long remain one of the greatest, most perplexing, seemingly intractable social problems in Nigeria (Adewuyi 2007).

The *problematique* of this chapter appears to be clear—who are the street beggars, and what are their distinguishing profiles in terms of origin, religion, age, sex, appearance and material conditions? Are they all Nigerians or do they include some intruding foreigners sauntering in from adjourning countries, and are they permanent or "hit-and-run" beggars seeking temporary relief in the penumbra of occasional dependency? More relevantly, what is our intellectual responsibility in this regard, and what is the responsibility of political leaders? Are beggars considered capable of self-renewal and automatic, if gradual, restoration to respectability?

Furthermore, is their demographic considered substantial enough to cause alarm, and is their exclusion from society considered a big enough loss to national productivity to warrant urgent attention? Of what cultural-psychological mode are the Hausa beggars themselves in terms of their general dispositions and specific attitudes to the things of this world? That is, do they see "development" as a participatory process in which they should be involved or are they content with sponging and parasitism as the only ways of living? This chapter attempts to illuminate these issues.

Street beggars—Who They Are

All of Nigeria's major cities, from Kaura-Namoda to Calabar and from Lagos to Nguru, are filled with street beggars. On the major roads and in the marketplaces, beggars constitute large crowds and innumerable hordes. They include hundreds of men, women and children without tenor or future, who bare their sexual passions on the dung sites by the roadsides, which they have made their permanent habitat. The following description is very apt:

> The crowds comprise of men and women of all ages and sizes, some crippled, some hale and hearty, all depending on their outstretched hands for their daily pittance … Among the faces like masks and with postules of scabies or eaten away with leprosy, among the rags which leave half-naked bodies which have long been innocent of any contact with water, among the beggars' crutches, sticks and bowls; there are some adorable children who smile happily at life …. (Fall 1981, 1–9)

To be sure, there is no known society that does not have its share of human derelicts. The issue, therefore, is not whether a society is socially stratified; the relevant questions are about the nature of social segmentation and how it comes about.

Sociologists distinguish several types of stratification, but these may be broadly grouped into two. The first and most popular type is not so much an institution in its own right as a by-product of other institutions—this is class-based, and classes in this category: "emerge from the interplay of a variety of factors related to the institutions of property and education and the structure of the national economy" (Marshall 1950, 31).

Most contemporary societies contain these types, their citizens being distinguished by social classes into high, medium and low, but with the opportunity to rise or fall along the rungs of the social ladder. This mobility is the distinctive feature of class as opposed to slavery-, estate- or caste-based societies. The second broad form is:

> expressed in terms of legal rights or established customs which have the essential binding character of law. In its extreme form, such a system divides a society into a number of distinct hereditary human species: patricians, plebeians, serfs, slaves and so forth. This (form of) stratification

> is, as it were, an institution in its own right, and the whole structure has the quality of a plan in the sense that it is endowed with meaning and purposes. (Marshall 1950, 31)

Marshall's paradigm provides a heuristic device to distinguish between the motley crowds found begging on Nigeria's roads.

The first set of beggars are class-based and consist of those I list here but discuss more lengthily elsewhere (Adewuyi 2007) as compulsive beggars, fine baras, tricksters, rag-day student beggars, mothers of twin babies, masquerades, eulogists, entertainers and physically disabled beggars, all of whom originate from non-Hausa segments of the populace. These beggars are mostly economically- and ceremonially-based and as such can respond to, and eventually fade away with, an increase in the gross national product and the more equitable distribution of economic and social goods (Adewuyi 2007).

The second group contains Hausa beggars. Beggars of Hausa origin, variously called almajiris, mabarata and professional beggars, come under Marshall's second classification as products of "rigid and established customs which have the essential binding character of law."

This discussion focuses on the Hausa beggars, being the generic type that defines begging as a social problem and in a quantity that could be called "enormous, " in distressed social and physical appearance that can evoke sympathy by which anybody can easily recognise them. Hausa beggars can be divided into two broad groups: children or pupil beggars and adult beggars, but for practical purposes both constitute the mean and ideal ends of the begging continuum.

Materials and methods

The data used in this study are quantitative and qualitative. Typically, quantitative data consist of literary works and other secondary materials and/or fresh information consisting of facts and figures generated first hand. Thus, this study draws immensely on mini-surveys and write-ups, both of which provided a huge and rich backdrop and beautiful embellishments.

Qualitative information has the capability to describe the characteristics of a large and heterogeneous population or its sample in depth, and possesses that unique ability to generate quick information. It also provides a good and reliable estimate of the range of opinions expressed on the issues of interest (Hyman 1955) and is therefore:

> useful for selecting communities (in this case beggars) with particular characteristics for intervention, or for providing baseline information relevant to the development of questionnaires for more quantitative study. (Vlassoff 1993, V)

The qualitative data used was generated in a longitudinal ethnographic survey carried out in a number of Hausa communities in northern Nigeria between 1993 and 1997 "Ethnography is the process of collecting data by direct inquiry in which the emphasis is on the description of the society studied rather than on the theoretical problem" (Mair 1975, introduction), and is therefore "a valuable method for understanding ideas and beliefs, practices and behaviours" (Davidson & Manderson 1993, 1).

Data Analysis and Presentation

Hausa beggars originate from a culture and disposition in which devotion to Koranic studies, rather than literacy in mathematics, computers and engineering, is believed to answer all of life's questions. It is a culture area where six-year-old boys are pushed away from home (and rarely return) to search for religious scholarship, and in doing so must glean survival by the roadside and end up not having any training or visible means of livelihood except the sophistry to beg. It is a place where beggars, like Hausa prostitutes (karuwai) and commodity merchant men, are administered within the Hausa structure of traditional administration, through the Hausa elite leaders, to facilitate rigid oversight and effective payment of taxation (Adewuyi 2007).

Hausa beggars—the Child Component

Children and adolescent pupils of Koranic schools in the entire terrain of northern Nigeria canvass for alms on a daily basis for their livelihood. The Arabic system of education is called almajirana, the pupil almuhajirun (plural almuhajirai) or perverted almajiri (plural almajiris), while almajiranci stands for the process of acquisition of Islamic education by going from place to place. Today, the connotations of these concepts have expanded beyond their denotations. This is why, for example, the word almajiri is now understood in the context of, or in relationship to, street begging more than scholarship. Koranic scholarship is premised entirely on the Koran and its memorisation, recitation, interpretation and propagation. It is disseminated by mallams (teachers) and alkalis (jurists). Arabic scholarship is not limited to Islamic northern Nigeria, but is also found in all predominantly Islamic societies of North and West Africa, Arabia and Asia. In Karachi, Pakistan, for example:

> Hundreds of young Muslim students sleep in the shadow of Mosques enduring the hard stone-floor and swarming clouds of flies … Starting as young as 8, these boys spend six hours a day memorising the Koran. They get no lessons in mathematics, geography, history or computers. Allah's will, as recorded in the Holy Koran, the teachers say, is all they need to understand the universe. (McGirk 2003)

Universality of Koranic Schools

Koranic education is a Hobson's choice for every Muslim Hausa boy as he has no other access to class, power or prestige except to get erudite in the Koran and become its revered teacher. It is in the search for this "golden fleece" that Muslim urchins enrol and migrate with mallams to cities where they beg for their livelihoods as a contingent survival arrangement.

The complete acceptance of Koranic education by the Muslim Hausa is a duty, and although data on the numbers of Koranic schools are fragmentary, those registered run into hundreds of thousands, covering the entire geographical terrain of Muslim northern Nigeria. As long ago as 1909 there were more than 20, 000 with an enrolment figure of about 150, 000 pupils (Coleman 1971, 135–137). By 1930, the figure had risen to 33, 426 and pupil-enrolment to 183, 374. By 1931, Islamic schools had risen by 6.06% to 35, 452 and pupils to 193, 294 (see Table 11.1 below), and by 1952 enrolment in registered Arabic schools had reached 657, 259 (Northern Regional Census 1952).

Table 11.1, Koranic Schools in Northern Nigeria (1931)

	1930		1931	
Province	**Number of Schools**	**Number of Pupils**	**Number of Schools**	**Number of Pupils**
Adamawa	1, 435	5, 461	1, 104	4, 639
Bauchi	4, 455	21, 774	4, 756	21, 039
Benue	490	4, 087	480	4, 240
Borno	4, 524	34, 000	881	35, 803
Ilorin	770	10, 231	978	11, 590
Kabba	176	1, 662	10, 357	2, 128
Kano	9, 633	39, 521	1, 167	45, 243
Niger	1, 012	4, 944	247	5, 180

Plateau	194	1, 484	6, 637	1, 631
Sokoto	6, 050	36, 912	4, 645	42, 334
Zaria	4, 750	23, 112	-	10, 413
Total	**33, 426**	**183, 374**	**35, 452**	**193, 294**

Source: Paden (1986)

Arabic schools and pupil-enrolment therein compared more favourably with Western scholarship in the 1930s. In 1930, there were a total of 366 elementary Western schools with an enrolment figure of 8, 116, and in 1931 a total of 306 such schools with an enrolment of 10, 099 (Paden 1986, 92). Thus, rather than increase or at least remain constant between 1930 and 1931, the number of Western-styled schools actually decreased by 22 or 14%, whereas registered Koranic schools increased by over 6% and enrolment by over 5%.

Far more escaped registration, being hidden away in the "impenetrable" rural enclaves where 70–80% live, and being dismantled each time government monitoring agencies raided them. So passionately do northern Muslims subscribe to Koranic scholarship that parents would send their children and wards unassisted to these schools for many seemingly unintelligent reasons:

> "karattu sai da bakunta"—Learning is better acquired away from home; it is better to study outside the reach of the loved, loving and distracting relations. "karattu sai da karachin abinci"—Learning can only be effective on an empty stomach; learning is hampered when there is enough to eat. (Last 1967; Sa'ad 1974)

Pupils escape from villages to the cities for several reasons:

> For sadaka, clothing and housing. They run away from squabbles at home or from the village where farmwork is too much of a burden, or when there is cin rani (draught) and some "neman da abin hannu" for scholarship and money. Most of them claim that without bara (gifts), the education received would not have albarka (blessing or usefulness) (Abba 1981, 5).

> Koranic education, in spite of its present deficiencies, still governs the educational life of most of the vast majority of people. (Aliyu 1972, 17)

Living Arrangements

A typical group of *almajiris* is made up of pupils of the same Koranic school. Evidently products of very poor socio-economic backgrounds, their ages range from six to eighteen. At night they huddle together to keep warm and store their belongings in the open veranda of the Mosque. Their belongings are scant, lacklustre and malodorous, oddments consisting of old clothes, caps, texts, tablets, alms bowls and a few worn-out sandals. They fasten strong ropes to the brims of their bowls to hang the empty bowl on the hand, neck, shoulder or any other convenient part of their body when begging and on the walls when not engaged. More interestingly, they also use the ropes as anti-food theft devices. For instance, if somebody decides to save their food for the next day, they tie their bowl to their leg or hand so they are woken if anyone tries to steal it.

Origin and Migratory Pattern

If the comprehensive census of schools and pupils is difficult to ascertain, segmented surveys give some ideas about their origins, migration patterns and modes of operation. Two micro-surveys of Zaria town by Mensah in 1977 and 1984 reported that about a quarter (24.5%) of the *almajirai* found in Zaria were born within the city. Over 75% were immigrants from the adjourning rural settings. Four-fifths (79.3%) of the parents of the kids were either unemployed or earning below poverty-line income. A more recent census by Shelleng (1991, 17) shows that almost three quarters (73.8%) of street kids in the Kaduna metropolis were *Koranic* school pupils, 90% of whom said that begging was their only means of survival.

Search for Survival

A recent study by the Women in Development Unit (WIDU) (1992, 25) emphasised the burden of *almajiris* survival:

> The *almajirai* are expected to feed themselves. They all do, except when they are lucky to hit it big by getting the leftovers from the mallam's wives. It is common to see groups of *almajirai* scavenging with dogs and vultures at refuse disposal points … sometimes to stay alive, they resort to begging for food rather than money. That is when begging for money runs them in direct competition with older beggars and psychotics who also depend on begging for their livelihood. The *almajiri* is therefore that hungry, scraggy-looking boy in tattered clothes all covered with dust, hugging an empty plate, his gateway to heaven, and for him, heaven is

something to bite, anything to bite that will not instantly kill. Go to Bauchi or any other big city for that matter, stop at tasha (motor park), buy some food to eat and see how they mob you.

Almajiri Adult-beggar Spiral

The search for sustenance rather than scholarship describes the daily routines of the almajirai and eats up most of the time meant for the study of the Koran. Some children, in order to make ends meet, resort to pilfering and other criminal activities when begging fails. Muhammed (1991) noted that the almajiri is a natural precursor to adult begging since adulthood behaviour flows unidirectionally from earlier experiences. Almajirana is a training ground that provides a child with a model of survival and a mechanism to pursue it. An almajiri learns to evoke sympathy in this process by self-abasement. His idiosyncrasies are many: dull composure, moribund appearance, lazy gait, aimless wandering and cringing, and rankya_dede mentality. In the words of Mohammed (1991):

> This is the main cause of Hausa-Fulani begging. They inculcate the habit of begging from childhood through the almajiri system and grow up with it. Once they are accustomed to begging, it will be a matter of time before they change into a new social life. The beggar must be sure he wears rags in order to attract attention and sympathy. It has become endemic in our society so much that if any member of the family becomes disabled, it is not a matter of shame for the family to encourage him to go out and beg, even if there are other members of the family who could cater for him or her.

Hausa beggars—Adult Men

Somehow, all children become adults if they survive long enough, but adults vary in the amount of class, prestige and power they command. The almajiris are no exception—they grow up to remain beggars. Evidently weighed down by burdens of age and oppressed by health problems, they trudge about, mount guards, slump lazily on their walking sticks or simply coalesce and encumber the sidewalks. As one passes by, what strikes even the least suspecting person is that the superfamilia_hominoidea are already at an advanced stage of social, physical and physiological atrophy. They look fatigued, ill, wretched, groggy, befuddled and filthy with a significant proportion presenting physical handicaps, the commonest of which are blindness, lameness, festering sores, many forms and degrees of congenital malformation, debility and dumbness.

They hibernate in virtually every available bus stop unprotected from the burning sun, drenching rain and sandy winds, which leave them further bedraggled through uncanny harshness and vicissitudes that are concordant with tropical extremities. Beggars that have degenerated into total sedentariness in overcrowded stranger-quarters, transit camps and uncompleted buildings fare even worse. They have equally converted such places to feculent ghettos where infections are transmuted and transmitted without abatement. Here they rot away, eaten up by curable and degenerative diseases, dying un-mourned and unmissed.

Ill health and disability, although major parameters in street begging, are not to be conceived in terms of physical sickness alone. A deep reflection indicates that above everything else, the social and psychological integrity of any persons that find street begging attractive has been severely impaired. The fact that some beggars suffer motor-nervous diseases like epilepsy and benign grades of mental illness can be ascertained quite easily through casual observation. However, the social-psychological underpinning of begging itself is completely disguised.

Taking to the street clearly indicates that most of the individuals involved are victims of societal tyranny, a consequence with its root in obscurantism. They have long been excluded from advanced knowledge and modern science and economically deprived and relegated to pathological social weaklings, having interiorised a perception of themselves as despicable runts, ne'er-do-wells that can only exist as inane parasites, merely hanging on to the fringes of society. Having failed to attain relevance in the noble departments of society, they have accepted that their only link to the rest of humanity is social parasitism. In a prologue to a discussion, Ohaeri (1990) told in poetry the wicked story of how "we" kicked them out:

> we are dealing with the truly homeless ones; the people of the streets, the ones we have abandoned; to the vagaries of nature; the children of our loins, our kindred; but we kicked them; out of our homes and humanity; onto the street ….

And Aliyu (1972, 13) also picked up a lamentation that:

> Beggars have found themselves at odd with society which has condemned them perpetually to suffer from the slings and arrows of outrageous fortune. Faced with harsh realities of life, deprived by lack of education for any kind of employment, weakened, disabled or crippled by disease, poverty or accident, denied of all social amenities, and treated as outcasts by society, they see and find themselves with no other choice or alternative but one which they are compelled to adopt, begging.

Female Hausa beggars

There is a huge female component of Hausa beggars although Hausa women are seldom recruited into the alms trade as are *almajiri*. Women are excluded from *almajiranci* for a plethora of reasons, and the need to get married and produce children immediately supersedes the need for long, formal (religious or secular) training. Unlike their male counterparts, even the few that receive religious education are by custom not required to seek it from place to place. Hausa women are also excessively "commodified" and not recognised or dignified more than household chattels. Even in matters as sacred as religion, women are not regarded as essential participants. Islam is regarded as essentially the men's religion with women having little or no part to play in it (Smith 1952, 2; Cohen 1966, 60). However, the fact that they do not participate in *almajiranci* is not to suggest that they are far too insulated to become beggars.

In fact, since it is impossible to swim in muddy water and make a boast to being clean, the moral force, the collective consciousness and the disposition of the Muslim Hausa society are so strongly in support of begging that street begging is an easy and natural alternative source of living for poor and powerless women, even more so than men. Everywhere in Hausaland, and for all purposes, women are treated as underdogs who exist for men to use, abuse and discard. So meretricious and pudendous, they are brought up to serve and look up to men, attending to their whimpers. They have no education or any visible means of living independently. Yet the men on whom they lean are in sorry conditions of indigence. Their brothers are *almajirai*, their fathers, husbands, uncles and nephews are beggars or wandering, scavenging *mallams*, and their mothers are dead, sick, totally secluded housewives, prostitutes at large or esurient beggars.

Since they are illiterate in Western scholarship, they are ignorant about their ordinary phenomenological health and nutritional needs, experience frequent divorce and therefore emanate from extremely ignorant, poor and powerless backgrounds which enforce street begging as their only way of life. In addition, some harmful ethno medical and cultural practices which are peculiar to the Muslim Hausa further compound their problems and deserve considerable attention.

Harmful Ethno medical and Cultural Practices

If young Hausa boys are forced into begging for survival in partial fulfilment of the requirements for the award of *ijaza* [certificate], young girls are pushed into it through child marriage and the attendant problems of childbearing which they are not physiologically prepared to shoulder. These practices are associated with cultural and ethno medical practices which the Hausa hold as sacrosanct.

The Hausa woman carries a morbidity burden that accompanies lactation. This is the practice of "roasting" every puerperal woman over a bed of hot coals and "steaming" her with hot water, presumably for calefacient effects. Also associated with this, she must be fed with "poisonous" gruel to "flush out impurities in her blood and boost her energy." The logic here is simple—a postpartum woman, in the Hausa ethno medical system, is regarded as extremely vulnerable to both *sanyi* (cold) and *rani* (heat). It is also believed that sediments of impurity lodge inside her which must be flushed out. She is therefore forced to warm up on a clay bed with a fireplace underneath (Trevitt 1973).

These practices portend serious health hazards. Mabogunje et al. (1987; 1988), Mabogunje (1989) and Ezem & Otubu (1980) report overwhelming numbers of Hausa women and new-borns seriously burnt by scalding water and charred by glowing coals. In addition, the gruel contains a large quantity (30 grams daily) of sodium carbonate, an acidulous chemical that hastens hyperactivity and eventually cardiac failure. Wall (1998, 352) noted that: "For the woman who sustains permanent cardiac damage as a result of this condition, progressive deterioration of heart function appears to be common."

The second burden is the hazard attendant to childhood and teenage pregnancy. By custom, Hausa girls commonly marry between the ages 12 and 14, sometimes as early as 9 or 10, and are sometimes affianced at a much younger age. Early betrothal and marriage are the rule rather than the exception because the same culturally-related reproductive prescriptions enforce that female reproductive capacity must come strictly under well-defined male control (Longhurst 1982; Rehan 1984; Wall 1998). This sometimes creates the need to "enlarge the vagina of a child-wife which is too small to permit her husband to have intercourse with her" (Tahzib 1985). This also carries the grim omen that such girls must get pregnant and become mothers while they themselves are still growing up physiologically.

Naturally, owing to extreme pressure on their pubescent tenderness, childhood pregnancy often results in serious morbid conditions. The greatest and most common of these is obstructed labour, which traditional barber-surgeons, who are principal stakeholders in Hausa ethno medical practice, often correct using obsolescent, unsterilized traditional surgery, *yakan gishiri* (Harrison 1980; Ityavyar 1984; Megafu 1985). Unfortunately, *yakan gishiri* often leads to serious haemorrhage, infection and injury to pelvic organs such as the urethra, bladder and rectum, as well as the vagina (Wall 1998, 353).

These injuries often lead to the development of obstetric fistulae (OFs), which consist of fistulae formed between the mother's bladder and vagina (vesico-vaginal fistula, VVF), and between the rectum and vagina (recto-viginal fistula, RVF), and complicated conditions of other pelvic organs such as the uterus, cervix, urethra and ureters.

The almost total restriction of this problem to the Hausa northern Nigeria should be noticed. Research by Wall noted that: "For Zaria town alone, a crude prevalence rate for obstructed labor is estimated at 1, 238 per 100, 000 births with an OF rate of 350 fistulae per 100, 000 deliveries" (1998, 356).

Apart from work done by several other physicians, Tahzib (1983; 1985) alone received 1, 443 cases in just one hospital, and Waaldijk (1989) repaired close to 10, 000 OFs. The latter found that about three-quarters (73%) of the patients with OFs were younger than 20, 52% developed fistulae with their first pregnancy, and over 33% occurred among girls aged 15 or younger, sometimes below 10. This cruel condition was worsened by procrastination in seeking medical care for sometimes as long as twenty years.

The fistulae ranged in size from very small (less than 1 mm) to "enormous" (greater than 5 cm). About 64% were at least 2 cm in diameter, the bladder-closing mechanism being involved in 69% of cases, while in 11% the urethra was completely destroyed. At any given moment, the OF estimate for Muslim northern Nigeria could be 500, 000 or higher when all out-of-hospital cases are also taken into account (Ampofo et al. 1990; Biela et al. 1976; Arrowsmith et al. 1996; Danso et al. 1996).

The material condition of the Islamic parts of northern Nigeria, in terms of comparative denudation, worsens perceptions and attitudes to modern healthcare facilities. Thus, the health-seeking behaviour of most Muslim Hausa women is cavalier and strong negative barriers undermine their doctor-patient contact. In this regard, a combination of negative cultural predilections and prohibitive communication barriers, in terms of distance, time and financial cost of reaching health centres, plays a major discouraging role.

> Because most Hospitals capable of performing fistula surgery are time-consuming, because fistula patients require longer hospitalisation than general surgery patients, because these women are almost always destitute

> and unable to pay for medical care, and because of the strict avoidance of male contact (most doctors are male) most women with obstetric fistulae are never treated. There are more than two million worldwide with this condition; perhaps as many as 250, 000 such women reside in northern Nigeria alone. (Wall 1998, 344–345)

About 67% of women with OF experience intrauterine wounds, distended bladders, eventual bladder rupture and total menstrual stoppage arising from hypothalamic aberration. The vascular ischemic injury that brings about fistula formation also causes severe tearing either in sporadic areas of the vagina or in the form of panvaginal lesions. This may produce a painful, stenotic, rigid, moistureless vagina that no longer permits sexual intercourse and makes fistula repair difficult (Wall 1998; Aimakhu 1974). Perhaps the most devastating of these problems is the social toll. Vaginal injuries make sexual intercourse painful and difficult, and constant urinal and sometimes fecal products make it unpleasant. Because of ignorance, these victims are accused of suffering venereal diseases, for which they deserve punishment. In consequence, friends, co-wives and neighbours often desert them to avoid "infection." Worse still, since OF occurs most often with the first pregnancy, foetuses involved in obstructed labour die, and OF requires modern surgery to which most women are disinclined or have no access, the morbidity is "incurable" and such women may never have any surviving children—a devastating blow in a family-oriented culture like (Islamic) northern Nigeria. Such girls are treated with blithe contempt, deserted by all, divorced with ignominy and dismissed back to their parents (Nwabugwu-Otesanya 1989).

But they fare no better in their families of orientation either. They are segregated, eating and sleeping all by themselves; they are prohibited from cooking for others or sharing utensils with them (Lawal 2004). They are rejected as "unclean, " quarantined and excluded from religious activities which finally kills whatever is left of their sense of self-worth, and expunges the possibility of spiritual absolution for their "sins" and psychological consolation for their affliction. Their untreated conditions continue, of course, to fester. Odour from them is ever strong and offensive, they being unable to resist the constant stream of urine and sometimes hydraulic faeces drizzling from their vaginas down their thighs and legs. With time, these illiterate, jobless, impoverished, childless, divorced, socially rejected, desolate, distraught women, reeking of putrescent products, are completely thrown to the margins of the society where they live a precarious existence, unable to earn a living except through begging.

Discussion of Findings

A huge body of ethnographic data reveals that street begging is the outcome of important ethno cultural processes and practices peculiar to the Muslim Hausa of northern Nigeria. These practices and processes relate to childbearing and social processes in which the Hausa boy-child must set out early in life and completely out of parental guidance and guardianship to seek Koranic education in distant lands among the anonymous Muslim *ummah*; and in which the Hausa girl-child must marry early in life to face the risky prospects of teenage pregnancy and its uncertain consequences.

These processes of bringing up children proceed along the normal, inescapable paths of human development from childhood through adolescence to adulthood, and are disguised paradoxically as so-called virtues that the Muslim Hausa hold in sincere esteem.

Islamic scholarship is the virtue of highest consideration among them. The object of emulation is not a Yoruba or Ibo boy proficient in computer engineering but a Koranic teacher fluent in Arabic and versed in the knowledge of Allah. If the type of scholarship they pursue is anachronistic and obsolete, their process of seeking it is a Neanderthal throwback that kills the masculinity in young and otherwise promising boys. Since they beg for their upkeep, they learn early not to compete in the marketplace or pick up industrial employment, but to put on a set of behaviours congruent with begging. It is not to be expected that such children, who live all their impressionable years as destitute alms-canvassers, by the roadside, without any adult chaperon or skill for earning a living, will develop into adults of consequence.

Similarly, or perhaps more fundamentally, a child-wife or adolescent-mother is already denuded into adulthood. It is worse that such women have no education or sellable skill that can enhance their participation in money-generating ventures, that they are secluded as housewives living in the hostile midst of older wives, and that all relations in both their family of orientation and procreation are poor and ignorant. It is worst that many of them and their children suffer many of the adverse consequences that follow childbirth such as burns, heart failure and fistulae. Again, it is inconceivable that women and children who suffer such terrible poverty will have any alternative to living other than begging.

Policy Intervention

From the intellectual point of view, the Hausa type and magnitude of begging is a massive social problem, and from the humanitarian angle one that must occupy the front burner in terms of national attention and solution. Happily, we know its cause and through this it becomes much easier to think of possible remedies.

The permanent, one-dose pill is the complete overhauling of the institutional complexes of the Islamic northern Nigeria with a view to making the family, economic, political and cultural subsystems more functionally responsible and less authoritarian. There must be an appreciable transformation of the normative patterns and "conscience collective" that give northern Nigerian poor families their weird uniqueness and society its authoritarian embroidery. The solution here must be necessarily catholic and heterotropic to be effective.

If the long-term solution targets total eradication, the short-term seeks rehabilitation; and if the former involves a major social-cultural shake up, the latter is largely concerned with resettlement. Rehabilitation will however take many forms, such as physical, medical, economic and social, and requires many processes.

There must be a national headcount survey to determine the number, history, state of origin, age, sex, disability patterns, present place of operation and health statuses of Hausa beggars. At the level of each state of the federation, rehabilitation centres and homes for senior citizens should be established and effectively run. A Beggars' Trust Fund should be established by an act of parliament into which employers, employees and charity organisations make regular mandatory contributions. Finally, the traditional system of Islamic education should be thoroughly overhauled to give way to, or at least accommodate, Western scholarship, and in this way put an end to street begging.

References

Abba, Isa. 1981. *Bara by Almajirai in Kano city in the 20th Century*. Paper presented at the Conference on the History of Kano. Bayero University, Kano, Nigeria.

Adewuyi, 'Tunji. 2007. *Street begging in Nigeria.* Nigeria: Spectrum Books and London: Safari Books.

Aimakhu, V. E. 1974. "Reproductive functions after the Repair of Obstetric Vesico-Vaginal Fistulae." *Fertility and Sterility.* 25: 586–591.

Aliyu, A. 1972. "Political and Administrative Implications of Rehabilitation of Beggars." In *Rehabilitation of Beggars in Nigeria*, edited by Okediji, F. O. Ibadan: University Press.

Ampofo, K., Otu, T. & Uchebo, G. 1990. "Risk Factors of Vesico-Vaginal Fistulae in Maiduguri, Nigeria: A Case—Control Study." *Tropical Doctor* 20: 138–139.

Ampofo, K. et al. 1990b. "Epidemiology of Vesico-Vaginal Fistulae in Northern Nigeria." *West African Journal of Medicine* 9: 98–102.

Arrowsmith, S. D et al. 1996. "Obstructed Labour Injury Complex: Obstetric Fistula Formation and Mulifaceted Morbidity of Maternal Birth Trauma in the Developing World." *Obstetrics and Gynecological Survey* 51: 568–574.

Bieler, E. U & Schnabel, T. 1976. "Pituitary and Ovarian Function in Women with Vesico-Viginal Fistulae after Obstructed and Prolonged Labour." *South African Journal of Medicin.* 50: 257–266.

Cohen, A. 1965. "Arab Border Villages in Israel." *Social Organization.* Manchester: University Press.

—. 1966. "Politics of the Kola Trade." *Africa* 36 (1): 18–36.

—. 1967. "Stranger Communities: The Hausa." In *The City of Ibadan*, edited by Lloyd, P.C. et al., 117–127. Cambridge: University Press.

—. 1969. *Customs and Politics in Urban Africa: A Study of Hausa Migrants in Yoruba Towns*. London: Routledge and Kegan Paul.

Coleman, J. 1971. "The Ibo and Yoruba Strands in Nigerian Nationalism." In *Nigeria: Modernization and the Politics of Communalism*, edited by Melson, R. & Wolpe, H. East Lansing: Michigan State University Press.

Danso, K. et al. 1996. "The Epideminology of Genito-Urinary Fistulae in Kumasi, Ghana, 1977–1992." *International Urogynaecology Journal* 7: 117–120.

Ezem, B. & Otubu, J. 1980. "A Complication of a Traditional Puerperal Practice in Nigeria." *International Journal of Gynaecology and Obstetrics* 18: 383–384.

Fall, Aminata Sow. 1981. *Beggars' Strike.* London: Longman.

Harrison, K. A. 1980. "Traditional Birth Attendants." *Lancet* 2: 43–44.

Ityavyar, D. A. 1984. "Traditional Mid-Wife Practice in Sokoto State, Nigeria." *Social Science and Medicine* 18: 497–500.

Last, M. 1967. *The Sokoto Caliphate.* London: Longman.

Lawal, A. 2004. "The Leaking Hopes." *Tell.* January 19, 42–44.

Longhurt, A. 1982. "Resource Allocation and Sexual Division of Labor: A Case Study of a Muslim Hausa Village in Northern Nigeria." In *Women in Development: Sexual Division in Rural Societies*, edited by Beneria, L. New York: Praeger.

Mabogunje, A. 1989. "Burn Injuries during the Puerperium in Zaria, Nigeria." *International Journal of Gynaecology and Obstetrics* 30: 133–137.

Mabogunje O.A, Khwaja M.S and Lawrie. J. H. 1987. *Childhood burns in Zaria, Nigeria Burns*1987. 13. Pp. 298–304.

Mabogunje, O. A. Khwaja M.S and Lawrie. J. H. 1988. "Burns in Adults in Zaria, Nigeria." *Burns* 14: Pp. 304–312.

Marshall, T. H. 1950. *Citizenship and Social Class.* Cambridge: University Press.

McGirk, T. 2003. "Cooler Surface, Seething Below." *Time.* September 15.

Megafu, U. 1985. "Factors Influencing Maternal Survival in Ruptured Uterus." *International Journal of Gynaecology and Obstetrics* 23: 475–480.

Mensah, E. 1977. "A Note on the Distribution of Beggars in Zaria." *Savanna: A Journal of the Environmental and Social Sciences.* Volume 6 No1. Pp. 73-76.

Mensah, E. 1984. "Children Beggars: A Case from Zaria, Nigeria." *Sociology* 34 (1).

Nduka, O. 1964. *Western Education and the Nigerian Culture: Background.* London: Oxford: University Press.

Nwabugwu-Otesanya, B. E. 1989. "Social Consequences of Vesico-Viginal Fistula: Zaria Experience." Paper presented at the first Women's Health Research Network in Nigeria General Meeting. Calabar September 5–8.

Ohaeri, J. 1990. "Destitution and Vagrancy in Nigeria, " Paper presented to the editorial sub-committee to Articulate National Mental Health Policy as part of Working Document for Editing Recommendation of the Asuni Panel on Rehabilitation of vagrant Psychotics and Destitute Persons.

Rehan, N. 1984. "Knowledge, Attitude and Practice of Family Planning in Hausa Women." *Social Science Medicine* 18: 839–844.

Sa'ad, A. 1974. "The Scholastic Community of Yola, Adamawa." Paper presented at the Faculty of Arts, Ahmadu Bello University, Zaria, Nigeria.

Shelleng, R. J. 1991. "A Study of Street and Working Children in Zaria Town." Thesis. Sociology. ABU, Zaria, Nigeria.

Smith, M. G. 1952. *Baba of Karo: A Woman of the Muslim Hausa.* London: Faber and Faber Ltd.

Tahzib, F. 1983. "Epidemiological Determinants of Vesico Vaginal Fistula." *British Journal of Obstetric and Gynaecology* 90: 387–391.

—. 1985. "Vesico Viginal Fistula in Nigerian Children." *Lancet* 2: 1291–1293.

Waaldijk, K. 1989. "The Surgical Management of Bladder Fistula in Women of Northern Nigeria." Nijinergen, Holland. Thesis.

Wall, L. L. 1998. "The Social Context of Maternal Morbidity and Mortality among the Hausa of Northern Nigeria." *Studies in Family Planning* 29: 341–359.

WIDU (Women in Development Unit, Zaria). 1992. *Child Abuse*. ABU, Zaria, Nigeria.

CHAPTER TWELVE

CLIMATE CHANGE AND SOCIAL PROCESSES IN RURAL NIGERIA

GODWIN ETTA ODOK

Introduction

The present defining human development issue is indeed climate change, and this has no doubt impacted social processes in different ways, especially in developing countries like Nigeria. In simple terms, climate change refers to changes in weather conditions over a prolonged period due to natural variability (natural forcing) or human activities (anthropogenic forcing). Climatic events in the last few years have settled all debates and uncertainties concerning climate change in Nigeria (Adelekan 2011). This chapter examines observed climate change involving structural alterations concerning processes of social interaction within rural Nigeria.

In recent times, no obsessions have been as overwhelming within academic and government circles as questions of climate change and sustainable development. This means that environmental and "green" concerns have assumed a central position in how development objectives are pursued and implemented. Development here is perceived as a sustained, socially engaged socio-structural transformation paradigm, which augments the productive capacity and economic returns of mass society, and provides scope for the socio-economic amelioration of the quality of life of mass society (Prah 2011). The greatest part of Nigeria is rural (Olawoye 2002), meaning that if any development programme must be different in Nigeria it must make a difference to the lives of the rural masses. The difference must be felt in all areas of social life, providing the perceptible and incremental growth of possibilities and opportunities in both material and non-material senses. It likewise means that the development must optimize the capacity of the rural mass society to intervene intelligently, creatively and knowledgeably on the environment in pursuit of its mode of livelihood.

It had been noted that a striking feature of developing Asia, unlike Africa, is that the development and transformation of Asian societies are noticeable, first and foremost, at the village or rural level (Prah 2011). The significance of this point is that in the transformation and development of agrarian society in Asia, the ultimate goal has been that social processes of change are those that transform the lives of the teeming rural underclass. Social processes in this sense refer to those "repetitive forms of behaviour" commonly found in a people's social lives (Ekong 1998).

With population growth, shifting cultivation and the colonial cash crop economy, forests and natural resources in rural Nigeria are depleting, leading to growing tensions among various groups. Consequently, this has resulted in competition. In its best description, this competition has transformed to heights where rules are flouted and competitors now seek to weaken or eliminate each other. The responsive pattern is thereby the maintenance of boundaries and territories. In this regard, competition, conflict and boundary maintenance have been highlighted as social processes that global climate change has encourages in recent times within rural Nigeria. Engaging discourses of political ecology framework, a common thread running throughout this chapter, is the role of "external, " "outside" or "global" forces in dissolving and displacing social bonds within rural Nigeria. These stress the embeddedness of "forests and natural-resources contestation" in historical contexts, social relations and linkages with wider economic and social settings.

This chapter begins with a brief methodological overview and proceeds to look at the two dominant dimensions of changing climate in rural Nigeria, after which an analysis of the social processes expedited by climate change in rural Nigeria are presented.

Methodology

Adopting a participatory rural appraisal (PRA) research approach, which comprises a literature review, interviews, observations and do-it-yourself activities (like the seasonal calendar in Agoi-Ibami, Iko-Esai and Butatong), this chapter looks at the impacts of climate change events on social interaction within rural Nigeria. Participant observation, semi-structured interviews and questionnaires are the main methods of data collection. Participant observation was chosen as a means to facilitate connection with the people, the collection of data that relates to sensitive issues, and to gain insights about daily activities and perceptions of the people being studied (Reenerg & Nielsen 2010).

The insights obtained were explored further in semi-structured interviews. Forty-three of such interviews were conducted with older, middle-aged and young men and women covering all socio-economic profiles in the selected villages. Transect walk, seasonal calendar and social well-being mapping were carried out, repeated over time and covering historical developments to map social memory, particularly regarding livelihoods and climate change (McIntosh 2000). All semi-structured interviews were digitally recorded. Observations and conversations during participant observation were written in notebooks. A questionnaire with 459 heads of households selected through a multi-stage sampling procedure was carried out.

The semi-structured interviews and the questionnaire were structured in such a way that for each category of questions the respondents were asked to assess their current situation. For instance, main income source, harvest yield, commencement/cessation of rainfall, field size, and so on. They were then asked to describe the main changes (if any) to their current situation over the past twenty-five years, and finally assess the main causes of these changes (if any). No explicit indication of the focus on climate factors was presented for respondents at this stage in order to minimize biases in their responses. At the end of the interviews and questionnaire sessions, the respondents were asked to assess their perceptions of climate change generally and the perceived impacts of this on their social interaction. When impacts were assessed as negative, the respondents were asked to explain their adaptive actions to respond to these impacts. All interviews were conducted with the help of interpreters.

Dimensions of Climate Change in Rural Nigeria

Humans, like other primates, constantly face the challenge of adaptation to the conditions of life on the earth. It is widely acknowledged that climate change is the most critical environmental challenge facing humanity at present (Chokor 2012). In broad terms, climate change refers to any change in climate over time, whether due to natural variability or as a result of human activity. More specifically, this involves change in climate conditions that arise from human activity, resulting in the release of greenhouse gases such as carbon dioxide (CO_2), methane (CH_4) and nitrous oxide (N_2O) to the atmosphere.

In Nigeria, the issue of climate change is usually considered from two dimensions (BNRCC 2011). The first dimension has been acknowledged by households and communities across the country, and also reported by the Nigerian Meteorological Agency (Anuforom 2010). This involves changes that have already been observed in climate parameters such as temperature, rainfall and extreme weather events.

The second dimension of climate change in Nigeria deals with changes expected in the future. In 2008, the Nigerian Meteorological Agency (Anuforom 2010) conducted an assessment of the Nigerian climate over the period 1941 to 2000 and demonstrated that between 1941 and 1970 only a few parts of the country around Sokoto and Maiduguri and in the southeastern region experienced the late onset of rains. However, from 1971 to 2000 they reported that the late onset of rains had spread to most parts, leaving only a narrow band in the middle of the country with normal conditions. In the same vein, their report showed that only a small part of the country in the southwest recorded the early cessation of rains between 1941 and 1970, whilst from 1971 to 2000 results confirmed that the early cessation of rains had covered most of the country. Hence, the combination of late onset and early cessation of rainfall shortens the rainy season in most parts of the country. Furthermore, according to them, between 1941 and 2000 annual rainfall decreased by 2–8 mm across most parts of the country, but increased by 2–4 mm in some other parts, mostly around Port Harcourt where the increase in rainfall rose significantly (NASPA-CCN 2011).

Accordingly, the report also confirmed that from 1941 to 2000 there was evidence of long-term temperature increase in most parts of the country. The main exception was in the Jos area where a slight cooling was recorded. On the other hand, the most significant increases were recorded in the extreme northeast, extreme northwest and extreme southwest regions where average temperatures rose by 1.4–1.9°C. Another observed evidence of climate change or warming in Nigeria as reported by BNRCC (2011) is the decrease in the occurrence of hail, with its total disappearance in the 1990s in the Jos plateau area where it used to be a common occurrence.

Expected climate change in Nigeria is determined using climate scenario analytic tools that provide long-term perspectives on expected changes in climate parameters. These climate scenarios are neither predictions nor forecasts (Anuforom 2010); instead, they provide useful information on how the future climate will be different from the present, based on a defined set of assumptions.

As part of the BNRCC Project, the Climate Systems Analysis Group at the University of Cape Town developed climate scenarios for Nigeria, employing an empirical approach using the statistical downscaling method (NASPA-CCN 2011). Trends in the past climate over Nigeria were investigated by analyzing the historical climate records from 40 NIMET stations for the period 1971 to 2000, and future climate change information was generated by downscaling two future climate projections from nine Global Climate Models. The two future climate projections were based on two scenarios known as A2 and B1, with A2 incorporating higher GHG emissions, and B1 incorporating lower GHG emissions (NASPA-CCN 2011). According to the projection, the higher global GHG emissions scenario (the A2 scenario) was selected as the strongest for Nigeria (BNRCC 2011).

Overall, the scenarios suggest a warmer climate in the future for Nigeria. For instance, the A2 scenario projects a temperature increase of 0.04°C per year from now until 2046–2065; this would then rise to 0.08°C per year after 2050. However, regional variations are expected accordingly. The coastal regions are projected to warm less than the interior regions because of the cooling effects of the Atlantic Ocean, and northern Nigeria is expected to be warmer than southern Nigeria. The highest increase (4.5°C by 2081–2100) is projected in the northeast region of Nigeria. This temperature distribution is consistent with the findings of the 2007 Intergovernmental Panel on Climate Change (IPCC) report (NASPA-CCN 2011).

The projected changes in rainfall vary across the country, with the A2 scenario suggesting a wetter climate in southern Nigeria but a drier climate in the northeast region of the country. For the 2046–2065 period, the projected change ranges from an average increase of 0.4 mm per day in the south (15 cm annually), to an average decrease of 0.2 mm per day (7.5 cm annually) in the north. These changes are consistent with the projected increase in temperature. The higher temperatures along the coast would increase evaporation from the ocean and produce more rainfall over the coastal region, provided there are mechanisms to trigger the precipitation process. On the other hand, a warmer climate in the semi-arid region (i.e. the northeast) would decrease the atmospheric humidity (moisture in the air), and thereby reduce the chance of cloud formation and rainfall.

Although projected annual rainfall increases in some parts of the country and decreases in others, all areas show increases in rainfall in some parts of the year at least. The scenarios show a peak increase in monthly rainfall in the 2046–2065 period of about 2 mm/day in the mangrove and rainforest zones, and about 1 mm/day in the savannah zones. In the mangrove, rainforest and tall grass (Guinea/Sudan) savannah, the scenarios project an earlier rainfall season onset and later cessation, resulting in a longer rainfall season by up to two weeks by the 2046–2065 period. In contrast, the scenarios project a shorter rainfall season over short grass (Sahel) savannah, with a potential decrease of greater than one week.

For the 2046–2065 period in the mangrove, rainforest and tall grass savannah, the scenarios suggest a small increase in extreme rainfall days (that is, days with more than 50 mm of rain). Over the Sahel, the A2 scenario suggests a small decrease in extreme rainfall days. However, the projected changes in temperature-based extreme events are pronounced over the entire country. For example, the scenarios suggest that by the 2046–2065 period the number of extreme heat days with the temperature reaching 38°C or more would increase by 7 days per year in the mangrove, 23 days per year in the rainforest, 41 days per year in the tall grass savannah, and 88 days per year in the short grass savannah. The scenarios also project significant increases in the number of heatwave days (number of days when the maximum temperature is greater than 35°C for three or more consecutive days) over the entire country; for instance, a 95% increase in the case of the northern short grass savannah zone.

Table 12.1. Summary of Key Trends in Climate Parameters for Nigeria by Ecological Zone

Climate Variable	Mangrove Zone	Rainforest	Tall Grass (Savannah)	Short Grass (Sahel)
Temperature	↑	↑	↑	↑
Rainfall Amount	↑	↑	↓	↓
Rainfall Variability	↑	↑	↑	↑
Extreme rainfall events—drought	Likely	Likely	↑	↑
Extreme rainfall events— storms and floods	↑	↑	Likely	Likely
Sea level rise	↑	NA	NA	NA

Legend: ↑ likely increase or increase; ↓ likely decrease or decrease; NA (not applicable)
Source: (NASPA-CCN 2011)

From the United Nations Framework Convention on Climate Change (UNFCCC) in 1992 to the Kyoto Protocol in 1997 and the Bali Action Plan ten years later, several multilateral environmental agreements have been developed to assist developing countries in adapting to climate change, especially in sub-Saharan Africa. These mostly facilitate innovation and diffusion of technology that can bolster the resilience of vulnerable communities to climate change, variability and extremes. For example, Article 4.5 of the UNFCCC urges developed countries who are party to the Convention (Annex I countries) to promote, finance and facilitate the transfer of environmentally sound technologies and know-how to developing countries (WCED 1987; World Bank 2010; World Bank 2011). Yet, despite their commitments, the difficulty of fulfilling this critical need has highlighted the importance of moving toward concrete actions. Today, the World Trade Organization's (WTO) agreement on Trade-Related Aspects of Intellectual Property Rights (TRIPS) provides potential opportunities to speed up the transfer of technology for adaptation (Yemiru et al. 2010). While addressing some concerns, significant challenges still need to be overcome in developing countries for adaptation technologies to deliver their full promise.

The need for this transfer of technology for adaptation lurks in the fact that global processes and crises are changing and deepening the risks already faced by poor and vulnerable people in rural communities, particularly those involved in agriculture (World Resources Institute 2005). As approaches to minimising the risks faced by these vulnerable people, social protection and climate change adaptation have much in common as they both seek to protect the most vulnerable and promote resilience in these communities (IDS 2007).

Postmodernists like Harvey (1989), Baudrilland (2000) and Virilio (2000) censured the implied inference of a universal approach as the natural outcome of climate change adaptation, as if there is no place for accommodating the existing multiplicity of approaches and cultures (Anwar 2008). In this way, climate change adaptation is treated as the logical extension of capitalism. The integrity of "outsider" climate change adaptation strategies within rural Nigeria is being threatened (Amin 2011), as the acceptance of capitalism as a handmaiden of climate change adaptation implies that the "profit motive" is its driving force within rural Nigeria.

Social Process Trajectory in the Context of Climate Change within Rural Nigeria

So far, climate change has accelerated three forms of social processes in rural Nigeria: competition, conflict and boundary maintenance. In simple terms, it is social processes that make human adaptation possible. Within rural Nigeria, forests and natural resources play a vital role in the culture and physical adaptation of the people. The forest not only defines the cultural traits of the people, it also defines their occupational specialisations

(NAI, CSO, The Forestry Ordinance 1915 Enactment). Occupation is thus closely related to tribal identity and contrasting occupations are a very common way to illustrate tribal differences. Crucially, this process of differentiation based on occupation within rural Nigeria also relates to other stereotypical traits such as body posture, skin colour, perceived intelligence, physical endurance and behaviour. This means that not only is occupational transgression, or doing the work of another tribal group, a challenge to tribal status, it is also a potential source of conflict (Coulthard 2008).

Drawing from the seasonal calendar and interviews data, it was established that traditional agricultural practices in rural Nigeria have been affected by climate change. Evidence prevails to show that there is always a central zone in the structure of the rural Nigerian society. This central zone accordingly impinges in various ways on members of the community and all those living within its ecological domain. Authentic “belongingness” to a community is therefore not defined in terms of just being located within an ecological space and adapting to an environment. Instead, membership is constituted by relationship to the central zone. The central zone is not, as such, a spatially located phenomenon of the realm of values and beliefs, especially in the means and relations of production. It is this centre of the order of symbolic and value beliefs which govern the society. With dwindling resources due to climate change events within rural Nigeria, the competition to access and retention within the central zone has become fierce. Respondents recognize and acknowledge that in recent times there have been role displacements, with the traditional central sphere loosing authority to an external arm of a central government, of which they have been suspicious “since the first whites arrived here to take our forests for conservation.”

To respondents, this external interference laid the foundation upon which subsequent interactions flowed. This sets the basic prerequisites for rational social action within rural Nigeria where community members now make rational calculations about the ways in which to attain their goals in the real world. In this way, strategies always evolve to ensure that others are controlled to remain outside the “central zone” of production. What became clear in all renditions was the understanding that local entities like forests, lands and biodiversity which climate change adaptation policies seek to protect are not physically present at negotiations. Hence, representations—words, symbols, utterances—are created to stand for what cannot be brought to the negotiation table. Respondents bemoaned that since their contact with the “outside world, ” the task of creating representations for forests and natural resource protection has largely been left to "outsiders." In order to adequately capture this plight in vivid terms, respondents underlined discourses from which social processes emerge within the milieu of climate change in rural Nigeria.

First, the position that was advanced resembles Michel Foucault's suggestion that discourses are statements that "define, describe, and delimit what it is possible to say and not possible to say (and by extension—what to do or not to do)" (Hajer 1995; Kress 1985). This means that in the context of climate change adaptation policy design, only statements that conform to establish discourses are considered "truthful" (Rajao 2013), implying that representations rely on the dominant discourses to be valid, and representations that do not fit into the dominant discourses are silenced (Foucault 2002).

In rural Nigeria, local social networks were found to be dominant channels of coping with climate-related disasters. In the rural town of Iko-Esai, for instance, a small group of villagers used to work together with a local facilitator to identify challenges facing their community and consider solutions together. In a discussion, an individual noted that the friendships they usually develop from such networks were very important: "… we talk to each other and tell each other information …." As a result of their experiences, the people had a disaster assistance network where responsibilities to check on each other and their neighbours during disasters were divided based on their experience in the relatively unique context of rural Nigeria. This example no doubt contrasts present-day climate change adaptation processes in rural Nigeria by being dynamic and locally driven.

In the case of present-day climate change adaptation in rural Nigeria, evidence prevails to insist that understanding local social processes is essential as sustainable adaptation measures must rely on a global network of localised actions. This reiterates the fact that adaptation needs to be context specific and locally based (Aalst et al. 2008; O'Brien et al. 2008; Mercer et al. 2008). This therefore suggests that rather than looking to a codified set of tools or approaches, a diverse and perhaps unexpected set of practices may be appropriate in the process of adaptation to climate change. A key lesson that emerged from these findings is around the important role of collective action and social networks in ensuring social cohesion in the face of daunting climate change challenges. It is therefore evident that the cultivation of social networks can enhance the community capacity to deal with climate-related disasters (Ireland & Thomalla 2011). This is because the creation of new social networks can provide new relations of support in times of climatic stress and facilitate the dissemination of new knowledge and practices for an uncertain context.

Contrary to Pieterse's (2010) view, in which indigenous or local knowledge is undermined, evidence from rural Nigeria coalesced to show that indigenous knowledge for forest management accumulates towards a diverse set of climate change adaptations that authorize important alternatives to the emerging norms of adaptation in rural Nigeria. Community members recognize the legitimacy and value of this local knowledge and practices, and they do not necessarily require that they be replicated elsewhere or "scaled up" to larger scale regional or global programmes. Respondents likewise acknowledged that the context of climate change adaptation efforts in rural Nigeria is undeniably shaped by ideas of hierarchical scale, with relations between development actors, funding agencies and policy makers fitting Howitt's (1993; 1998; 2002) model of relational scale formations. However, the relevance of indigenous knowledge is visibly displayed in manners that, though the knowledge may be considered disparate and disconnected, is significant in responding to a global challenge like climate change.

The emphasis of interest worth highlighting is the point that development in its true sense is always of necessity embedded in the local. This implies that global discourses of development are always simultaneously local discourses and practices, and that the subject is the starting point for change (Gibson-Graham 2005; 2006). This further stresses that it is in a process of re-subjectivisation that real change becomes possible. For instance, it is commonly believed in rural Nigeria that one of the first steps to altering the social structures that create rural poverty is to alter how the people see themselves and what actions they believe are possible (Olutayo 2009; Olutayo & Omobowale 2007). This is because the capacity to deal with climate change rests just as much on what is believed to be possible. For adaptation to be effective, sustainable and appropriate, it will rely upon many people taking action to alter the ways they manage their livelihoods, run their households, conduct their businesses or construct the organisations they are part of. This will also require that people in both the developed and developing worlds seek different ways to "go onward in a different mode of humanity or not at all" (Plumwood 2007, 1; Gibson-Graham 2011).

Conclusion

Considering the growing political, academic and local awareness of the necessity of adaptation to climate change in rural Nigeria, understanding that adaptation to extreme climatic events within rural Nigeria is defined by "varied sensitivities, " as exhibited by different groups of actors, is crucial. This implies that adaptation to climate change will never be a homogenous process agreed upon by all members of societies, but one influenced by competition, conflict and boundary maintenance. Acknowledging this must be a first step for governments, donor agencies, researchers and civil society if climate change adaptation at the rural level is to be facilitated, supported and understood. This also reinvigorates the fact that human actions are limited or determined by the "environment, " meaning that human beings become what they are at any given moment not by their own free decisions, taken rationally and in full knowledge of the conditions, but under the pressure of circumstances which delimit their range of choice and which also fix their objectives and the standards by which they make choices. This describes social interaction and climate change adaptation in rural Nigeria—that individuals' behaviour in adapting to extreme climatic events is never entirely free but always determined by forces outside the community.

This chapter has illustrated the heterogeneity in adaptation to climate change by focusing on social processes (competition, conflict and boundary maintenance), by which rural households in Nigeria construct increasingly diverse adaptive actions to survive and improve their standards of living. It should be noted, however, that the chosen approach, based on the in-depth analysis of three forest-dependent communities, limits the generalisability of the data for the entire country. Indeed, it seems that other rural communities in Nigeria are embracing cooperation and assimilation, social processes absent in Agoi-Ibami, Iko-Esai and Butatong. Hence, social processes of climate change within rural Nigeria can only be understood in context, which requires that the scale and agency of social interaction and decision-making are clearly defined. This is generally less problematic at the micro scale where the range of agents, contexts and interests is less diffuse (Adger et al. 2009).

On the other hand, this does not mean that place-based, micro-scale and context-specific studies may not provide insights of a more generic nature about conditions that enhance or constrain adaptive capacity (Adger & Barnett 2009). Instead, understanding the general importance of the role of forest resources in adaptation to climate change brings out the importance of "beliefs" and "values" in the operation of society. This is because the state of things in society depends largely on "how" and "what" we think about nature. The capitalist tendency of competition and striving for material comfort expressed through conspicuous consumption has indeed led humans to relentlessly exploit the environment. The analysis of this study has also brought out the structural-functional view of society as a system with interrelated parts in which what affects one part affects the others, and consequently puts the entire system at a disequilibrium.

References

Adelekan, I. O. 2011. *Climate Change, Weather Extremes and Society.* The Seventeenth Faculty Lecture, Faculty of the Social Sciences, University of Ibadan, May 25, 2011.

Adger, N. W., Dessai, S., Goulden, M., Hulme, M., Lorenzoni, I. & Nelson, D. R. 2009. "Are there Social Limits to Adaptation to Climate Change?" *Climatic Change* 93 (3–4): 335–354.

Adger, W. N. & Barnett, J. 2009. "Four Reasons for Concern about Adaptation to Climate Change." *Environment and Planning* 41 (12): 2800–2805.

Anuforom, A. C. 2010. "Demonstration & Assessment of Climate Change in Nigeria & Development of Adaptation Strategies in the Key Socio-Economic Sectors: Metrological Approach." A Paper presented at the National Stakeholders Workshop on "Developing National Adaptation Strategy and Plan of Action for Nigeria, " Abuja. 22 March 2010.

BNRCC (Building Nigeria's Response to Climate Change). 2011. Climate Change Adaptation Strategy Technical Reports, Nigeria (CCASTR). A Compendium of Studies Commissioned and Published by Building Nigeria's Response to Climate Change Project. Coordinated by Nigerian Environmental Study/Action Team (NEST), Ibadan, Nigeria.

Chambers, R. 1983. *Rural Development: Putting the Last First.* London & New York: Longman.

Chokor, B. A. 2012. "A Review and Critique of Global Initiatives on Climate Change and Its Management with Special Reference to Developing Countries." *Climate Change and Sustainable Development in Nigeria*, edited by Illiya, M. A. & Dankani, I. M., 7–28. Ibadan: Crown F. Publishers.

Ekong, E. 1988. *Rural Sociology: An Introduction and Analysis of Rural Nigeria.* Uyo: Dove Educational Publishers.

Foucault, M. 2002. *The Order of Things: An Archeology of the Human Sciences.* London: Routledge.

Gibson-Graham, J. K. 1996. *The End of Capitalism as We Knew It.* London: University of Minnesota Press.

—. 2005. "Surplus Possibilities: Postdevelopment and Community Economies." *Singapore Journal of Tropical Geography* 26: 4–26.

—. 2006. *A Postcapitalist Politics.* Minneapolis and London: University of Minnesota Press.
—. 2011. "A Feminist Project of Belonging in the Anthropocene." *Gender, Place and Culture* 18 (1): 1–21.
Hajer, M. A. 1995. *The Politics of Environmental Discourse: Ecological Modernization and the Policy Process.* Oxford: Oxford University Press.
Howitt, R. 1993. "A World in a Grain of Sand: Towards a Reconceptualisation of Geographical Scale." *The Australian Geographe*. 24: 33–44.
—. 1998. "Scale as Relation: Musical Metaphors of Geographical Scale." *Area* 30 (1): 49–58.
—. 2002. "Scale and the Other: Levinas and Geography." *Geoforum* 33: 299–313.
Kress, G. 1985. *Linguistic Processes in Sociocultural Practice.* Oxford: Oxford University Press.
NASPA-CCN (National Adaptation Strategy and Plan of action on Climate Change for Nigeria). 2011. *Draft for Stakeholder Review.* Prepared by the Building Nigeria's Response to Climate Change (BNRCC) Project.
Olawoye, J. 2002. "Contemporary Challenges for Rural Sociologists in Nigeria." In *Currents and Perspectives in Sociology*, edited by Uche C. Isiugo-Abanihe, Austin N. Isamah & 'Jimi O. Adesina. Ibadan: Department of Sociology, University of Ibadan.
Olutayo, A. O. 2009. *The Irony of Knowledge in Africa's Development.* Monograph. Department of Sociology, University of Ibadan, Ibadan.
Olutayo, A. O. & Omobowale, A. O. 2007. "Production, Processing and Marketing of Export Crops for Rural Development: The Case of Cocoa in Nigeria." In *African Development Perspectives Year Book 2007*, edited by Wohlmuth, K., Eboue, C., Gutowski, A., Jerome, A., Knedlik, T., Meyn, M. & Mama, T. Berlin: Lit Verlag.
Pieterse, J. N. 2010. *Development Theory.* London: SAGE.
Plumwood, V. 2007. "A Review of Deborah Bird Rose's Reports From a Wild Country: Ethics of Decolonisation." *Australian Humanities Review* 42: 1–4.
Prah, K. K. 2011. "Culture: The Missing Link in Development Planning in Africa." In *Philosophy and African Development: Theory and Practice*, edited by Lansana Keita. Dakar: council for the Development of Social Science Research in Africa.
Rajao, R. 2013. "Representations and Discourses: The Role of Local Accounts and Remote Sensing in the Formulation of Amazonia's Environmental Policy." *Environmental Science and Policy* 30: 60–71.

Reenerg, A. & Ostergaard, N. J. 2010. "Cultural Barriers to Climate Change Adaptation: A Case Study from Northern Burkina Faso." *Global Environmental Change* 20: 142–152.

WCED (United Nations World Commission on Environment and Development). 1987. *Our Common Future*. Oxford, UK: Oxford University Press.

World Bank. 2010. Monitoring Climate Finance and ODA. *Issues Brief 1*. World Bank, Sustainable Development. Vice Presidency, Environment Department, Washington, DC.

—. 2011. *World Development Indicators*. Washington, DC: World Bank.

World Resources Institute. 2005. *World Resources 2005: The Wealth of the Poor, Managing Ecosystems to Fight Poverty.* Washington, DC: World Resources Institute.

Yemiru, T., Roos, A., Campbell, B. M. & Bohli, F. 2010. "Forest Incomes and Poverty Alleviation under Participatory Forest Management in the Bale Highlands, Southern Ethiopia." *International Forestry Review* 12 (1): 66–77.

CHAPTER THIRTEEN

CHALLENGES OF WOMEN ENTREPRENEURS IN RURAL INFORMAL ECONOMIC ACTIVITIES: IMPLICATIONS FOR SUSTAINABLE RURAL DEVELOPMENT IN OGUN STATE, NIGERIA

OLABISI SHERIFAT YUSUFF

Introduction

Women entrepreneurship is one of the most important inputs in the economic development of a country (Chants 2007). The growth of entrepreneurship results from certain environmental conditions and socioeconomic and cultural inputs. Women entrepreneurs have been designated as the new engines for growth and the rising stars of the economies in developing countries, bringing prosperity and welfare (Vossenberg 2013). Their role in economic growth and social change continues to dominate recent policy debates on development (Staub & Amine 2006), and the growth of the proportion of women entrepreneurs in the informal economies of developing countries has drawn the attention of both the academic and the development sectors. Donors, international public institutions, national and local governments, NGOs, private companies, charities, knowledge institutes and business associations have initiated programs or policies to promote and develop women's entrepreneurship.

An important resource is the Global Entrepreneurship Monitor project, which estimates that more than 187 million women are engaged in entrepreneurial activity (GEM 2012). They initiate programs for capacity building of entrepreneurial skills, strengthening women's networks, provide finance and training, or design policies that enable more and stronger start-ups and business growth. They all claim that female entrepreneurship is essential for growth and development. Some even argue that women entrepreneurs' contributions tend to be higher than the entrepreneurial activity of men (Minniti 2011).

While the role of women entrepreneurs in the informal economy is significant in developing countries, certain conditions hinder women's entrepreneurial developments and such roles have remained invisible to policy makers. Females in Nigeria's informal sector seem to be invisible, along with their contributions and needs, given that the prevailing social system has a patriarchal context in which women seek and access social opportunities (Nyamnjoh 2005). Women's informal economic activities constitute the single most important source of employment in rural Nigeria. The informal sector is the only way to earn a living for people who are self-employed outside the formal economy (Fapounda 2012).

Before commencing, however, it is necessary to define what is meant by informal entrepreneurship. Given that entrepreneurship has long been a problematic and elusive concept and, as Anderson & Starnawska (2008) state, "entrepreneurship means different things to different people, " an appropriate working definition is employed as somebody actively involved in starting a business or is the owner/manager of a business (Harding 2006; Richardson, Rhona & Finnegan 2004), with informal work defined as monetary transactions not declared to the state for tax and/or benefit purposes but which are legal in all other respects (European Commission 2007).

Women in Nigeria account for about 50% of the nation's population. Rural women form the majority (more than 70%) of this total population, playing essential and dynamic roles in rural economic activities. They are actively involved in agriculture which is the basic sector of the rural informal economy (Nnoyelu & Gadzama 2001). Yet, their participation in developmental issues is very low because their personalities, interest, ideas and activities have not received the attention commensurate with their energy (Jibowo 2003). Rural women are relegated to the background in all facets of life (United Nation Development Fund for Women 2005).

A World Bank report (2008) shows that women in developing countries are groaning under the weight of an unjust culture, beliefs and the overbearing influence of a male-dominated society, especially in Nigeria where women are denied access to land ownership. The principles guiding the ownership of economic resources like land and property strengthened the stereotype of a male-dominated society in which women are suppressed or downtrodden (Oyenechere 2005). However, sustainable development can only be achieved with the full participation of women. Unfortunately, lack of access to entrepreneurial resources has affected their contributions to economic development and growth. There are various constraints that challenge the informal economic activities for women in the course of discharging their roles. These include poor access to market information, technology and finance, poor linkages with support services, and an unfavourable policy and regulatory environment. Added to the above is the difficulty confronted by small businesses in accessing bank credits, but the most serious and damaging problem threatening the state of entrepreneurship in Nigeria is a lack of government interest and support for small enterprises (Ariyo 2005; Chu, Hung & Benzing 2008).

If entrepreneurship is accepted as a key driver of economic growth and an essential component of national development, then a better understanding is needed of those factors which inhibit rural women's entrepreneurship activities in Nigeria. Therefore, examining challenges that affect and confront female entrepreneurial activities in the rural informal economy is very important for sustainable development (Ozar 2002; Usman 2008). Starting a business is difficult under the best of circumstances, and is even more so in sub-Saharan Africa with its complex environmental factors. With regard to transitional and developing economies, Smallbone & Welter (2001) gloomily describe the external environment as "hostile in social, economic, and political terms." In this study, we argue that the clear identification and progressive reduction of such barriers will be positive steps forward, encouraging more women to become entrepreneurs in rural areas and better supporting those who already operate as entrepreneurs, thereby reducing their risk of failure.

It is the aim of this study to examine the challenges of rural female entrepreneurs in the informal economy in the Ado-Odo Local Government areas of Ogun state. It has the following objectives: (1) to identify the types of informal economic activities women engage with in the informal economy; (2) to identify the environmental constraints faced by women in their informal entrepreneurial activities; and (3) to make recommendations geared towards the improvement of female informal entrepreneurial activities. The significance of this work is that through this research we will obtain better insights into the dynamics of persistent gender inequalities and the challenges of women's informal entrepreneurial activities in Ogun state. It is hoped that this study will aid policy formulation on informal sector activities and poverty alleviation of women entrepreneurs in the informal economy, which will in turn contribute to the improvement of the welfare of rural women.

Literature Review

In all countries of the world, women continue to be the primary caregivers for their children and family dependents, even if they work outside the home. In developing countries in particular, many women also operate as the family's sole breadwinner, seeking paid employment outside the home or starting their own businesses. According to annual surveys by the Global Entrepreneurship Monitor Consortium (GEM 2005), the economic contribution of women workers is very considerable in sub-Saharan Africa, where many women form the backbone of their nation's economy. Yet this vital economic contribution often goes unmeasured or unreported by the government.

Most female-owned businesses in sub-Saharan Africa that operate in the informal sector are necessity-based, and best described as micro- or small-scale enterprises (GEM 2012; McDade & Spring 2005). They are often run out of the home because women entrepreneurs do not have the necessary funds to acquire business premises (McDade & Spring 2005; ILO 2006). Although a convenient arrangement, the lack of physical space eventually acts as a brake on business growth. Other problems facing women who want to start or grow their own businesses have been documented by Fick (2002), Chamlee-Wright (2002), Akinola (2005), Kibas (2005) and the International Labour Organisation (ILO) (2006). They include lack of accurate market information, lack of operating funds and lack of property to use as collateral.

Woldie & Adersua (2004) reported that aspiring women entrepreneurs face additional barriers to success arising from negative social attitudes. Prejudice against women entrepreneurs is experienced much more severely in Africa than in developed Western nations, arising from deeply-rooted, discriminatory cultural values, attitudes, practices and the traditions of patriarchal cultures. Local prejudice is expressed through differential attitudes towards women in general, and through different standards and expectations for their social behaviour in particular. While social attitudes are not the only factors hindering female entrepreneurship, they are recognized by Gartner (1985) as critical factors. Moreover, negative attitudes in Nigeria were reported by Woldie & Adersua (2004) as posing the greatest challenge to women entrepreneurs.

United Nations (2006) reports indicate that women entrepreneurs continue to face many challenges, including government rules and regulations, gaining access to finance and building an ICT infrastructure that enables efficiency and growth. Others include poor financial management, liquidity problems, management inexperience and incompetence, problems in coping with inflation and other external economic conditions. Also important are poor or non-existent books and records, sales and marketing problems, staffing, difficulties with unions, the failure to seek expert advice, limited social and business networks, a low level of demand in the local economy, and the value and system of tenure for housing. Constraints in access to finance, lack of work experience and skills and lack of role models are also part of the problems faced by women in their entrepreneurial activities.

Ambert, Katja & Thomas (2007) see environmental problems which women in the informal economy are likely to face as including health and safety risks, dangerous working conditions, gendered violence, and an increased susceptibility to HIV/AIDS. In Africa, informal occupation exposes women to extremely harsh conditions for very limited reward.

The 2009 World Bank report indicates that in Africa many women entrepreneurs work in difficult situations compared to their male counterparts. Factors like political instability, poor infrastructure, high production costs and non-conducive business environments affect more women entrepreneurs than men in this region. Limited access to key resources like land and credit and the socio-cultural environment also act as serious impediments. In the era of globalisation, changing patterns of trade and evolving technologies necessitate skill enhancement that many women entrepreneurs in the continent are yet to possess. Yet, in the African countries they face numerous barriers preventing them from realizing the full potential of the economic contributions of their enterprises. Several environmental indicators are identified as the major factors.

Bumpus (2008) states that another problem faced by women entrepreneurs is occupational mobility glitches. Occupational mobility—shifting from one product line to another—is considered by women entrepreneurs as disadvantageous. Taking a chance to venture out on their own is considered a risky proposition, which can be indulged by the family members once (but not again) if a woman wants to be more adventurous. Women are also at a financial disadvantage when creating a second product line. Many women have to borrow from the men in their lives to start up the first venture. However, money for a second venture is often not as likely to be forthcoming from the same source. Many women entrepreneurs have to experience the troubling "assistance" of support agencies. Harassment in government departments and indifferent and discriminating attitudes of officials of all small-scale industry related departments, such as taxation, labour and power, are some of the problems that women entrepreneurs have to deal with.

Interestingly, in one study in South India by Das (2007), female entrepreneurs did not feel that having their own business affected their roles as a spouse, parent or homemaker. However, it should be noted that all these women had someone to help them with their household chores—either a part-time or a full-time maid. Part of the reason for a lower level of role conflict may also be the high amount of spousal support that these women had. Over 74% of women said that their spouses were either happy or very happy that they owned their own businesses. Another factor that may have contributed to the high degree of spousal support might have been the stable, satisfactory nature of their marriages. It may be noted that most of the women had been married for a long time, with over 80% stating that they were "satisfied" or "very satisfied" with their marital life (De Groot 2001).

Another recurring obstacle is a perceived lack of time or competing demands on time. This is because women are responsible for so many different domestic chores and the raising of children. They do not have enough free time to develop either their entrepreneurial skills or to develop an existing business. The lack of free time does not allow them time to travel to support institutions, banks and other finance houses for advice and information on credit, to attend training programmes to acquire skills, or to seek out better customers or suppliers. This lack of free time has been observed in a number of studies across different countries, such as Cote d'Ivoire, Ethiopia, Mali, Morocco, Senegal and Zimbabwe. The results suggest that lack of time is a barrier to most women, in most economies, independent of the level of development.

Okojie (2002) argues that poverty is a major factor that hinders female entrepreneurial development. Poverty, according to him, incapacitates women economically, indirectly subjecting them to a state of destitution, powerlessness and even violence. These conditions negatively affect female entrepreneurial development. Furthermore, education and manpower, lack of equipment and appropriate technology, cultural restrictions, weak land rights, erroneous ideas about women and credit, entrepreneurial attitudes, misplaced focus and marketing are other major obstacles that hinder female entrepreneurial development (Food and Agricultural Organization 1989; Idemudia-Elabor 1991). In the view of Oyekanmi (2004), women in Africa are gendered in terms of access to and control of strategic resources that would have positive impacts on their lives.

In addition, men are perceived to be the entrepreneurs (Ahl 2009). Moreover, insightful studies show that even among female enterprise owners, women entrepreneurs seem to choose their trade by accident and prefer to diversify into new areas rather than expand their present enterprises, thus making them more susceptive to risk and difficulties in developing entrepreneurially than male traders, who prefer augmenting their business instead of venturing into new domains (ILO 1995). The extant literature points out that women are perceived as weak, passive, irrational, gentle and of kind dispositions, having no innovative behaviours. These attributes are antithetical to entrepreneurial development as entrepreneurs need to be innovative, rugged and aggressive (Akpa 2007; Babalola 2009).

Jahed, Kulsum & Akther (2011) found that women entrepreneurs in Bangladesh also suffer from the myth of their not being effective organizers. They are believed to be best suited to housekeeping. This has created difficulties for women to become true entrepreneurs. A study on female entrepreneurs by ESCWA (2009) found that due to the prevailing social norms, female entrepreneurs were prevented from managing their businesses independently. These norms restricted their mobility, and thereby affected interaction with others. Because of this patriarchal bias, their role prescriptions, ambition, self-confidence, innovativeness, achievement motivation, and risk-taking ability, which are essential for an entrepreneurial career, are inhibited.

Women entrepreneurs also face restrictions hampering their mobility. Some of the women entrepreneurs complain that government clerks and private dealers harass them. As a result, many operate on the "comfort zone movement"; that is, they tend to operate only among clients that they know. Products are sold to relatives and friends and suppliers tend to be family friends.

Institutional Theory—A Sociological Perspective

Institutional theory takes a sociological view of reciprocal interactions between institutions (such as business entities) and society. This theory is adopted for this research because it provides explanations on the reciprocal nature between business entities and society. According to Scott (2001), institutions are social structures that have gained a high degree of resilience among scholars. Institutions are embedded in country-specific institutional arrangements (Amine & Staub 2009) and differences between country institutions affect both the level of entrepreneurial activity, and the nature and amount of innovation taking place in each country (Busenitz, Gomez & Spencer, 2000). Scott (2001) identified three different systems or "pillars" that support social institutions—namely, the regulatory, normative and cognitive systems. In the regulatory system, formal and informal rules are set, monitored and enforced if necessary by means of laws, regulations and government policies which promote or restrict behaviours within a country (Busenitz, Gomez & Spencer 2000).

The normative system consists of "normative rules that introduce a prescriptive, evaluative, and obligatory dimension into social life" (Scott 2001). In contrast, the cognitive system recognizes "the shared conceptions that constitute the nature of social reality and the frames through which meaning is made" (Scott 2001). Thus, individuals' cognitive structures and social knowledge combine to represent a nation's cognitive environment. This sociological view of institutions includes consideration of conditions prevailing in the market environment, so it is well suited to the study of entrepreneurship. In rural areas of Nigeria there are several factors that inhibit female rural entrepreneurship development, the most important of which is the total neglect of the roles of rural women. Given that researchers have established theoretical links between entrepreneurship, environmental factors and institutional systems, this chapter considers institutional theory to be an appropriate theoretical explanation for analysing the barriers facing women in rural economic activities.

The above review of the literature on women's entrepreneurship in developing countries presents a complex picture of critical environmental barriers, social challenges and practical problems that women must overcome if they want to become entrepreneurs or expand their informal economic activities in rural areas.

Methodology

This research utilizes only the qualitative method of data collection, because there is no available data for informal economic actors as a result of its itinerary nature. Qualitative methods of data collection were therefore found to be appropriate for this type of work.

The study area was the Ado-Odo Local Government area of Ogun state, chosen for its rural nature. Atan, Owode, Ketu, Igbesa and Alapoti villages were chosen using the purposive method, being purely rural in nature. Ten women in rural economic activities were purposively selected in each village—the choice of ten women in each village was purely for convenience. The total number of female respondents interviewed was 40. Only two focus group discussions (FGDs) were carried out in Igbesa and Atan in this study.

The researcher had earlier contacted women at Igbesa and Atan markets. The discussions were fixed on Sunday evening at the head of the market's houses. Eight women were included in each of the focus group discussions. In both in-depth interviews (IDI) and focus group discussions

(FGDs), responses were recorded and notes were taken. All responses from in-depth interviews and discussions were later transcribed and translated into English. Using institutional theory, responses were grouped into sub-themes. The responses were analyzed through content analysis and ethnographic summary.

Discussions of the Findings

Regulatory System and Women Entrepreneurs

Elements in the regulatory system that affect entrepreneurs include the laws, regulations and government policies which support or restrict the creation of a new enterprise (Busenitz, Gomez & Spencer 2000). These are inheritance laws and the ownership of property, lack of access to capital and lack of access to micro-loans. Women entrepreneurs who own and operate rural informal activities do not comprise an homogeneous group. They operate a diverse form of informal economic activities. The majority of respondents were small-scale farmers. They were asked about the inheritance laws that guide the ownership of farmland, and the majority indicated that they have no legal rights to ownership. Several reasons were given for this. Some of the respondents pointed out that they were not indigenes of that community and they married from other villages. Some claimed that they were working on their husband's farm, while the indigenes of those villages claimed that they farm on family lands, but have no legal rights to them. The responses recorded below illuminate this issue.

> Acquiring farmland is not an easy thing around this place. I got married from another area to this place. My husband had no farmland. He had to lease from another family. Farming is not an easy thing around this place at all. *Awon omo onile* (Indigenous owners of farmland) are our major problems here. They are constantly harassing us for more money and threatening to sell our farmland. (Female/IDI/42yrs/June 2013)

> This farmland belongs to my late father. I know I had no legal rights on this land, though it belonged to my late father. In this community, men are seen as the legal inheritors of farmland. My brothers can sell the land anytime, because they believed that a woman should do and possess whatever she wants to possess in her husband house. I had to relocate to my home village when my husband died. This land was only given to me temporarily. So it can be taken anytime. (Farmer/ IDI/55yrs/July 2013)

> When you want to buy farmland from indigenous farm owners as a woman, you are asked to bring your husband or your brother. You are then advised on what to plant on the land. The farm owners will tell you to plant only food crops. People have interpreted it to me that you cannot plant cash crops which will bring in more money. These food crops are for subsistence and the little you are able to sell is to enable us have some money. This means that we cannot go far or acquire wealth in these farming activities. (Farmer/50yrs/FGD/May 2013)

The responses above show the various ways in which women are hindered in their farming activities in rural areas. Women farmers have no other option than to rely on using their husbands' or relatives' land or renting property from others. Eventually, however, the ability to access real farmland becomes an essential condition for women to expand their farming activities. Ekejuiba (1991) already found that land has become monetized, and that individual's ownership is correspondingly encouraged at the expense of usufructuary rights. This made the position of rural women who were divorced and widowed more insecure as this vital means of production becomes more difficult.

Inadequate Access to Financial Capital

Financial capital has long been recognized as the most critical element of new venture creation and subsequent successful performance (Marlow & Patton 2005). Many micro businesses are under-capitalized because owners cannot meet the collateral requirements necessary for obtaining commercial loans. Even if they succeed in meeting requirements, these loans often turn out to be very costly (Yusuff 2010). Thus, while access to capital can be difficult for both men and women, it is usually much more difficult for women entrepreneurs. A general lack of experience and exposure restricts women from venturing out and dealing with banking institutions (United Nations 2005). It is not surprising then that access to capital is one of the most frequently cited environmental barriers to business entry for African women entrepreneurs (International Labour organization 2006). Women in rural communities are especially vulnerable to these types of regulatory discrimination. In many cases, they do not have collateral for a traditional bank loan, they may not have any savings and they seldom own land. Any one of these factors alone or in combination makes it difficult, if not impossible, to raise venture capital to start or expand a business (Center for Women's Business Research 2005; ILO 2006).

Below are some of the responses given by women respondents.

> We do not have access to bank loans. Where do we get guarantors or collaterals to obtain loans? We do not have lands of our own or building properties of our own. Our trading is only for subsistence. In fact, even if the banks are ready to give us loans, our husbands will not be in support of us taking loans from banks. We only rely on our monthly contributions to augment our trade. No bank will be ready to give us loans. In fact, they consider us as poor people here. (34yrs/trader/IDI/September 2013)

> We learnt that Micro Finance gave out some loans to people trading in cities. We do not have such here. No, there is no Micro Finance that had come to approach us to take loans. In fact, take a look at our villages around here, did you see any Micro Finance Office? The government did not recognize us here. We have been forgotten. The only way we raise capital here is through *esusu.* I engaged in *esusu* with my other friends. I also engage in a labouring job like the peeling of cassava and frying of garri when I am not in the market. (Trader/32yrs/FGD/May 2013)

> As for bank loans, we traders believe that it is not meant for us. There are several reasons why we believe this. We are not formally educated. Understanding the procedure and terms of loans may be difficult for us. Again, it is not every day that the market booms, and there are several days that we may not sell in the market. Our trade is only on a small-scale level, and even then we pay lots of money to *iya oloja*, *omo onile*, local governments, and even area boys. We also need to take care of our children. The support of our husbands is very little at home, so the little profits we make from our sales go to settle all these areas. Then how do we repay with all these problems if we take bank loans? (Trader/ 48yrs/ FGD/September, 2013)

The responses above show that there are many factors hindering rural informal economic activities for women, such as the micro-scale of women-owned businesses, their literacy levels, the psychological perception of themselves which Horner (1969) called fear of success, and neglect by micro finance houses precluding them from obtaining capital through bank loans.

Normative System, Cognitive System and female entrepreneurial activities

In sub-Saharan Africa, men becoming entrepreneurs constitutes a legitimately acceptable behaviour, whereas women that engaged in entrepreneurial activities are seen as aberrant, and wanting to break away from tradition. These perceptions are mostly based on the association of entrepreneurship with traditional male stereotypes (Aidis, Welter, Smallbone & Isakova

2007). Though women becoming entrepreneurs may be acceptable in some areas, such as farming communities, women as successful entrepreneurs are widely regarded as illegitimate and unacceptable, especially if they outshine their husbands (Njeru & Njoka 2001).

Women entrepreneurs in rural informal economies face problems attributed to socio-cultural factors because some cultures and social traditions play significant roles in determining who becomes an entrepreneur. For instance, among the Yoruba of southwest Nigeria, women are not expected to be involved in occupations that would take them outside their matrimonial homes; rather, they are expected to manage the family and be submissive to their husbands (Ehigie & Umoren 2003). Rural women entrepreneurs were asked about the attitudes of their spouses towards their informal economic activities as women are not supposed to leave home, but stay and take care of their husbands. The responses received were quite different from the above opinions.

Women respondents were asked about the support of their husbands towards making a living in trading outside the home. The majority stated that they had their support, and did not feel that having their own business affected their roles as mothers and businesswomen. The majority of the respondents indicated that things have changed and no man supports any woman staying at home without working. The responses below illuminate this issue:

> I met my grandmother and my mother working. Why should I stay at home not working? My husband did not feel threatened that I am working. There is no conflict between my husband and me because I am working. Moreover, it is not in our culture for women not to work. Women who refuse to work are called "*Alabodo*" (a lazy woman who prefers sex and food only). Our men here do not even like women who do not work, unless there is agreement between husband and wife that his wife should be a full-time homemaker. (Trader/32 yrs/IDI/May 2013)

> My husband supports me in this trade because of my contributions at home. If he does not want me to trade, how will he pay for the school fees of our children here? Again, many men nowadays seek financial support from their wives because of the high level of unemployment in the country. Our men do not have jobs again. In fact, most of them stay idle at home. (Trader/40yrs/FGD/July 2013)

> People in the community will always advise you to start some trading. It is not even good for women now to stay at home. Even if you stay at home, you still need to find some work to do. Among the *alehas* (those in purdah), the majority produce goods at home like washing soap, *kunu*, *wara*, and bean cakes among others. The only difference here is that they

> do not go to markets themselves, but give these goods to their sons or daughters to sell for them. (Trader/45yrs/IDI/July 2013)
>
> I always planned my travelling to purchase goods in Lagos when it is not the turn for the man to stay with me. This means that cooking and taking care of our husband will be the duties of the other wives. (Trader/35yrs/FGD/May 2013)

The contrary responses obtained on the societal support for the informal economic activities may have to do with the level of their micro enterprises. Njeru & Njoka (2001) earlier argued that women becoming entrepreneurs may be acceptable in some areas, such as farming communities, but that women as successful entrepreneurs are widely regarded as illegitimate and unacceptable, especially if they outshine their husbands. More research is needed in this area among successful women entrepreneurs to confirm or reject the opinions of the authors.

Conclusion and Recommendations

Women entrepreneurs continue to face problems in rural areas. Based on an institutional theory-driven analysis of environmental barriers affecting women entrepreneurs in rural informal economic activities, the analysis of responses shows that the conditions of rural areas are not conducive for female entrepreneurial development. Many environmental barriers of different types persist in discouraging them. Changes are needed in all three institutional systems (regulatory, normative and cognitive) for a more conducive environment to develop that will favour entrepreneurship in general and women entrepreneurs in particular. Sustained efforts to promote change in the regulatory environment will require planning and implementation on several fronts simultaneously. For example, political leadership at the highest level is needed to bring about changes in laws to improve the social status of rural women. After the demise of Better Life Programmes for women, there have been no deliberate goals or programmes to elevate the status of female entrepreneurs in rural areas.

There is a need to overcome the constraints to tap the productive potential of women and enhance their contribution to rural development. The impossibilities of owning farmland and using real property as collateral are major reasons that women in rural areas in Nigeria cannot obtain bank loans. Without loans they are unable to acquire more property and achieve business growth. Thus, a vicious circle persists which will require widespread government intervention to rectify.

Fear of success and the illiteracy levels of female entrepreneurs are other key issues that affect rural female entrepreneurial development. Government intervention should include promoting acceptance of the new belief that women be both allowed and encouraged to undertake self-employment as entrepreneurs, modifying current prejudicial beliefs and discriminatory behaviours that hold them back from aspiring higher, and encouraging the abandonment of old stereotypes about women's limited abilities to contribute to society. The large-scale promotion of attitude and behavioural change in rural areas does not necessarily require the use of sophisticated or expensive mass media, as in developed countries. Low-cost media include outdoor billboards and posters, mobile units equipped with video and sound equipment, radio advertising, and promotional events in rural areas.

The need for access to property is particularly acute among women working in the agricultural sector where land is essential for the cultivation of crops and animal pastures. Governments in some African nations are addressing this lack of property by issuing land certificates. Women in rural areas need to own land that can be used as collateral for bank loans to start or expand a business. Thus, national governments must modify laws and rules governing the ownership of property and land to qualify women for access to commercial sources of funds.

Lack of access to capital is a problem for both men and women. While there has been significant growth in micro-loan institutions in Nigeria, especially in cities, there is an intense need for them in rural areas. Therefore, the numbers of micro-loan institutions operating in urban areas need to increase, and a more intense marketing of financial services toward women is needed in rural areas.

Change in the cognitive environment of the sub-Saharan region requires the provision of adequate educational and training programmes for females. Some analysts believe that it will be possible to leap-frog traditional stages of education and training by introducing technology that is not only sophisticated in function but also very simple to use and cheap to buy.

Limitation of the Study

Using environmental and institutional analyses we have identified a broad range of factors that persistently constrain the activities of women entrepreneurs in rural areas in Nigeria. Problems exist in the regulatory, normative and cognitive environments and involve complex issues of social legitimacy. However, the result of this study is not generalizable because of the small population involved and the small villages chosen in the study area. There is a need for further research involving a large segment of the population across rural areas in Nigeria and quantitative data collection that will give the actual numbers of women inhibited by institutional and environmental barriers for proper planning/goals towards sustainable entrepreneurial development.

References

Aidis, R., Welter, F., Smallbone, D. & Isakova, N. 2007. "Female Entrepreneurship in Transition Economies: The Case of Lithuania and Ukraine." *Feminist Economics* 13 (2): 157–183.

Ahl, H. 2009. "Why Research on Women Entrepreneurs needs new Directions." *Entrepreneurship Theory and Practice* 30: 595–621.

Akinola, G. O. 2005. "Gender Factor in the Structure and Conduct of the Cocoa Industry in Nigeria." *South African Journal of Business Management* 36: 7–22.

Akpa, A. 2007. "Challenges of the Nigerian Entrepreneurs in the Twenty-First Century." A paper presented at the maiden annual college of management sciences seminar, university of Mkar.

Ambert, C., Katja, J. & Thomas, L. 2007. "HIV, AIDs and Urban Development Issues in sub Saharan Africa. Beyond sex and Medicines: why getting the Basics Right is part of the Response." Paper prepared for Swedish International Development. Agency, Stockholm. www.sida-.se/jsp/sida (accessed September 2010).

Amine, L. S. & Staub, K. M. 2009. "Women Entrepreneurs in sub–Saharan Africa: An Institutional Theory Analysis from a Social Marketing Point of View. Entrepreneurship and Regional Development." *An International Journal* 21 (2): 183–211.

Babalola, S. S. 2009. "Women Entrepreneurial Innovative Behaviour: the Role of Psychological Capital." *International Journal of Business and Management* 4 (11): 184–192. www. Ccsenet.org/journal.-html (accessed April 25, 2010).

Busenitz, L. W., Gomez, C. & Spencer, J. W. 2000. "Country Institutional Profiles: Unlocking Entrepreneurial Phenomena." *Academy of Management Journal* 43: 994–1003.

Chamlee-Wright, E. 2002. "Savings and Accumulation Strategies of Urban Market Women in Harare, Zimbabwe." *Economic Development and Cultural Change* 50: 979–1005.

Center for Women's Business Research. 2005. www. http://nfwbo.org (accessed September 2012).

Chant, S. 2007. "The Informal Sector and Employment." In *The Companion to Development Studies*, edited by Vandana, D. and Potter, R. London: Hodder-Arnold.

Chu, Hung M., Kara, O. & Benzing, C. 2008. "An Empirical Study of Nigerian Entrepreneurs: Success, Motivations, Problems and Stress." *International Journal of Business Research* 8 (2): 102–116.

Ehigie, B. O. & Umoren, U. E. 2003. "Psychological Factors Influencing Perceived Entrepreneurial Success among Nigeria Women in Small-scale Business." *Journal of International WomenStudies* 5 (1): 78–93.

Ekejuiba, F. 1991. *Women in the Context of Nigerian Rural Development.* Ed. Ijere. Women in Nigerian Economy. Enugu: Acena Publishers.

European Commission. 2008. "Evaluation on Policy: Promotion of Women Innovators and Entrepreneurship." DG Enterpriseand Industry. ENTRO4/093-FC-Lot 1EC.

Fapounda, T. M. 2012. "Women and the Informal Sector in Nigeria: Implications for Development." *British Journal of Arts and Social Sciences* 4 (1): 35–46.

Fick, D. S. 2002. *Entrepreneurship in Africa: A Study of Success.* Westport, CT: Quorum Books.

Gartner, W. B. 1985. "A Conceptual Framework for Describing the Phenomenon of New Venture Creation." *Academy of Management Review* 10: 696–706.

Food and Agricultural Organization. 1982. Role of Women in Agricultural Production. Rome: FAO.

Global Entrepreneurship Monitor. 2012. GEM 2011 Global Report. http://www.gemconsortium.org (accessed December 2012).

Harding, R. 2006. *Global Entrepreneurship Monitor*. UK: London.

Horner, M. 1969. "A Bright Woman is Caught in a Double-Bind." *Psychology Today* 62 (2): 36–48.

Jibowo, A. A. 1993. *Essentials of Rural Sociology*. Abeokuta, Nigeria: Gbemi Sodipo Press Ltd.

Kibas, P. B. 2005. "Challenges Facing Women Entrepreneurs in Africa." http://www.fnst.org (accessed February 2013).

McDade, B. E. & Spring, A. 2005. "The 'New Generation of African Entrepreneurs': Networking to Change the Climate for Business and Private Sector-led Development." *Entrepreneurship & Regional Development* 17: 17–42.

Minniti, M. 2011. "Female Entrepreneurship and Economic Activity. European." *Journal of Development Research* 22: 294–312.

Njeru, E. H. N. & Njoka, J. M. 2001. "Women Entrepreneurs in Nairobi: The Socio-cultural Factors Influencing their Investment Patterns." In

Negotiating Social Space: East African Micro Enterprises, edited by Alila, P. O. & Pedersen, P. O., 141–56. Trenton, NJ and Asmara, Eritrea: Africa World Press.

Nnoyelu, C. & Gadzama, E. 2001. "Effective Roles for Women in Agriculture in Sub Programmes." FACU, Ibadan. 1–9.

Nyamnjoh, F. B. 2005. "Fishing in Troubled Waters: Disquettes and Thiofs in Dakar." *Africa* 75 (3): 295–324.

Okojie, C. E. 2002. "Globalization and the Women Enterprises Opportunity and Challenges." UNIFEM women enterprises Forum. Lagos.

Onyenechere, E. C. 2009. "Constraints of Rural Women in Informal Economic Activities in Imo State, Nigeria." *African Development* 34 (1): 83–101.

Oyekanmi, F. A. 2005. "Gender Issues in Globalization; An Overview of the Situation in Africa." Paper presented at the lecture series of the Department of Sociology, Lagos State University.

Richardson, P., Rhona, H. & Finnegan, G. 2004. "The Challenges of Growing Small Businesses: Insights from Women Entrepreneurs in Africa." SEED Working Paper No. 47. Series on Women's Entrepreneurship Development and Gender Equality. WEDGE- ILO.

Scott, W. R. 2001. *Institutions and Organizations*. Thousand Oaks, CA: Sage.

Smallbone, D. & Welter, F. 2001. "The Distinctiveness of Entrepreneurship in Transition Economies." *Small Business Economics* 16: 249–62.

Staub, K. M. & Amine, L. S. 2006. "Women Entrepreneurs in Africa: Ready to Go!" Paper presented at the 3rd International Entrepreneurship Conference at the United States. International University of Nairobi, May 31 to June 2, in Kenya.

United Nations Development Fund for Women. 2005. "Progress of The World Women: Women, Work and Poverty." New York.

Vossenberg, S. 2013. "Women Entrepreneurship Promotion in Developing Countries. What Explains the Gender Gap in Entrepreneurship and how to Close it." Working paper No2013/08.MAASSTRICH School of Management.

Woldie, A. & Adersua, A. 2004. "Female Entrepreneurs in a Transitional Economy—Businesswomen in Nigeria." *International Journal of Social Economics* 31: 78–93.

World Bank 2008. World Development Report 2008. Agriculture for Development.

World Bank. 2007. Doing business: Comparing business regulations. http://www.doingbusiness.org (accessed February 14, 2012).

CHAPTER FOURTEEN

SOCIAL STRUCTURE, PROPERTY RIGHTS AND DEVELOPMENT IN NIGERIA

NURUDEEN ALLIYU

Introduction

While property as an infrastructural requirement for development in any nation may be of interest to many scholars of development bias, access to and control of property are of significant importance to those interested in the gender aspect of development. An understanding of the interaction between property, the development process and social relations of production would not be sufficient without adequate knowledge of the social structure of the society that makes up the pattern of social interaction through which culture is formed. The focus of this chapter is therefore on the interaction between property (with special attention to women) and the social structure of southwest Nigeria, predominantly occupied by the Yoruba sub-ethnic group, and how this impacts the overall development of the area and women.

Women and Property

What constitutes "property" differs greatly from one culture to another, and is still very significant in understanding social phenomena in any society. Its significance has to do with its role in the economy upon which other superstructures are erected. The whole idea about "having" and "not having" is all about property or means of production. The haves are the bourgeoisies and the have-nots are proletariats in a capitalist society, but being propertied or property-less is not only a bourgeois and proletariat affair. This issue of property is also not gender neutral. While women have access to property in some societies, they have little or no access in others. This has implications for the role of women *vis-à-vis* the role of men in any society. It also has implication for the status of men and women and all gender relations generally. Property can therefore be seen as a vital indicator of the balance of power between men and women. Thus, the greater the access of both sexes to property equitably in the society, the more likely they are to equally contribute to development.

Any imbalance in access to property by either sex would definitely lead to power imbalance and the lower contribution to development from the less powerful. The relationship between women and men, especially in a patriarchal society, is structured by access to and control over transmission of property. The relationship as read in the literature has been described as that of male-superiority and female-inferiority, a relationship of men (the haves, the propertied) and the women (the have-nots, the property-less). The significance of property as a factor in men-women relationships is reported by Pina-Cabral's account of two Portuguese rural Parishes wherein women of the landed (propertied) peasantry marry and enjoy an elevated position, being called "female boss." By contrast, landless (property-less) women are rarely married, producing children out of wedlock and being dependent on the wealthy for their livelihood (cited in Hirschon, 1984, 4). It is evident, according to Whitehead (1984), that property could not primarily have been a relation between people and things, but a relation between people and people—a social relation, and specifically gender relations. The discussion on "women" and "property" in this chapter shows the social character of property.

In Whitehead's survey of African non-class societies and other areas, "women and men have important roles in production and each sex has acknowledged rights to commercial property including land—the major means of production" (1984, 183). Similarly, Fadipe (1970) said of the Yoruba in Nigeria that "a sense of individual property is not confined to those of the male sex, individual property among boys has its correspondence among girls." Furthermore, "the fact that a woman has a right to accumulate property to which her husband has no claim is another evidence of the strength of the sentiment of individual property among the Yoruba" (1970, 194).

For Muntembe (1982), the situation is also similar. He argued that in the pre-colonial era when African societies were less differentiated, women in many areas were not only productive but also had access to property at the commercial level as identified above, and some states even backed it up with constitutional law. The constitution of the Federal Republic of Nigeria, for instance, confers on both sexes the right to freedom from discrimination (including access to property). There seems, therefore, to be a sort of equivalence in both sexes' access to land.

Whitehead (1984, 183) however contends that "those ideologies of equivalence in the gender's access to land and other tangible resources (property) have to be understood in the context of the implication of other aspects of the commercial property system (laws)." This is very significant because it is women's access to property as documented in the literature that it is more often than not vicarious, in both patriarchal and matriarchal societies. The legal or constitutional backing to protect women against discrimination in access to property is also more often than not unexecuted (Olawoye et al. 1991; Kabir 1990; Whitehead 1985; 1984; Aidoo 1988; Strathern 1984).

The foregoing suggests that the mechanism of appropriating property in most societies goes a long way to determining the nature and ownership of property control over its transmission. The Yoruba in Nigeria, for instance, have a clear conception of private property, and as such individual property means more to them than commercial property. Fadipe (1970) identified the following as a means of acquiring property among the Yoruba:

(a) Possession brought about by the expenditure of energy and labour of a hitherto unappropriated object, such as the building of a house or clearing land for farming purposes. Acquisition in war, whether of a human being or an inanimate object, may also be brought under this heading.
(b) Legal transfer, either by sale and purchase, by gift or by inheritance.
(c) Possession (which is not contested) for a certain length of time.
(d) Prior discovery and laying hold of any material object relatively scarce in time or place.

All the means of appropriation of property identified above are not restricted to any sex. In fact, Yoruba women enjoy autonomy and independence such that they are not only powerful in the business sector but also politically prominent, which was the case in pre-colonial as in post-colonial Nigeria.

The degree and nature of influence over any mechanism of appropriating property in any social formation by either sexes, but particularly women, are better looked at by Sexton's account of two communities of the highlands of Papua New Guinea. Strathern, quoting Lonaine Sexton (1984), described the Daulo women's mechanism of appropriating property, control and transmission:

> Their women have developed their own savings and exchange system called Pidgin Wok meri (women's work/enterprise). Small groups drawn from the co-resident lineage wives of a village protect their savings from the depredations of their husbands by banking them collectively. They use the capital for business ventures and for exchange with similar women's groups …
>
> Established groups sponsor "daughter" groups in other villages by making them loans that are eventually repaid when they become "mothers" themselves … Daulo men also respond to women's efforts, they respect women's claim to dispose of some of the cash income [property] and further support groups with expert advice, acting as book-keepers and truck drivers.
>
> (Strathern 1984, 159–169)

On the contrary, the Hagen women are equated with wealth that flows between men and as such are treated as objects (things) rather than subjects (persons). Strathern reports that:

> Some of the commonest female names are term for shell valuables in the 1960s. I heard fathers refer to their daughters as trade stores that is, business ventures, women are also acknowledged sources of sustenance, likened to the sweet potatoes they grow. Men may thus compare women with valuables they exchange with one another; and with the investment potential that lies in the ties created by the woman marrying from one clan into another; and with the very products of female labour. Nor do women find anything odd or objectionable in such equations (*meaning that they have been ideologically brain washed through socialisation—[often through women] to accept the situation as natural)*. It is not people in general who are likened to wealth, but women in particular. We would seem to have an obvious case for considering that Hagen women are classified as "property." (Strathern 1984, 163, my emphasis).

Women as Property

The case of Hagen women presented above is not peculiar to them, and is also found in many other societies. The implication is that the women described as "property" cannot acquire property, not to mention the control and/or transmission of such afterwards. "In ancient Israel also, children, along with wives, concubines, slaves and animals were all the property of the male, to do with whatever he chose" (Gray 1982; see also Harris 1984).

For Harris (1984), women are more commodities to be given into marriage. She narrates a biblical example of this as the occasion when Abraham sent his servant to find a wife for his son Isaac. The servant spoke to Rebekah's father and brother and their response was: "Behold, Rebekah is before thee, take her and go, and let her be thy master's son's wife, as the Lord hath spoken" (Genesis 24: 51).

It is important to note here that:

(1) Rebekah, her father and her brother had not met either Abraham or Isaac at this stage.
(2) Rebekah had not uttered a word in the deal of whom she would marry.
(3) Rebekah's mother was not consulted let alone had a word to say about her own daughter
(4) All the men from both Isaac's and Rebekah's families decide the issue when it is obvious that it is Rebekah who is to marry a complete stranger.

In another situation, and still depicting women as property, Harris (1984) also shows that a father could offer his daughter as a prize like any other common good. Her reference is also drawn from the Bible: "And Caleb said, He that smiteth Kirjath-Sepher, and taketh it, to him will I give Achsah my daughter to wife. And Othniel the son of Kenaz, Caleb's younger brother, took it: and he gave him Achsah his daughter to wife" (Judges 1: 12–13).

It should be taken from the above instance that:

(1) Women (be it wife or daughter) are portrayed here as being of such little worth that they might be given away with outmost disregard for their person and discrimination.
(2) Women are also portrayed as "things" to use in the men's home as the man pleases in what so ever form ranging from sex, domestic and farm works and child reproduction.

Engels also corroborates the above submissions in his famous book *The Origin of the Family, Private Property and the State*. For him, the wife is described as *oikurema* (a thing for housekeeping) among the Euripides: "And apart from the business of bearing children, she was nothing more to the Athenian than the chief housemaid" (Engels 1983, 64).

Apart from the various uses a woman can be subjected to as property, Harris (1984) further observes that women (particularly daughters) could also be violated by men if the father is paid some monetary reward in this regard, and the case is settled. This is summarized in the book of Deuteronomy 22 as follows:

> If a man find a damsel that is a virgin, which is not betrothed and lay hold on her, and lie with her, and they be found. Then the man that lay with her shall give unto the damsel's father fifty shekels of silver, and she shall be his wife; because he hath humbled her, he may not put her away all his days. (Deuteronomy 22: 28–29)

It is worth noting that:

(1) Women are not only seen as property, but the process of acquiring one, as described above, shows the level of disdain, disrespect and disregard men have for women.
(2) A violated daughter need not be worried about, but the father must be paid.
(3) The mother is not an issue for consideration in this matter.

All the above instances could be described as comprising the ideological foundation (rooted in religious beliefs) for the superiority of the male over female. And since the "Lord" has spoken concerning some of the issues above, any attempt to challenge the status quo has been very difficult, particularly for women. Advancement in knowledge has however proved that the status quo can indeed be changed for the better.

Women, Property and Development in Southwest Nigeria

Property, within a capitalist social formation, is based on the idea of "private ownership." This, according to Hirschon (1984), confers on the individual the right to use and dispose, and to the extent that women are seen and related to as property it is given that they are "privately owned." Men in such a society are therefore likely to own all valuable properties, including women, and where such "properties" own a property, she is most likely to be under the direct influence of the overall owner of "properties." The men, in this case, may even determine the types of property owned by women.

Against this background, attempts were made to investigate the situation in Lagos and Ogun states (male dominated societies) on how women acquire property for development. Table 14.1 below presents the detailed processes of property acquisition by the respondents.

The continuous reference to the Yoruba is predicated on the fact that:

(a) the study was done in Yoruba land (i.e. Lagos and Ogun States.
(b) 74.9% of the respondents are Yoruba, and
(c) property rights seem to be granted to both sexes in Yoruba land.

Table 14.1. Respondents' Sources of Property

	PROPERTY TYPE							
	Land		Cars		Small Business		Houses	
SOURCES	Freq.	%	Freq.	%	Freq.	%	Freq.	%
Inheritance	42	76.4	02	9.1	03	3.0	04	22.2
Gift	03	5.5	03	13.6	03	3.0	00	00
Personal	02	3.6	06	27.3	68	68	01	5.6
Husband	05	9.1	10	45.5	25	25	12	66.6
Husband Family	01	1.8	01	4.5	00	00	01	5.6
Own Family	02	3.6	00	0.0	01	1	00	00
Others	-	-	-	-	-	-	-	-
TOTAL	55	100	22	100	100	100	18	100

Source: Field Returns

The study was restricted to the four types of property in the above table because of their capacities for use in generating further capital. They are factors in the production processes of any capitalist setting. And to the extent that the relationship between men and women in the control of societal wealth, production processes or capitalism is negatively skewed against women, it is given that women who acquire the above could be termed "propertied."

Land, in rudimentary economics, is described as a factor of production. Although economists argue that it includes all natural resources, such as mineral deposits like oil, the concern here is the actual land itself. Fifty-five out of 195 respondents in the table above claimed they have land as property, 22 have cars/lorries, 100 have businesses and 18 have houses. About 76.4% of the respondents who claimed to have land got it through inheritance. This seems to reveal that the notion of property such as land is based on the individual having specific rights. This is particularly true among the Yoruba people who constituted about 74.9% of the respondents. According to Fadipe (1991, 194): "… The Yoruba child is given at an early age every opportunity to acquire a sense of individual property … (This) is not confined to those of the male sex … what has been said about individual property among boys has its correspondence among girls."

Fadipe further argues that the strength of the sentiment of individual property among the Yoruba is evidence of the right of a woman to acquire/accumulate property to which her husband has no claim. The high figure of respondents who inherited land may be due to the fact that land is abundant in the rural areas, and as Fadipe claimed "no adult member of the community (Yoruba) who has need of land goes without it."

Contrariwise, 3.6% of respondents claimed to have acquired land through personal effort, having nothing to do with inheritance. They might have purchased the land, particularly where it is very scarce. This idea of transfer by sale actually started in Lagos long before the cession of the Island in 1861 to the British Crown (Fadipe 1991).

About 5.5% got their land as a gift from other people, as in Africa such generosity is natural. Another 9.1% claimed that their husbands were the source of the land. However, the involvement of the husband in getting the land is not clear. Somehow, the husband could have been instrumental in the women's effort to get the land. It is, however, not uncommon for men to buy things for women and, of course, husbands buy things for wives in African societies. The remaining 1.8% and 3.6% claimed that their husband's and their own families were the sources of their land.

Vehicles are essential means of transportation in Nigeria today. Much more than that, they enhance business performances particularly for those who may have to transport their goods from one place to another. In addition, they are a perceived symbol of success of anything one is engaged with in Nigeria. So, any individual who has one or more they personally use for whatever purpose is assumed to be somehow successful.

Forty-five percent of the 22 women who claimed they have cars/lorries indicated that their husbands are the source of the vehicles. This is far higher than the 9.1% who claimed their husband is the source of their lands. It is also lower than the 76.4% who claimed they inherited lands. One can therefore say that husbands in Nigeria are more likely to buy vehicles for their wives instead of land. This may be true particularly among the Yoruba people who may be regarded as somehow ostentatious in their styles of living. However, among the women who engage in lumbering businesses, some claimed that it is sometimes a joint venture between them and their husbands—while they sell the planks, the husbands buy the logs/timbers as timber contractors.

On this premise, the provision of vehicles, particularly lorries, to transport both the timber and the planks might have been through the husbands of such women. This is not to say that some did not acquire cars/lorries on their own as 27.3% of 22 women claimed they got them personally, although with their husbands' consent. Gifting is another source for some respondents. About 13.6% of the 22 women who claimed they have cars/lorries got them this way, although who exactly provided them was not specified. Yet another 9.1% inherited theirs, and the husband's family is the source for about 4.5% of the 22 who have them. None mentioned their own families as the source.

In the categorization of properties acquired by the respondents, four types were identified:

(a) Registered industry (manufacturing) 10.2%
(b) (i) Land for production purposes
    (ii) Houses for commercial purpose 16.4%
(c) Indigenous business (dealing in local goods) 34.4%
(d) Modern business (dealing in foreign goods) 39%.

From the foregoing, the total percentage of the respondents working as business/commercial properties dealing in indigenous/modern goods and manufacturing industries is 83.6%. This seems to be in consonance with the United Nations Development Fund for Women in developing countries report, which stated that 70% of small enterprises are run by women (UNIFEM 1988). Indeed, the International Labour Organisation estimated that about 16 million women were engaged in the informal sector in sub-Saharan Africa in 1990 (ILO 1990). Soetan (1995) posits that "small scale enterprises (SSEs) are increasingly representing an important source of income for women in Nigeria." For her, "SSEs are found in the informal sector of urban centres as well as the non-farm sector of rural areas."

The above assertions seem to lend credence to the percentage of the respondents (83.6%) that have commercial/properties. When asked if the figure for women in the informal sector has to do with low academic performance, the respondents argued that it may have been so in the past, but now "women are more in the informal not because they do not go to school Ha! Graduates are even more within us." However, among the one hundred women who claimed they have business enterprises, about 68% of them also claimed that they acquired the business enterprise through personal efforts. It is however indicated that men do assist the women in business: "In my own case men do not hinder us from getting money"; "my husband did not hinder me, he even assisted me a lot."

Yet another respondent has this to say:

> In the past our husbands forbade us working on our own, we should just be giving birth to children. We had to beg to be allowed to work. When they

> agreed, they watch time for us so that you come back on time say by 4 p.m. to cook food and take care of home. But now we help ourselves with lots of resistance to this attitude of men.

From the above, there is no doubt that the propertied women who have business enterprise exert lots of resistance to the patriarchal-dominant attitude of men. It is also evident that men do support women and husbands do support wives in this case. What is significant, however, is that the first two respondents above were younger women below 40, while the third is over 50. The difference between these two categories of women may be due to some obvious, gradual but positive changes in the perception of women in the society. In a situation where efforts are consistently made to improve such perception by all concerned, it is most likely that greater equality will occur.

While 68% attribute the source of their business enterprise to personal effort, about 25% attribute theirs to their husbands. It is not impossible that those in this category are more likely to be the sole wives of their husbands, as the propertied women who belong to a polygynous setting complained that: "… If we ask our husband to give us something, if he is to give us two things, it is with struggle that he will give one."

Polygamy for these women has not really been helpful for their business enterprises. In effect, in a society where polygamy is still highly practiced, it is more likely that it will continue to constitute a serious source of concern for the businesswomen, particularly those already trapped in it. It may even threaten the family's survival where women in the informal business enterprise have been the major providers (Soetan 1995).

The two sources above seem to be the major sources of acquiring commercial properties by the respondents. The other sources were through inheritance (3%), gifts (3%) and their own families (1%). These sources are not very significant going by the percentage of the respondents in these categories. Finally, none of the respondents attribute the source of their business enterprise to the husband's family.

House ownership is one of the most cherished cultural acquisitions in Nigeria, apart from the properties discussed above. This is particularly true among the Yoruba in southwestern Nigeria. Indeed, according to Lawal (2000, 2): "It is a barometer for measuring success and status level. It is also used as a form of investment or object for procuring financial facilities for further investments."

It is therefore not strange to see in the above table that about 22% of the 18 respondents (who claimed they have houses) actually attribute it to inheritance. It is customary to the Yoruba, for example, to invest in or equip their children for the future by providing them with the means of production, such as land or houses in the urban centres. If houses were as abundant as land, it is probable that more of the respondents would have had houses through inheritance. Nevertheless, the percentage is still higher than the 9.1% that inherited cars and the 3% that inherited small business enterprises.

Surprisingly, 66.6% of the respondents who claimed to have houses attributed this to their husbands. This is even higher than 45.5% of the 22 who claimed that they have cars/lorries. The active involvement of husbands in the property acquisition of their wives, particularly cars/lorries and houses, is common. On the issue of houses, an investigation was carried in the qualitative study as to why some women acquire property in their husbands' names. The respondents gave such diverse reasons as:

> I can't build a house of my own in my husband's name. Why? I am the person doing all the work, and I am not the only one he married.
>
> It may be so in the past but now we do not agree to that again. We will use our name to build house. What we have belongs to our children, our husband has many wives. Family is so many, so why would I not buy my things in my name. Tell me! More so no peace in the house. A woman who has one husband may buy property in her husband's name but not we that are many in our husband's house.

The above statement seems to reveal the actual attitude of women to property nowadays, particularly those who are married to a polygamist. The monogamist may have a contrary attitude since they (i.e. the women), their future and children are much more "secured" than the women married to a polygamist.

Based on the above attitude one would have expected a situation where many of the respondents would have attributed their source of houses more to personal efforts rather than husbands when a majority of the respondents are from polygamist households. Rather, 5.6% of the women claimed personal effort as the source of their houses, and 66.6% claimed husbands as the source. The seeming contradiction between the attributes demonstrated in the quantitative study and the figure shown in the quantitative data seems to be clarified by Adedokun's study in 1990 of 400 Yoruba husbands and wives in Ibadan. She noted that even though the perception of the male as provider is still prevalent, empirical evidence shows that: "78% of educated working wives reported that they help their husbands in their duty as provider. The wives reported frequent full or part payments for school fees. The uneducated wives reported that they help but it was less frequent" (Adedokun 1990, 72).

In effect, it is not unlikely that some of the respondents were simply doing/playing gender stereotyping of women as submissive even when completing the questionnaires. The following comment seems to corroborate this claim:

> It is not possible for a woman to buy a car (property) without the husband's consent. If you (a woman) want to give honour to whom honour is due to, you have to inform your husband about such big thing. If you do not, God does not like such attitude.

In fact, according to Soetan (1995), although male superiority is still maintained through psychological and cultural (religious) means, equality is gradually being established through women's economic self-expression.

Lastly, 5.6% of these who claimed they have a house attribute it to their husband's family. None attributed it to their own family or it's being a gift.

Property rights as catalyst for change in women's statuses and development

Measuring how property is acquired by women in the study area necessitates asking them about the fate of widows in the society. In this regard, the respondents were asked—In the case of the death of a husband in your community, what happens to a wife (or wives)? Their responses are presented in table 14.2 below.

Table 14.2. Husbands' death and implication for Wife/wives

Fate	n = 195	%
Inherited by another family member	46	23.6
Remain with the husband's family unmarried	20	10.3
Return to her own family unmarried	05	2.6
Live wherever she desires	100	51.2
No response	24	12.3

More than half (51.2%) of the respondents said that widows in their communities could choose to live wherever they desired after the death of their husbands. Another 10.3% are of the view that widows could also choose to remain in the husband's family unmarried to any member of the family. This was not possible before, particularly when widow inheritance was very common. Even though the practice of widow inheritance is decreasing, about 23.6% of respondents argued that widows could still be inherited in their communities. Also, 2.6% claimed that the possibility of a widow returning to her own family also exists.

Apart from other factors that may influence widow inheritance, it was gathered from the respondents through the qualitative instruments that the family, the status of the widow and the property combine to determine their fate in a patriarchal society. The family, for instance, plays overriding roles, especially where there is no will and there are lots to share among the members of the family from the deceased estate. If there are liabilities to share the family hardly intervenes. However, the role of the family in this issue of inheritance also depends on how good or bad the family is. The role of the family may be limited greatly if there is a will administered by a legal practitioner. Such a will does not consider the wife or wives as part of the property to be shared since if the dead were alive they would definitely not want to share them (though they are a "property" to him) with any other man.

The status of the wife/wives also plays a very crucial, if not the most important, role in this issue of widow inheritance. Below are two cases recorded under high and low statuses.

Status and Inheritance in Southwest Nigeria

High Status	Low Status
Me, for example when my husband died, my husband's younger brother could not approach me for such inheritance because he knows "his power" could not carry me. *Emi kii se eru e*—I am not his "property" at all. Even before my husband died I used to give him money so, such a man cannot be bold enough to approach me for inheritance or marriage.	Widow inheritance is not happening again as such. What I feel that is causing it is when the woman has lot of children and she cannot take care of them. In such a situation, the family might force her to re-marry within the family. It might not be of her own wish that she should marry the brother of her husband. But because of her situation, she may have no option but to submit herself totally to the man who wants to marry his brother's wife.

The implication of the above cases is that the higher the status of a widow, the lower the chances of her being inherited and vice-versa.

Concluding Remarks

Obviously, it is very clear that the social structure that sustained the low status of women, reducing them to mere property, has slowly but surely been challenged in southwest Nigeria, as evidenced by the new status acquired by the women. This has improved their power to negotiate, access and control a significant part of their lives compared to women in other places. Their rights to property have not only improved their quality of life, they have also increased their contributions to the development of their society from household level to national level, going by their predominance in the informal sector of a developing economy such as Nigeria.

References

Adedokun, L. 1990. "Women, Colonialism and Change: Research into Tasks and Social Behaviour to Marriage. Ed. Olurode, Lai." *Women and Social Change in Nigeria.* Lagos: Unity Publishing and Research Co. Limited.

Aidoo, A. K. 1988. "Women and Food Security: The Opportunity for Africa." *Development* 2 (3).

Fadipe, N. A. 1970. *The Sociology of the Yoruba*. Ibadan: Ibadan University Press.

Gray, E. D. 1982. *Patriarchy as a Conceptual Trap.* Messacluise Hs: Round Table press.

Harris, K. 1984. *Sex, Ideology, and Religion: The Representation of Women in the Bible.* New Jersey: Bames and Noble Books.

Hirschon, R. 1984. *Women and Property—Women As Property*. New York: Croom Helm London and Canberra St. Martin's Press.

Kabir, Z. S. 1990. "Law and Marital Problems in Kano State." *The Muslim Women* 1 (2).

Lawal, H. O. 2000. "Housing Finance in Nigeria (1990–2000): A Review of Policies, Problems and Prospects." Masters in Business Administration. Thesis. Management and Accounting. Obafemi Awolowo University, Ile-Ife, Nigeria.

Muntembe, M. S. 1982. "Women and Agricultural Change in Railway Region of Zambia: Dispossession and Counter Strategies, 1930–70." *Women and Work in Africa.* Boulder: Westview Press.

Olawoye, J. E. & Olarinde, S. E. 1991. "Socio-Cultural and Legal Barriers Hindering the Full Participation of Women in the Development

Process." *Economic and Democratic Reforms in Nigeria Development.* Lagos: SID and FEF.

Soetan, F. 1991. "Women, Small Scale Enterprises and Social Change: Implications of Changes in Industrialization Strategy." *Nigerian Women in Social Change*. The Programme in Women Studies. Edited by Afonja, S. & Aina, B. Obafemi Awolowo University, Ile-Ife, Nigeria.

Strathern, M. 1984. "Subject or Object? Women and the Circulation of Valuables in Highland New Guinea." *Women and Property—Women As Property.* Edited by Hirschon, R. New York: Croom Helm, London and Canberra, St. Martin's Press.

Whitehead, A. 1984. "Men and Women, Kinship and Property: Some General Issues." *Women and Property—Women as Property.* Edited by Hirschon, R. New York: Croom Helm London and Canberra, St. Martin's Press.

Whitehead, A. 1985. "Effects of Technological Change on Rural Women: A review of Analysis and Concepts." *Technology and Rural Women.* Edited by Ahmed, I. London: Allen and UNWIN.

INDEX